AF584698

W I L D E R N E S S
G A L L A T I N
F O R E S T
Hermit Lake
Big Butte Lake
Gravel Lake
Anchor Lake
Rubble Lake
Erratic Lake
Widowed Lake
Summerville Lake
Jorden Lake
Crazy Mountain
Lake Elaine
Green Lake
Trail Lake
Wright Lake
Fritter Lake
Lennon Lake
Shrew Lake
Whitcomb Lake
Creek
10800
10200
10400
9800
9400

HOUGHTON MIFFLIN

SOCIAL STUDIES

MARYLAND STUDIES

Visit Education Place®
www.eduplace.com/kids

 HOUGHTON MIFFLIN BOSTON

MARYLAND

Maryland Databank

These Latin words are part of a prayer. They mean "with favor wilt thou compass us as with a shield."

This man represents a farmer.

A fisherman represents the natural resources of Maryland's waterways.

The Great Seal of Maryland centers around a Coat of Arms used by Lord Baltimore.

1632 refers to the year in which the king of England granted the Maryland Charter to Lord Baltimore.

Baltimore's family motto means "Strong deeds, gentle words."

Maryland Facts

Population, 2000	5,296,486
Land Area	9,775 square miles (25,317 square kilometers)
Economy	**Agriculture:** Dairy, poultry, corn, tobacco, soybeans, and nursery products **Industry:** Service industry, government, seafood, mining, electronic equipment, transportation, food products, publishing
Motto	"Strong deeds, gentle words"
State Nickname	The Old Line State

Maryland Symbols

State Flower
Black-Eyed Susan

State Flag
Maryland State Flag

State Reptile
Diamond-back Terrapin

State Dog
Chesapeake Bay Retriever

State Bird
Baltimore Oriole

State Tree
White Oak

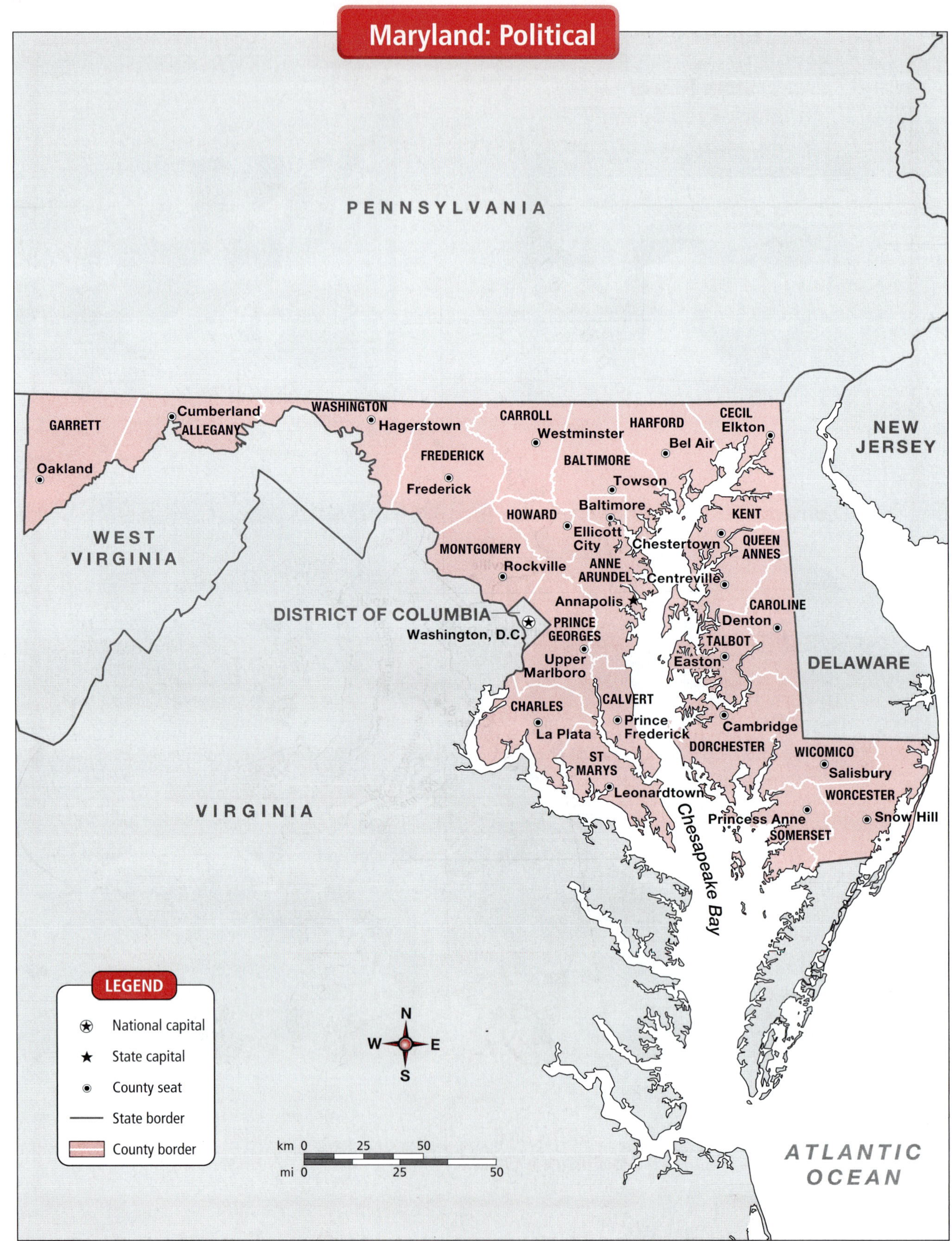

Maryland: Political
PENNSYLVANIA
NEW JERSEY
DELAWARE
WEST VIRGINIA
VIRGINIA
DISTRICT OF COLUMBIA
Washington, D.C.
GARRETT
Oakland
ALLEGANY
Cumberland
WASHINGTON
Hagerstown
FREDERICK
Frederick
CARROLL
Westminster
BALTIMORE
Towson
Baltimore
HARFORD
Bel Air
CECIL
Elkton
HOWARD
Ellicott City
MONTGOMERY
Rockville
ANNE ARUNDEL
Annapolis
KENT
Chestertown
QUEEN ANNES
Centreville
CAROLINE
Denton
TALBOT
Easton
PRINCE GEORGES
Upper Marlboro
CALVERT
Prince Frederick
CHARLES
La Plata
ST MARYS
Leonardtown
DORCHESTER
Cambridge
WICOMICO
Salisbury
WORCESTER
Snow Hill
SOMERSET
Princess Anne
Chesapeake Bay
ATLANTIC OCEAN
LEGEND
National capital
State capital
County seat
State border
County border
N
S
E
W
km 0 25 50
mi 0 25 50

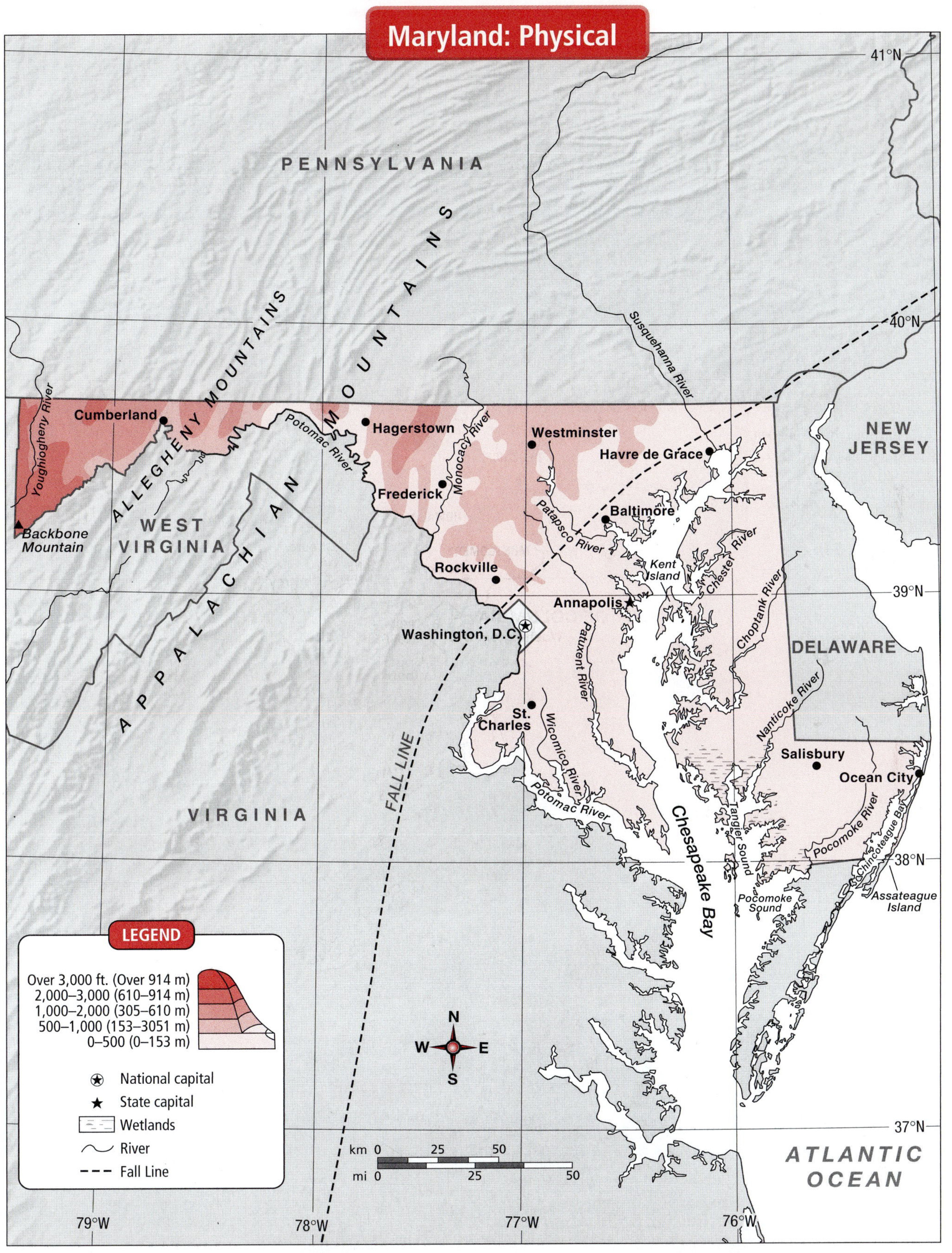
Maryland: Physical
PENNSYLVANIA
NEW JERSEY
DELAWARE
WEST VIRGINIA
VIRGINIA
ATLANTIC OCEAN
ALLEGHENY MOUNTAINS
APPALACHIAN MOUNTAINS
FALL LINE
Chesapeake Bay
Cumberland
Hagerstown
Westminster
Havre de Grace
Frederick
Baltimore
Rockville
Annapolis
Washington, D.C.
St. Charles
Salisbury
Ocean City
Backbone Mountain
Kent Island
Youghiogheny River
Potomac River
Monocacy River
Patapsco River
Susquehanna River
Chester River
Choptank River
Patuxent River
Wicomico River
Nanticoke River
Pocomoke River
Chincoteague Bay
Tangier Sound
Pocomoke Sound
Assateague Island
41°N
40°N
39°N
38°N
37°N
79°W
78°W
77°W
76°W
LEGEND
Over 3,000 ft. (Over 914 m)
2,000–3,000 (610–914 m)
1,000–2,000 (305–610 m)
500–1,000 (153–3051 m)
0–500 (0–153 m)
National capital
State capital
Wetlands
River
Fall Line
N
W
E
S
km 0 25 50
mi 0 25 50

Maryland: Precipitation

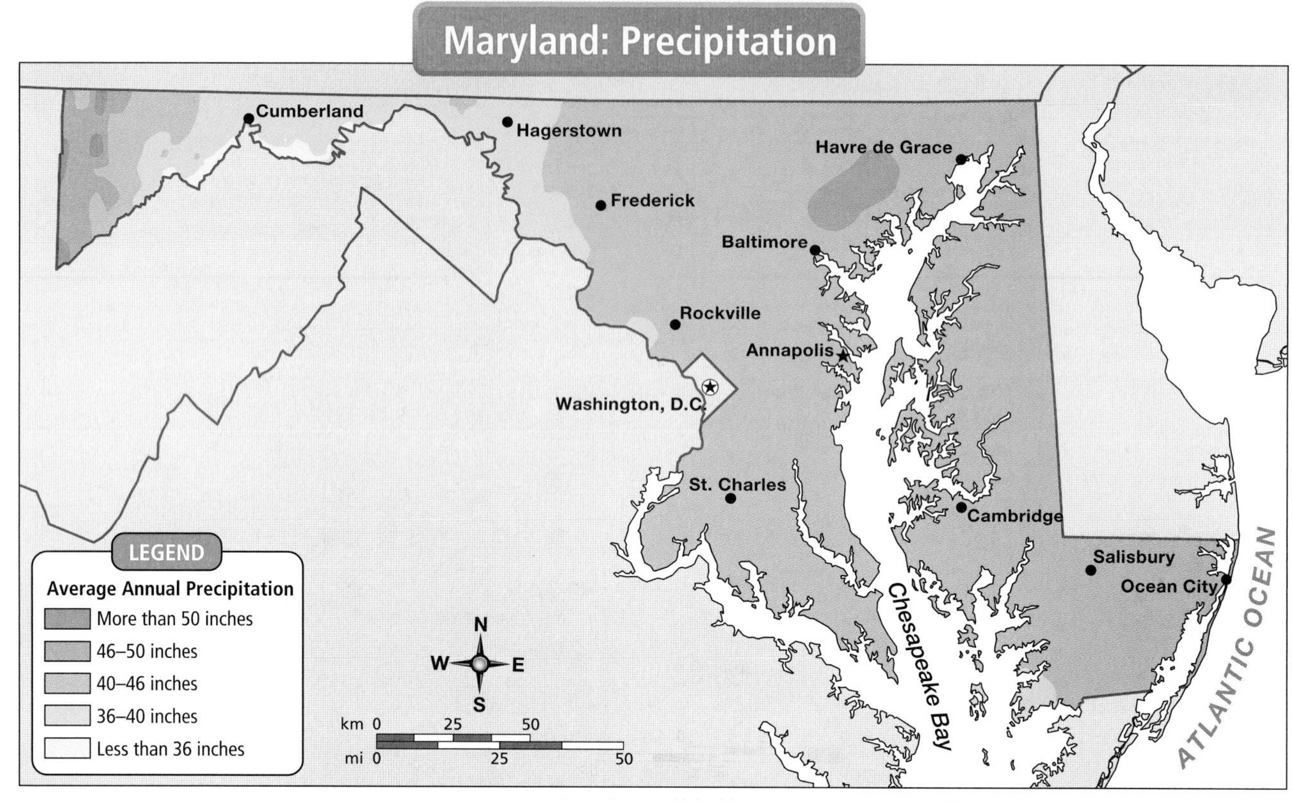

Average January Temperature

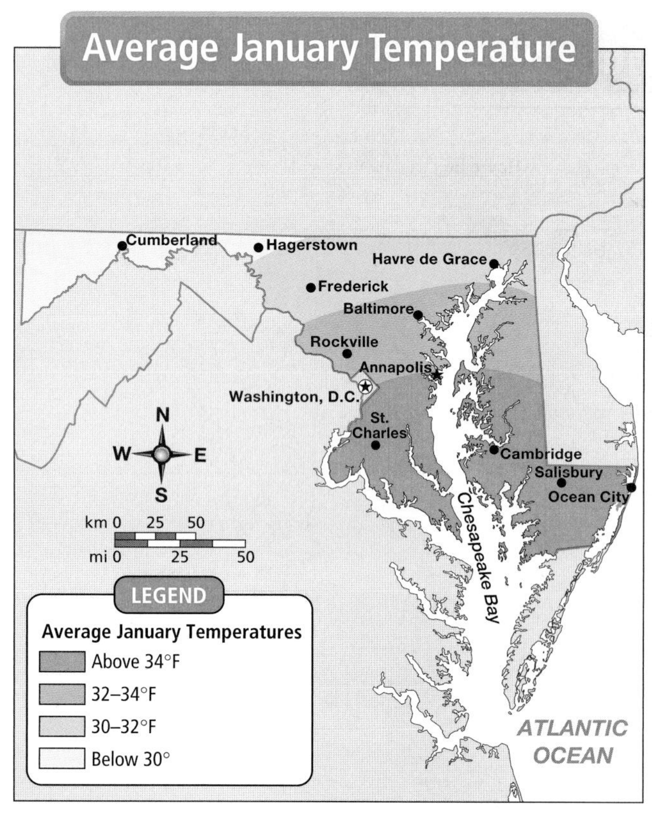

Average July Temperature

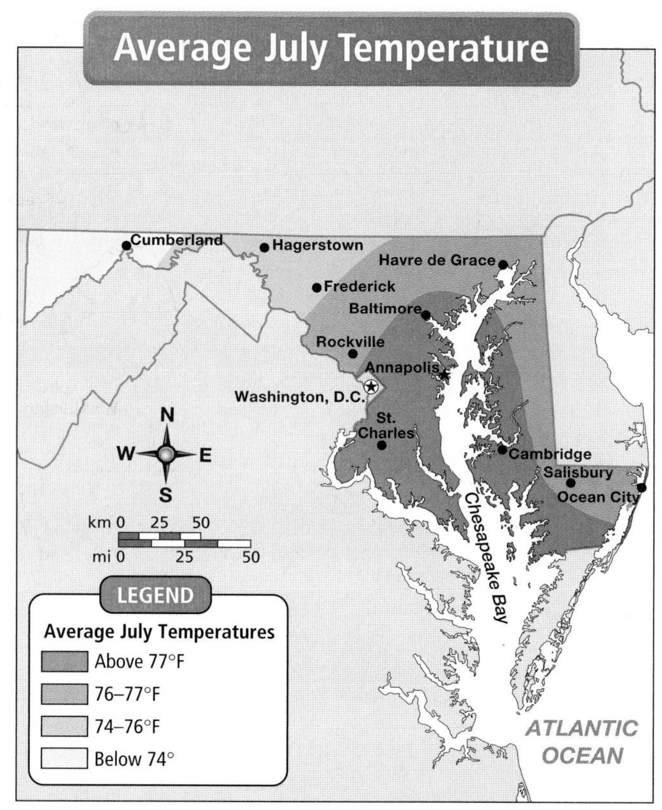

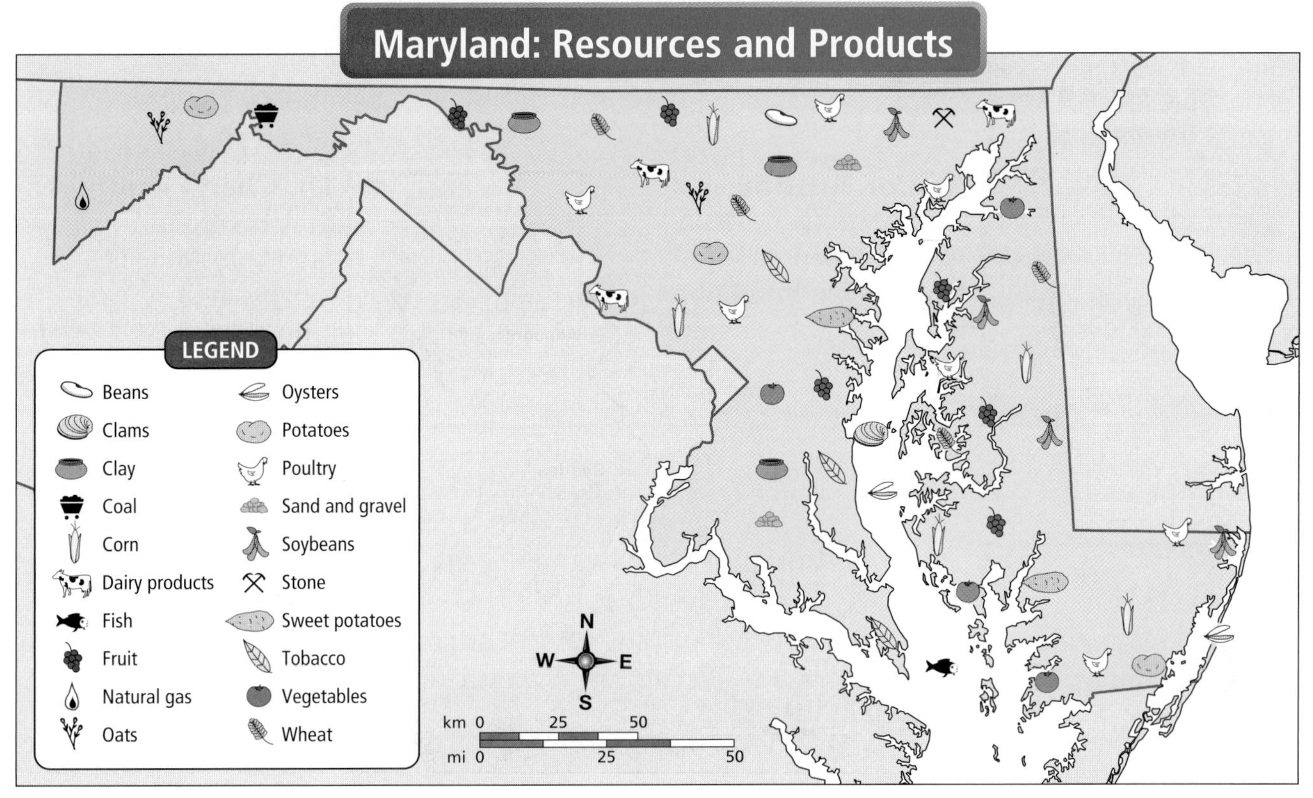
Maryland: Resources and Products
LEGEND
Beans
Clams
Clay
Coal
Corn
Dairy products
Fish
Fruit
Natural gas
Oats
Oysters
Potatoes
Poultry
Sand and gravel
Soybeans
Stone
Sweet potatoes
Tobacco
Vegetables
Wheat
N
W
E
S
km 0 25 50
mi 0 25 50

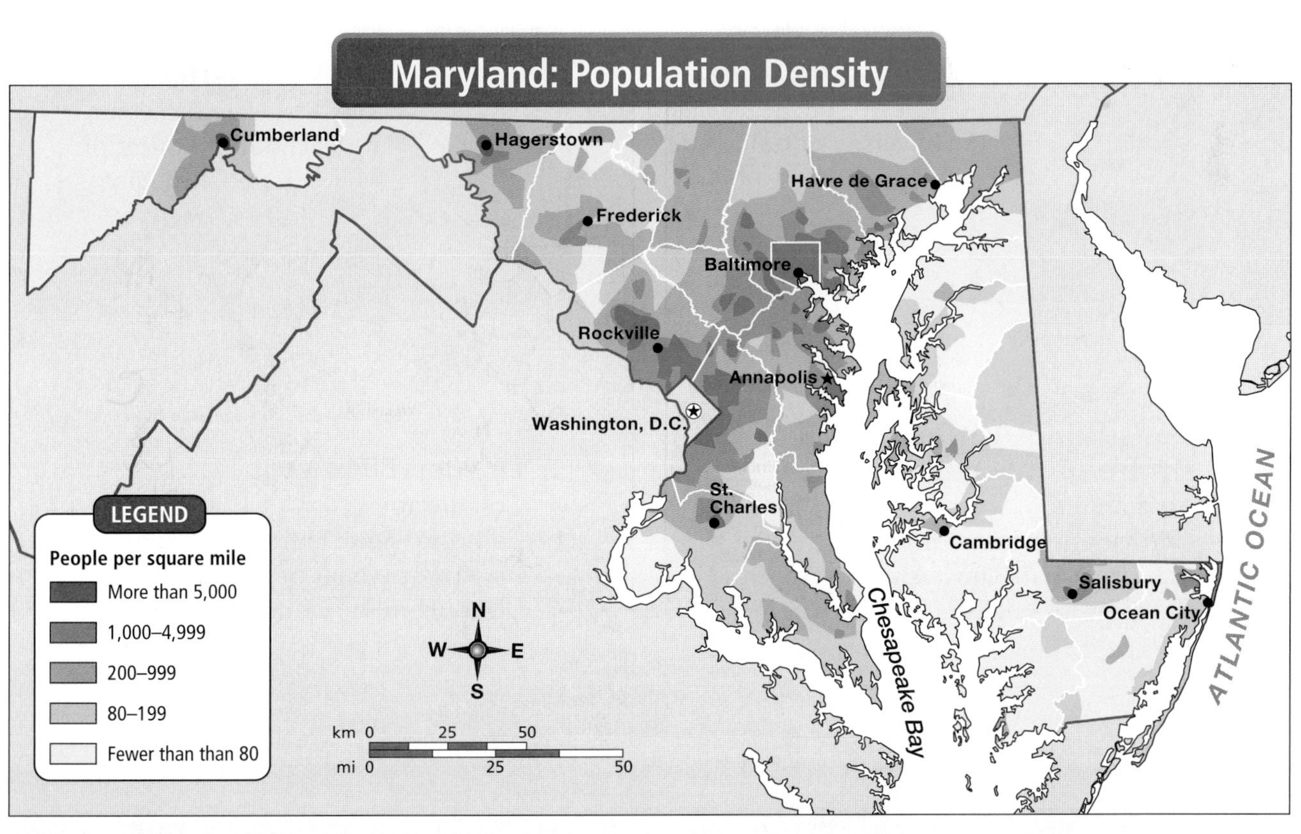
Maryland: Population Density
Cumberland
Hagerstown
Havre de Grace
Frederick
Baltimore
Rockville
Annapolis
Washington, D.C.
St. Charles
Cambridge
Salisbury
Ocean City
Chesapeake Bay
ATLANTIC OCEAN
LEGEND
People per square mile
More than 5,000
1,000–4,999
200–999
80–199
Fewer than than 80
N
W
E
S
km 0 25 50
mi 0 25 50

AUTHORS

Senior Author
Dr. Herman J. Viola
Curator Emeritus
Smithsonian Institution

Dr. Cheryl Jennings
Project Director
Florida Institute of Education
University of North Florida

Dr. Sarah Witham Bednarz
Associate Professor, Geography
Texas A&M University

Dr. Mark C. Schug
Professor and Director
Center for Economic Education
University of Wisconsin, Milwaukee

Dr. Carlos E. Cortés
Professor Emeritus, History
University of California, Riverside

Dr. Charles S. White
Associate Professor, School of Education
Boston University

Consulting Authors

Dr. Dolores Beltran
Assistant Professor
Curriculum Instruction
California State University, Los Angeles
(Support for English Language Learners)

Dr. MaryEllen Vogt
Co-Director
California State University Center for the Advancement of Reading
(Reading in the Content Area)

HOUGHTON MIFFLIN SOCIAL STUDIES

MARYLAND STUDIES

HOUGHTON MIFFLIN BOSTON

MARYLAND

Consultants

Philip J. Deloria
Associate Professor
Department of History and Program in American Studies
University of Michigan

Lucien Ellington
UC Professor of Education and Asia Program, Co-Director
University of Tennessee, Chattanooga

Thelma Wills Foote
Associate Professor
University of California, Irvine

Stephen J. Fugita
Distinguished Professor
Psychology and Ethnic Studies
Santa Clara University

Charles C. Haynes
Senior Scholar
First Amendment Center

Ted Hemmingway
Professor of History
The Florida Agricultural & Mechanical University

Douglas Monroy
Professor of History
The Colorado College

Lynette K. Oshima
Assistant Professor,
Department of Language, Literacy and
Sociocultural Studies and Social Studies Program Coordinator
University of New Mexico

Jeffrey Strickland
Assistant Professor, History
University of Texas Pan American

Clifford E. Trafzer
Professor of History and American Indian Studies
University of California, Riverside

Teacher Reviewer

Dr. Kara Libby
Prince George's County Public Schools
Upper Marboro, Maryland

© 2006 Houghton Mifflin Company. All rights reserved.

No part of this work may be reproduced or transmitted in any form or by any means, electronic or mechanical, including photocopying and recording, or by any information storage or retrieval system, without the prior written permission of Houghton Mifflin unless such copying is expressly permitted by federal copyright law. Address requests for permission to reproduce Houghton Mifflin material to School Permissions, Houghton Mifflin Company, 222 Berkeley St., Boston, MA 02116.

Printed in the U.S.A.

ISBN: 0-618-550364

123456789-VH-13-12 11 10 09 08 07 06 05

Contents

UNIT 1 The Land and Settlement of Maryland

CHAPTER 1 Maryland's Land and Early People

CHAPTER 2 Colonial Maryland

UNIT 2 Independence and Growth

CHAPTER 3 Revolution and Independence

CHAPTER 4 Maryland and The Nation

UNIT 3

A Changing State

CHAPTER 5 The Civil War

CHAPTER 6 The Twentieth Century

UNIT 4 Maryland Today

CHAPTER 7 The Government in Maryland

CHAPTER 8 Maryland's Economy

UNIT 5 Maryland and the East

CHAPTER 9 Exploring the East

References

Citizenship Handbook

Resources

Skill Lessons

Take a step-by-step approach to learning and practicing key social studies skills.

Map and Globe Skills

Graph and Chart Skills

Study Skills

CANADA
MAINE
VERMONT
Montpelier
Augusta
NEW HAMPSHIRE
Concord
Lake Ontario
NEW YORK
Buffalo
Albany
Boston
MASSACHUSETTS
Lake Erie
ATLANTIC OCEAN
Hartford
CONNECTICUT
Providence
RHODE ISLAND
PENNSYLVANIA
NEW JERSEY
New York
Pittsburgh
Harrisburg
Trenton
Philadelphia
MARYLAND
Baltimore
Annapolis
Washington, D.C.
Dover
DELAWARE
N E S W
km 0 50 100
mi 0 50 100

LEGEND
State capital
National capital
Large city
Apple-growing areas
Peach-growing areas
Cherry-growing areas
Grape-growing areas

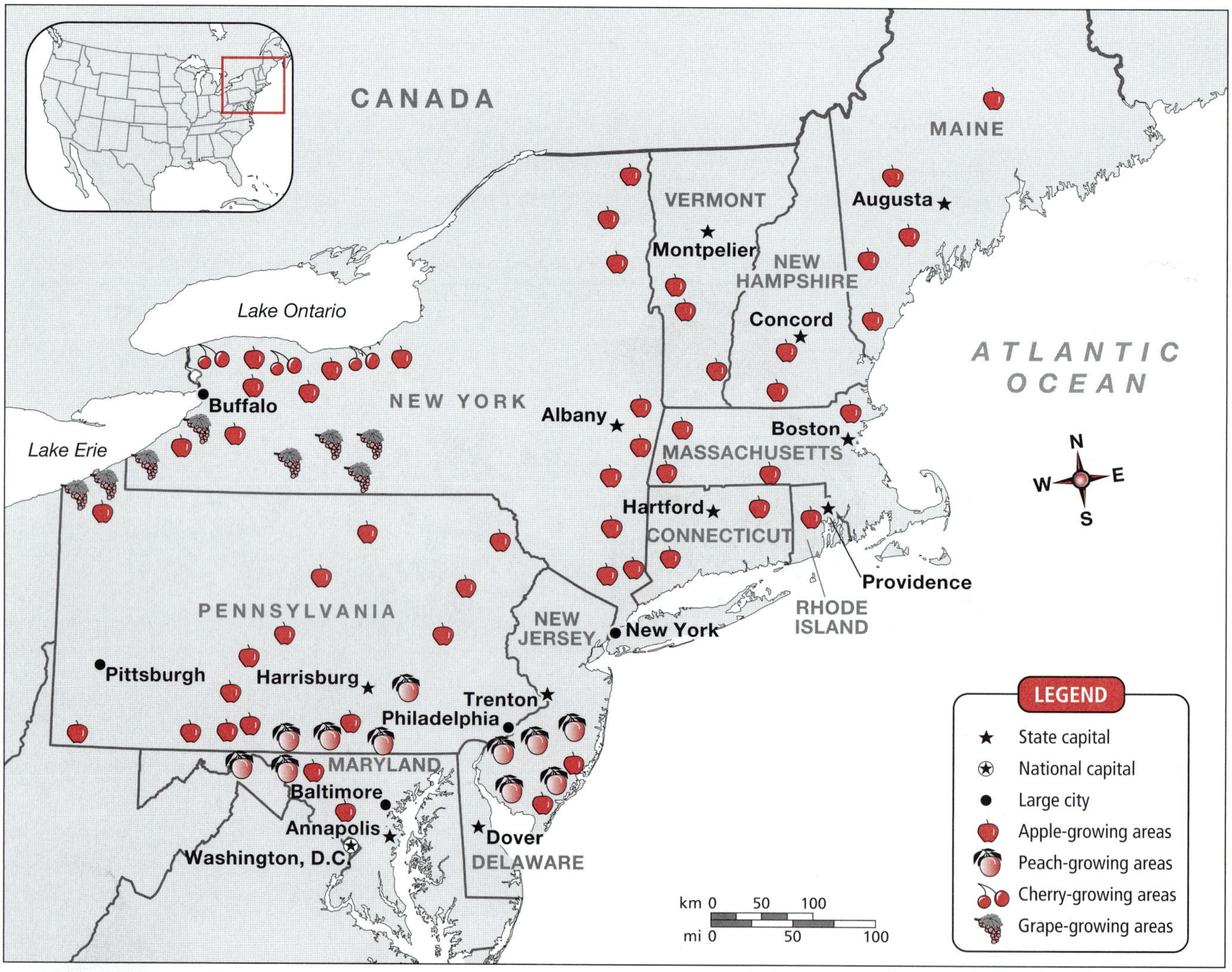

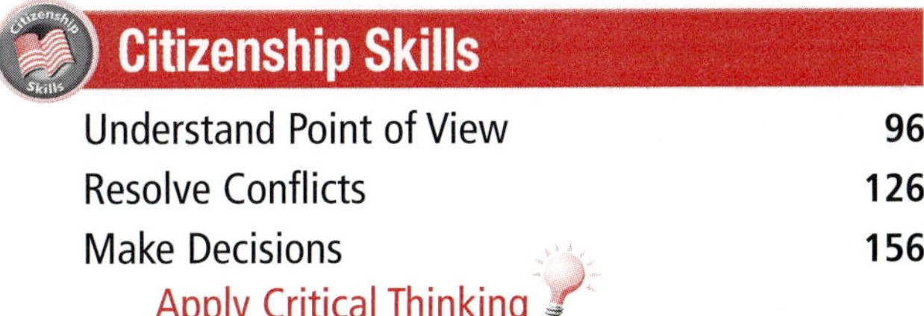

Citizenship Skills

Reading and Thinking Skills

Reading Skills/Graphic Organizer

About Your Textbook

1 How It's Organized

Units The major sections of your book are units.

Each starts with a big idea.

Chapters Units are divided into chapters, and each opens with a vocabulary preview.

Get ready for reading.

Four important concepts get you started.

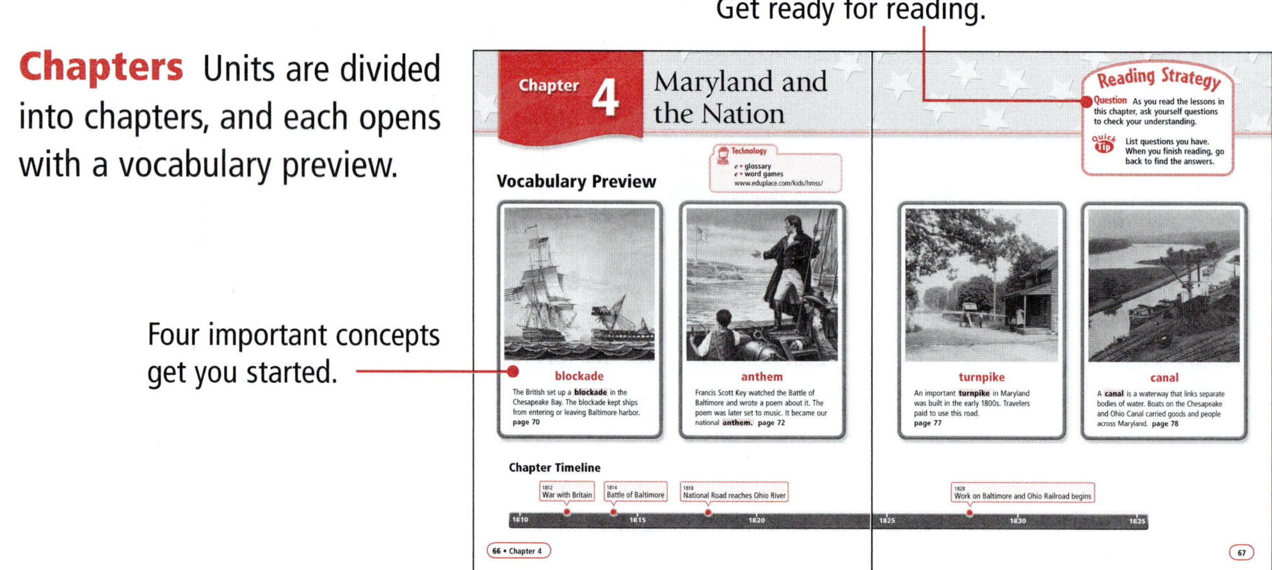

2 Core

Lessons Lessons bring social studies to life and help you meet your state's standards.

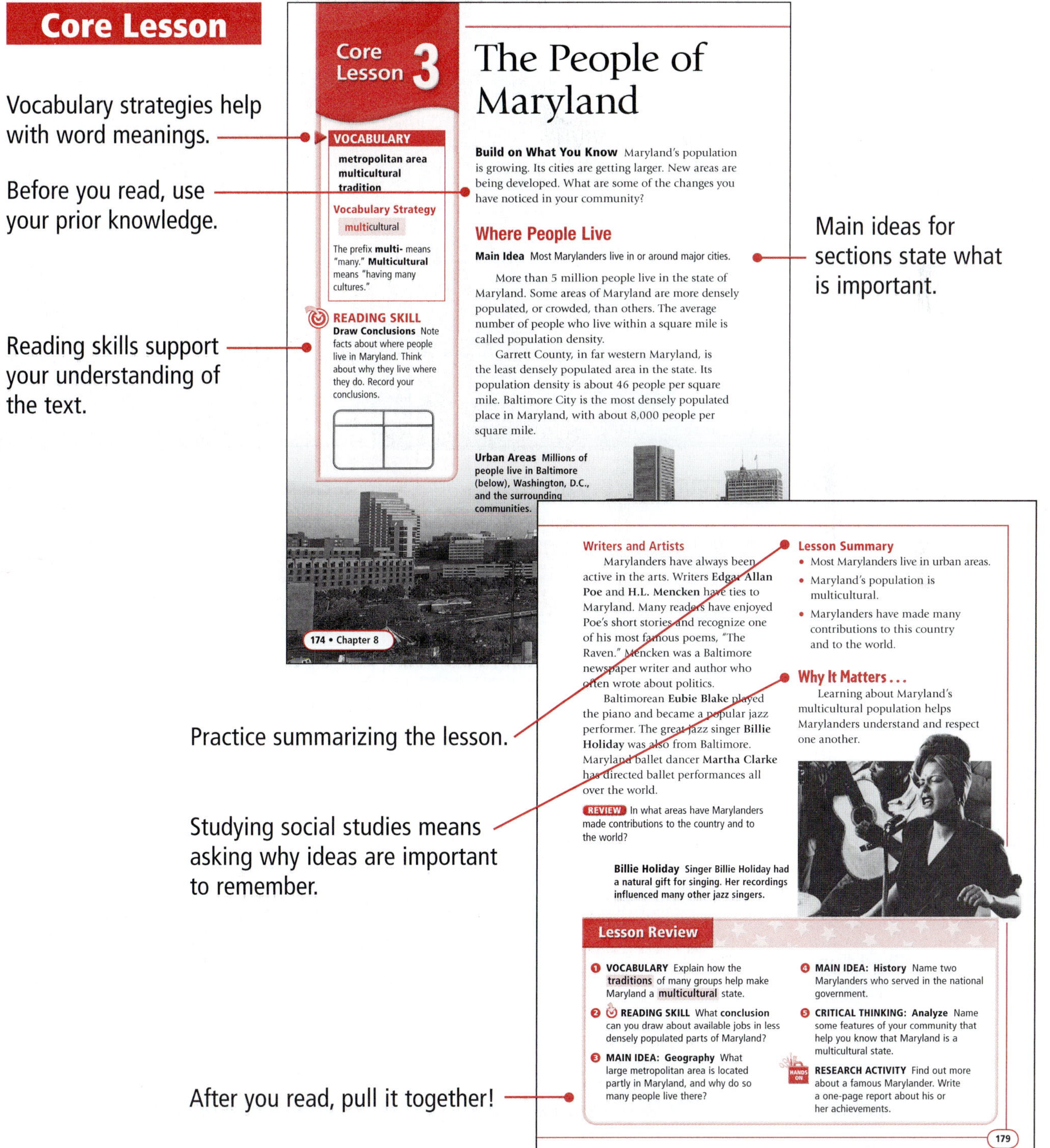

Core Lesson

Vocabulary strategies help with word meanings.

Before you read, use your prior knowledge.

Reading skills support your understanding of the text.

Main ideas for sections state what is important.

Practice summarizing the lesson.

Studying social studies means asking why ideas are important to remember.

After you read, pull it together!

Core Lesson 3

The People of Maryland

VOCABULARY

metropolitan area
multicultural
tradition

Vocabulary Strategy

multicultural

The prefix **multi-** means "many." **Multicultural** means "having many cultures."

READING SKILL

Draw Conclusions Note facts about where people live in Maryland. Think about why they live where they do. Record your conclusions.

Build on What You Know Maryland's population is growing. Its cities are getting larger. New areas are being developed. What are some of the changes you have noticed in your community?

Where People Live

Main Idea Most Marylanders live in or around major cities.

More than 5 million people live in the state of Maryland. Some areas of Maryland are more densely populated, or crowded, than others. The average number of people who live within a square mile is called population density.

Garrett County, in far western Maryland, is the least densely populated area in the state. Its population density is about 46 people per square mile. Baltimore City is the most densely populated place in Maryland, with about 8,000 people per square mile.

Urban Areas Millions of people live in Baltimore (below), Washington, D.C., and the surrounding communities.

174 • Chapter 8

Writers and Artists

Marylanders have always been active in the arts. Writers **Edgar Allan Poe** and **H.L. Mencken** have ties to Maryland. Many readers have enjoyed Poe's short stories and recognize one of his most famous poems, "The Raven." Mencken was a Baltimore newspaper writer and author who often wrote about politics.

Baltimorean **Eubie Blake** played the piano and became a popular jazz performer. The great jazz singer **Billie Holiday** was also from Baltimore. Maryland ballet dancer **Martha Clarke** has directed ballet performances all over the world.

REVIEW In what areas have Marylanders made contributions to the country and to the world?

Lesson Summary

- Most Marylanders live in urban areas.
- Maryland's population is multicultural.
- Marylanders have made many contributions to this country and to the world.

Why It Matters . . .

Learning about Maryland's multicultural population helps Marylanders understand and respect one another.

Billie Holiday Singer Billie Holiday had a natural gift for singing. Her recordings influenced many other jazz singers.

Lesson Review

1. **VOCABULARY** Explain how the traditions of many groups help make Maryland a multicultural state.
2. **READING SKILL** What conclusion can you draw about available jobs in less densely populated parts of Maryland?
3. **MAIN IDEA: Geography** What large metropolitan area is located partly in Maryland, and why do so many people live there?
4. **MAIN IDEA: History** Name two Marylanders who served in the national government.
5. **CRITICAL THINKING: Analyze** Name some features of your community that help you know that Maryland is a multicultural state.

HANDS ON **RESEARCH ACTIVITY** Find out more about a famous Marylander. Write a one-page report about his or her achievements.

179

3 Skills

Skill Building Learn map, graph, and study skills, as well as citizenship skills for life.

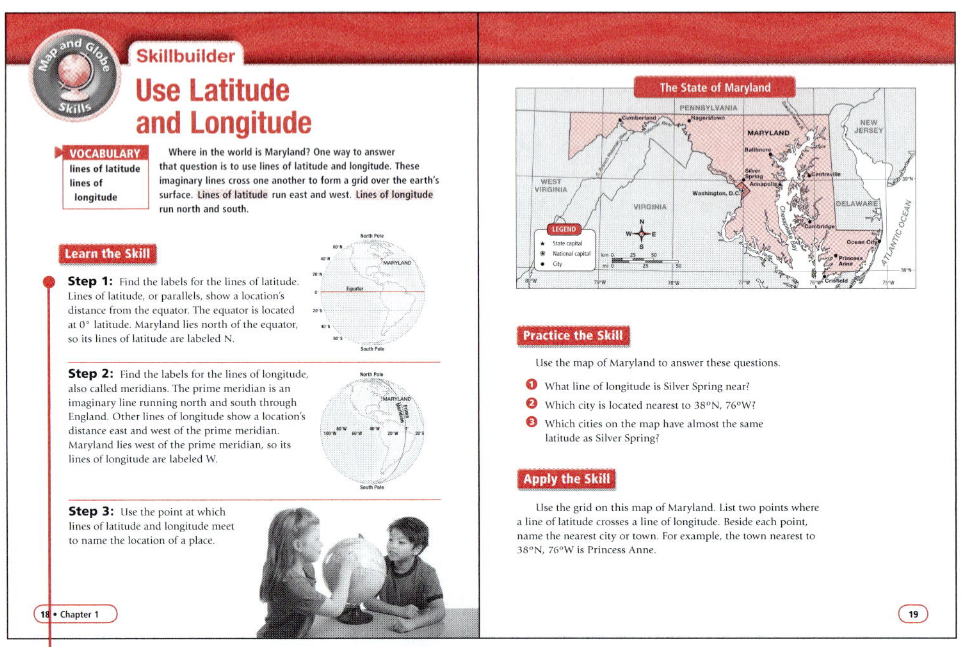

Skill lessons step it out.

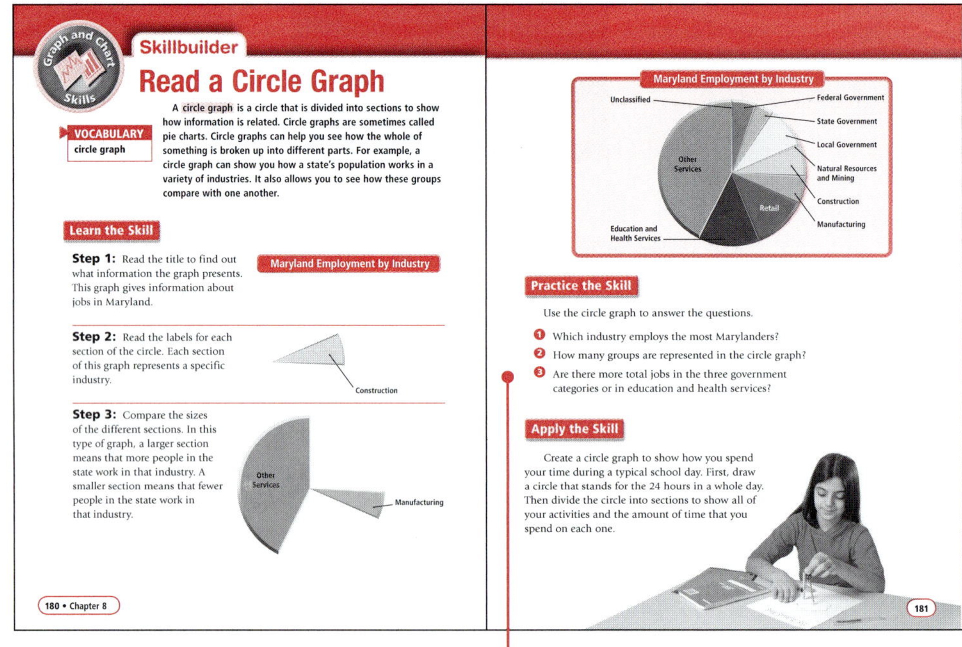

Practice and apply a social studies skill.

4 References

Citizenship Handbook

The back of your book includes sections you'll refer to again and again.

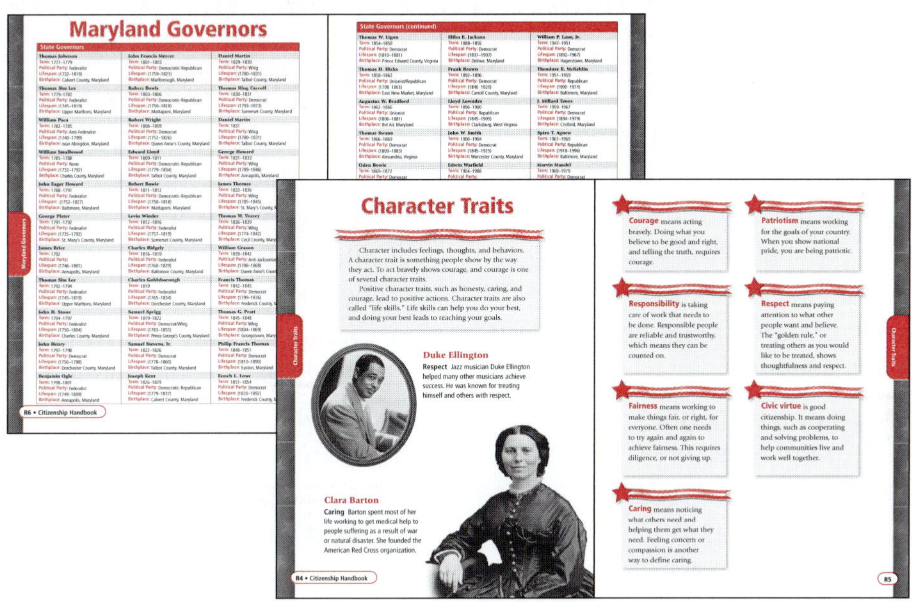

Resources

Look for atlas maps, a glossary of social studies terms, and an index.

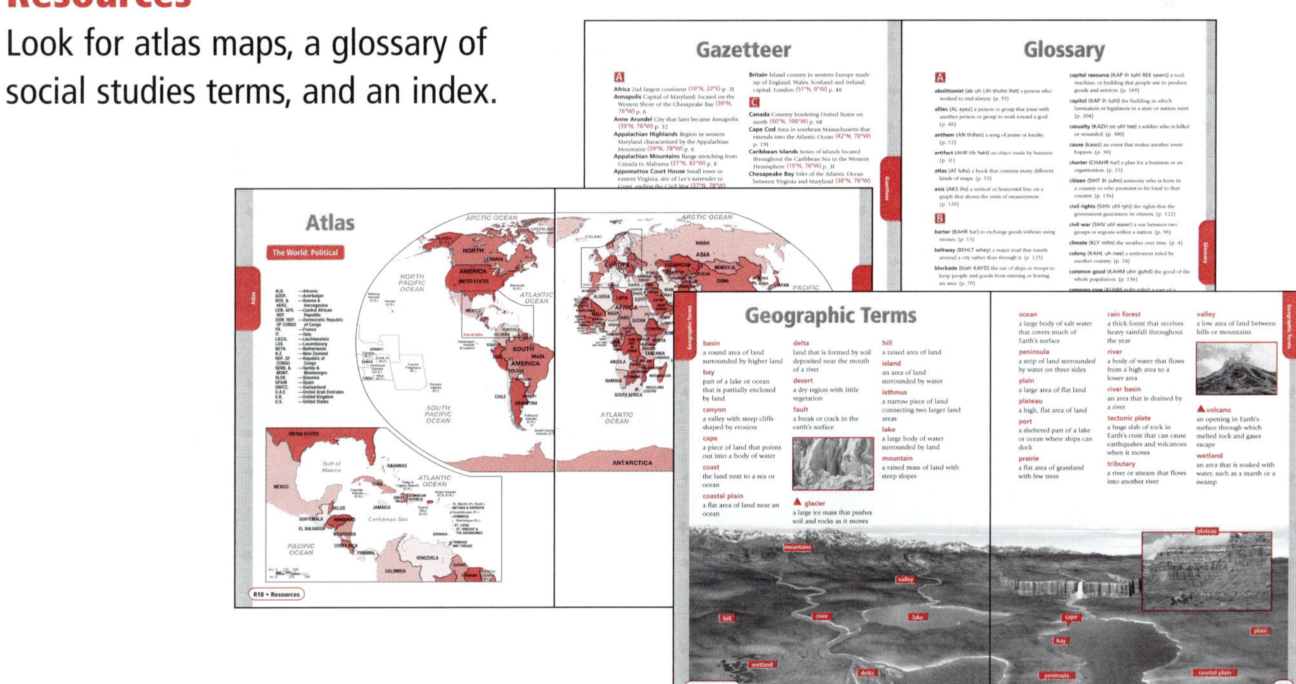

Reading Social Studies

Your book includes many features to help you be a successful reader. Here's what you will find:

VOCABULARY SUPPORT

Every chapter and lesson helps you with social studies terms. You'll build your vocabulary through strategies you're learning in language arts.

Preview
Get a jump start on four important words from the chapter.

Vocabulary Strategies
Focus on word roots, prefixes, suffixes, or compound words, for example.

Vocabulary Practice
Reuse words in the reviews and skills. Show that you know your vocabulary.

READING STRATEGIES

Look for the reading strategy and quick tip at the beginning of each chapter.

Predict and Infer
Before you read, think about what you'll learn.

Monitor and Clarify
Check your understanding. Could you explain what you just read to someone else?

Question
Stop and ask yourself a question. Did you understand what you read?

Summarize
After you read, think about the most important ideas of the lesson.

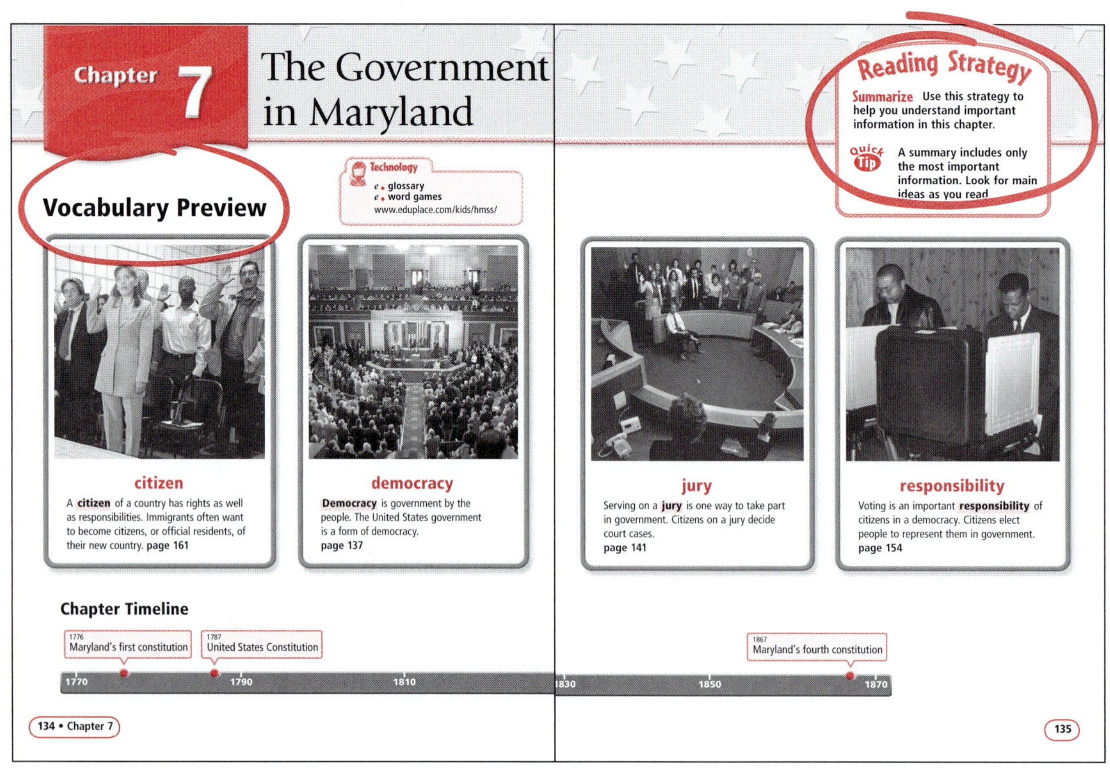

Chapter 7 The Government in Maryland

Vocabulary Preview

Technology
e• glossary
e• word games
www.eduplace.com/kids/hmss/

citizen
A **citizen** of a country has rights as well as responsibilities. Immigrants often want to become citizens, or official residents, of their new country. **page 161**

democracy
Democracy is government by the people. The United States government is a form of democracy.
page 137

jury
Serving on a **jury** is one way to take part in government. Citizens on a jury decide court cases.
page 141

responsibility
Voting is an important **responsibility** of citizens in a democracy. Citizens elect people to represent them in government.
page 154

Reading Strategy

Summarize Use this strategy to help you understand important information in this chapter.

Quick Tip A summary includes only the most important information. Look for main ideas as you read

Chapter Timeline

1776 Maryland's first constitution
1787 United States Constitution
1867 Maryland's fourth constitution

1770 1790 1810 1830 1850 1870

134 • Chapter 7

135

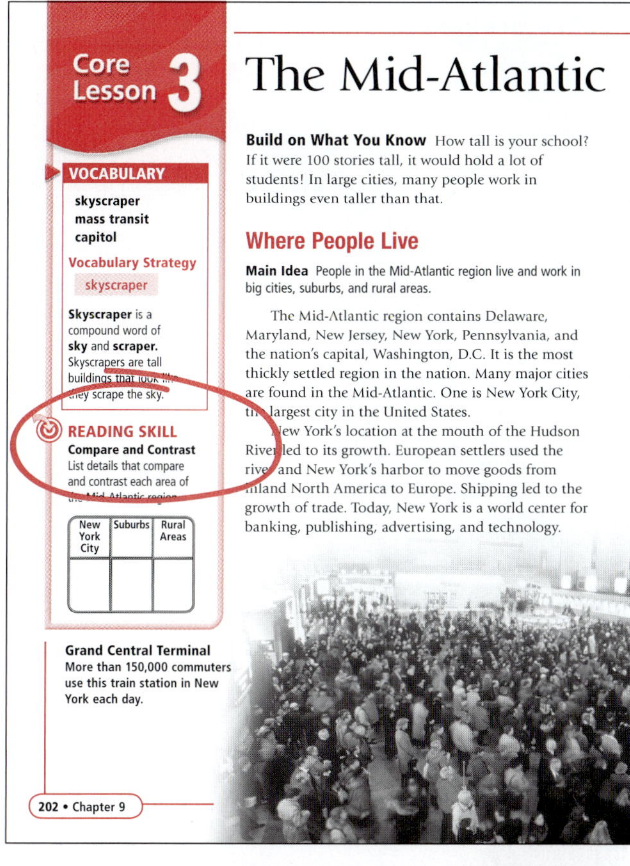

Core Lesson 3

The Mid-Atlantic

VOCABULARY

skyscraper
mass transit
capitol

Vocabulary Strategy

skyscraper

Skyscraper is a compound word of **sky** and **scraper.** Skyscrapers are tall buildings that look like they scrape the sky.

READING SKILL

Compare and Contrast List details that compare and contrast each area of the Mid-Atlantic region.

New York City	Suburbs	Rural Areas

Build on What You Know How tall is your school? If it were 100 stories tall, it would hold a lot of students! In large cities, many people work in buildings even taller than that.

Where People Live

Main Idea People in the Mid-Atlantic region live and work in big cities, suburbs, and rural areas.

The Mid-Atlantic region contains Delaware, Maryland, New Jersey, New York, Pennsylvania, and the nation's capital, Washington, D.C. It is the most thickly settled region in the nation. Many major cities are found in the Mid-Atlantic. One is New York City, the largest city in the United States.

New York's location at the mouth of the Hudson River led to its growth. European settlers used the river and New York's harbor to move goods from inland North America to Europe. Shipping led to the growth of trade. Today, New York is a world center for banking, publishing, advertising, and technology.

Grand Central Terminal More than 150,000 commuters use this train station in New York each day.

202 • Chapter 9

Public and Private Services

State governments are public institutions. That means they serve the state's people and communities. State services for the public include education, fire and police protection, and highways. States pay for public services by collecting taxes. A tax is a fee paid to the government. States may tax the money people earn, the property they own, and the things they buy.

State services are public. Services provided by a group or individual are private. For example, New Jersey builds public roads for everyone to use. However, private companies sell the cars and trucks that travel on the roads.

REVIEW What are the three branches of state government, and what do they do?

Lesson Summary

- The Mid-Atlantic has many large cities surrounded by suburbs.
- New York City, a financial and industrial center, is the biggest city in this region.
- Rural regions of the Mid-Atlantic support farming, mining, and tourism.
- State governments divide power among three branches.

Why It Matters . . .

Millions of people live and work in the Mid-Atlantic region. Workers in this region provide goods and services to the entire nation and the world.

Lesson Review

1. **VOCABULARY** Match each vocabulary term with its description.
   skyscraper capitol mass transit
   (a) transportation for many people; (b) very tall building; (c) building in which legislators meet
2. **READING SKILL Compare and contrast** public and private services.
3. **MAIN IDEA: Culture** In what ways is living in a city different from living in a rural area?
4. **MAIN IDEA: Geography** What is one difference between a capital city and other cities?
5. **CRITICAL THINKING: Infer** Why do you think more people rely on mass transit in a city than in a suburb?

HANDS ON **CURRENT EVENTS ACTIVITY** Read about what is happening in one Mid-Atlantic state. What is one major issue the state's government is dealing with?

205

READING SKILLS

As you read, organize the information. These reading skills will help you:

Sequence
Cause and Effect
Compare and Contrast
Problem and Solution
Draw Conclusions
Predict Outcomes
Categorize (or) Classify
Main Idea and Details

COMPREHENSION SUPPORT

Build on What You Know

Check your prior knowledge. You may already know a lot!

Review Questions

Connect with the text. Did you understand what you just read?

Summaries

Look for three ways to summarize–a list, an organizer, or a paragraph.

UNIT 1

The Land and Settlement of Maryland

Why do people move to new places?

"*Here are . . . plains, valleys, rivers, and brooks, all running most pleasantly into a fair [beautiful] bay. . .*"

Captain John Smith, describing the land around Chesapeake Bay, 1606

Leonard Calvert

c. 1606–1647

Leonard Calvert traveled far from his home in Ireland to start a new colony on the Chesapeake Bay. **page 30**

History Makers

Anne Arundell

1615–1649

Maryland settlers named a town after Anne Arundell, the wife of Cecil Calvert. The town became Annapolis. **page 39**

Matthias De Sousa

Dates unknown

During the 1600s De Sousa started a business providing furs for hat-makers in England. He later became involved in Maryland's government. **page 35**

Chapter 1 Maryland's Land and Early People

Vocabulary Preview

wetland

This **wetland** near Chesapeake Bay is an important part of Maryland's natural environment. Wetlands are home to all kinds of animals and plants. **page 5**

artifact

Scientists can examine an **artifact** to learn how people lived long ago. Artifacts may include spear tips, fishing hooks, and other things that early people made. **page 11**

Chapter Timeline

About 11,000 years ago
People living in Maryland

12,000 years ago

8,000 years ago

Reading Strategy

Predict and Infer Use this strategy before you read.

Look at the pictures in the lesson to predict what it will be about.

natural resource

The good soil near Maryland's rivers is a **natural resource** that Maryland Indians depended on. They grew crops such as corn. **page 12**

longhouse

Maryland Indian families often lived together in a **longhouse.** They used wood poles and bark to build these shelters. **page 16**

About 3,000 years ago
People begin living in villages

About 1,000 years ago
People begin to farm in Maryland

4,000 years ago — Today

Core Lesson 1

Land and Water of Maryland

VOCABULARY

- **climate**
- **landform**
- **elevation**
- **wetland**
- **region**

Vocabulary Strategy

landform

Think about the meaning of the two smaller words in the compound word **landform.** A **landform** is a **form,** or shape, of the **land,** such as a mountain or a valley.

READING SKILL

Main Idea and Details Write the main idea from the section "Chesapeake Bay" and add details to support it.

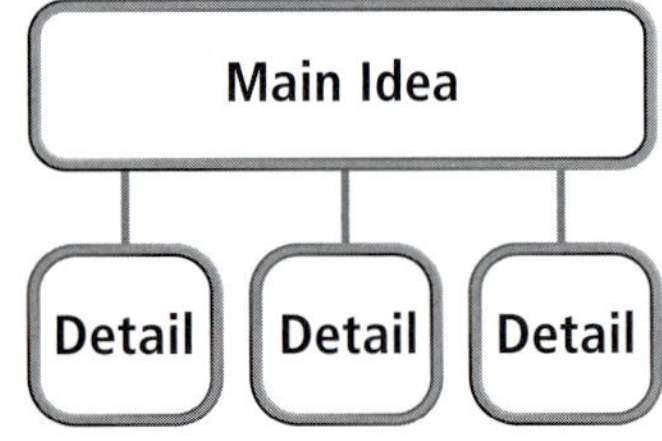

Build on What You Know How would you describe the land where you live? Is it flat or hilly? Can you see mountains or the ocean? The physical features of Maryland take many forms.

Land and Water

Main Idea Maryland has many kinds of land and water features.

Maryland is a state in the middle of the Atlantic coastline. It has much natural beauty and a pleasant climate. A **climate** is the weather in a place over time. Maryland's landforms include mountains, hills, valleys, and plains. A **landform** is a feature of the earth's surface.

The Potomac River and the Chesapeake Bay are Maryland's main bodies of water. The Potomac is Maryland's longest river. It forms part of the state's southwestern border with Virginia and West Virginia. The Potomac empties into the Chesapeake Bay. A bay is a small body of water set off from a larger body of water. The Chesapeake Bay is set off from the Atlantic Ocean. Beaches in eastern Maryland border the ocean.

The Chesapeake Bay The Chesapeake Bay divides Maryland into two large areas—the Eastern Shore and the Western Shore.

The Great Falls Many waterfalls mark the fall line on the Potomac River.

From Mountains to Shore

Elevations across Maryland vary widely. **Elevation** is the height of a landform above sea level. Sea level is the level of the surface of the world's oceans.

Maryland's highest elevations are in the western part of the state. As you go east, mountains change to rolling hills. Even farther east, the state becomes much flatter when you cross the fall line. The fall line is a line of waterfalls that divides the hilly and flat sections of the state. Beyond the fall line, to the east, the flat land around the Chesapeake Bay is just above sea level.

The Chesapeake Bay

The Chesapeake Bay is one of Maryland's most important physical features. The shoreline of the Chesapeake Bay is over 3,000 miles long. It includes wetlands. A **wetland** is land that is covered by water for part of the year, such as a marsh or swamp.

Most of Maryland's rivers empty into the Chesapeake Bay. The fresh water from the rivers meets with the salt water from the Atlantic Ocean. This provides the Chesapeake Bay with an unusual environment.

REVIEW How is the land in eastern Maryland different from the land in western Maryland?

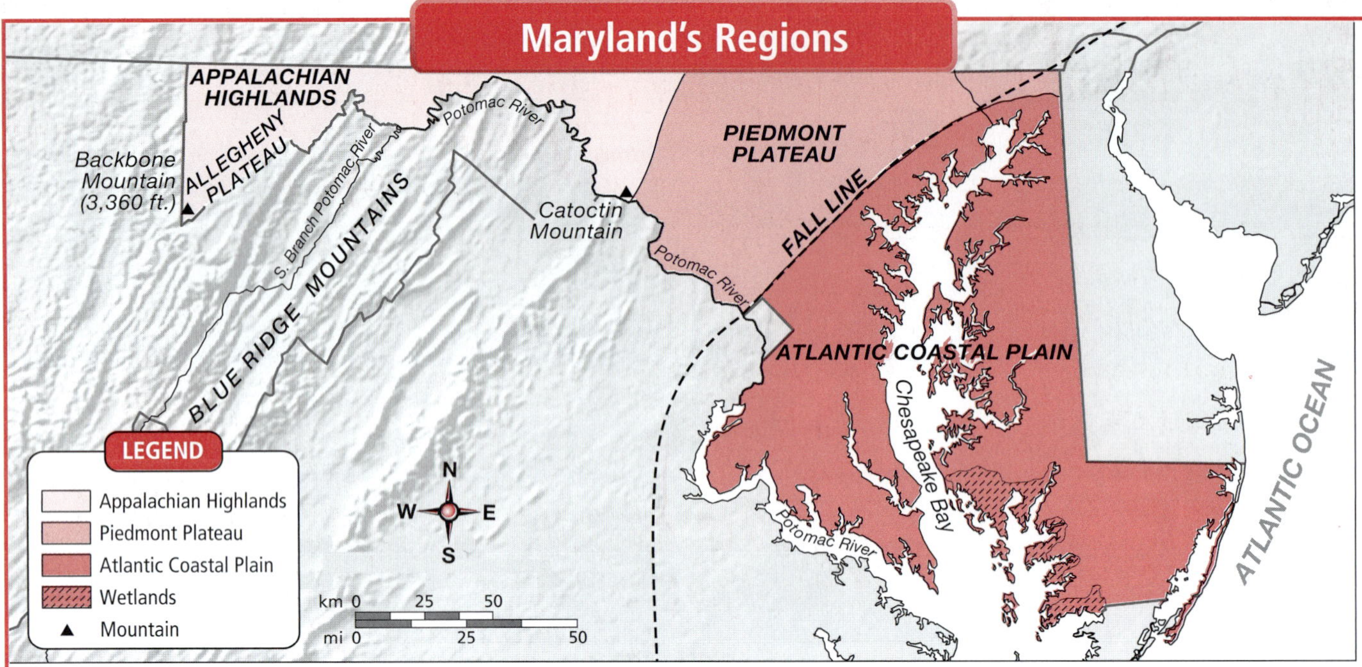

Three Regions, Three Climates The farther west you go in Maryland, the higher the elevation, and the cooler the climate.

SKILL **Reading Maps** Which of Maryland's regions is the largest?

Maryland's Regions

Main Idea Maryland has three major natural regions.

Maryland can be divided into three natural regions. A **region** is an area that shares various features, such as landforms or climate. Maryland's three natural regions are the Appalachian Highlands, the Piedmont Plateau, and the Atlantic Coastal Plain.

The Appalachian Highlands

The Appalachian Highlands stretch across western Maryland. The Allegheny Plateau is a raised area in western Maryland. East of the plateau are the Blue Ridge Mountains.

Between the mountain ridges in this region are deep valleys. Because of their elevation, the Appalachian Highlands have the coolest climate in Maryland.

The Piedmont Plateau

East of the Appalachian Highlands lies the Piedmont Plateau. Land in the Piedmont Plateau is hilly, but lower than the land in the Appalachian Highlands. In fact, *piedmont* means "foot of the mountain." The eastern boundary of the Piedmont Plateau is the fall line. The climate there is milder than it is in the western mountains.

Farming in Montgomery County Many farms such as this one produce crops and dairy products on the Piedmont Plateau.

The Atlantic Coastal Plain

The southeastern half of Maryland makes up the Atlantic Coastal Plain. The Chesapeake Bay divides the plain into two parts, the Eastern Shore and the Western Shore. Land on the Eastern Shore is mostly flat. Land on the Western Shore is more hilly.

Water is a major physical feature of this region. Smaller bays and streams cross the land along the Chesapeake Bay. Almost a quarter of the Eastern Shore is wetlands.

The waters of the Chesapeake Bay and the Atlantic Ocean help keep the weather from becoming very hot or very cold. The Atlantic Coastal Plain has the mildest climate in the state.

REVIEW Compare and contrast the climates of Maryland's three regions.

Between the Ocean and the Bay Maryland's Ocean City is on a barrier island that separates the Atlantic Ocean from the Chincoteague Bay.

Lesson Summary

Maryland's Regions

Region	Geography
Appalachian Highlands	mountains, valleys, cooler climate
Piedmont Plateau	hills, valleys, fall line, milder climate
Atlantic Coastal Plain	low, flat or rolling land, bays, wetlands, very mild climate

Why It Matters . . .

Physical features such as climate and landforms help determine how and where Marylanders live, work, and play.

Lesson Review

1. **VOCABULARY** Describe Maryland's physical features using the following words:
   elevation **wetland**
2. **READING SKILL** Name specific **details** that tell about this **main idea:** Maryland has many kinds of land and water features.
3. **MAIN IDEA: Geography** What are the sources of the water in the Chesapeake Bay?
4. **MAIN IDEA: Geography** Name Maryland's three natural regions.
5. **MAIN IDEA: Geography** Compare Maryland's three natural regions.
6. **CRITICAL THINKING: Synthesize** Describe the land and water features where you live.

ART ACTIVITY Make a map of the natural region in which you live. Show its main landforms and bodies of water.

Skillbuilder

Review Map Skills

VOCABULARY
- legend
- compass rose
- map scale

Globes and maps show the surface of the earth. A globe is a model of the earth, so it is round. A map is a flat picture of all or part of the round earth.

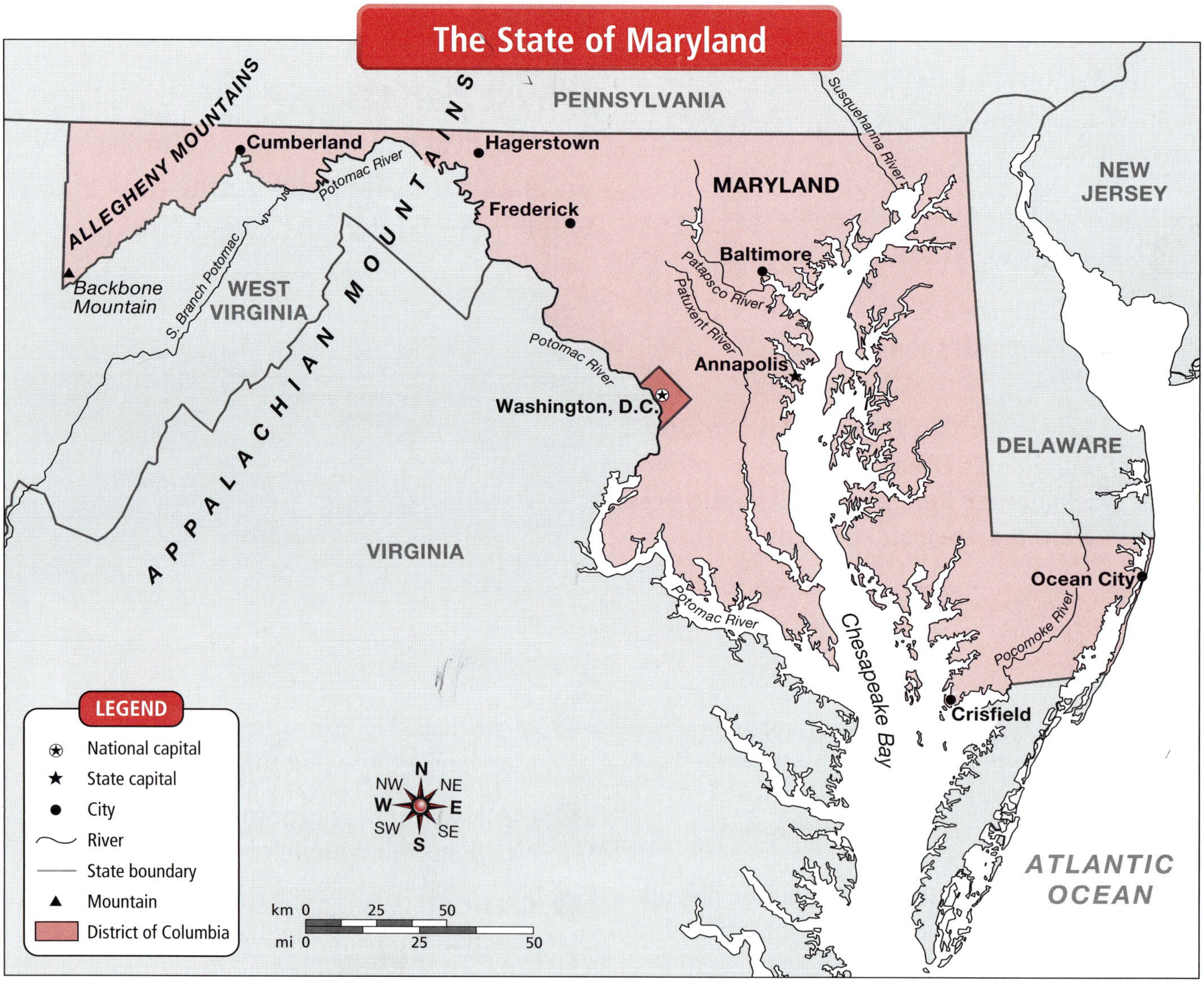

The State of Maryland

PENNSYLVANIA
ALLEGHENY MOUNTAINS
Cumberland
Hagerstown
Potomac River
Susquehanna River
MARYLAND
NEW JERSEY
Frederick
Baltimore
Backbone Mountain
S. Branch Potomac
WEST VIRGINIA
APPALACHIAN MOUNTAINS
Patapsco River
Patuxent River
Potomac River
Annapolis
Washington, D.C.
DELAWARE
VIRGINIA
Ocean City
Potomac River
Chesapeake Bay
Pocomoke River
Crisfield
ATLANTIC OCEAN

LEGEND
- National capital
- State capital
- City
- River
- State boundary
- Mountain
- District of Columbia

N, NE, E, SE, S, SW, W, NW

km 0 25 50
mi 0 25 50

Learn the Skill

Step 1: Read the map title to find out what the map shows.

The State of Maryland

Step 2: Study the map legend. The **legend** explains what the colors, symbols, and lines on the map stand for.

LEGEND

- National capital
- State capital
- City
- River
- State boundary
- Mountain
- District of Columbia

Step 3: Use the **compass rose** to find main directions such as north, south, east, and west. The compass rose also shows intermediate directions such as northeast, southwest, northwest, and southeast.

Step 4: Use the **map scale** to find the distance between locations.

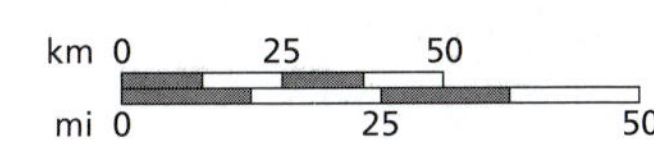

Practice the Skill

Use the map on page 8 to answer these questions.

1. What symbol stands for the state capital? What is the capital of Maryland?
2. Is Annapolis north or south of Baltimore?
3. About how many miles are between Cumberland and Hagerstown?

Apply the Skill

Choose any starting point on the map on page 8. Write step-by-step instructions to tell someone how to get from one place to another.

Core Lesson 2

The First People of Maryland

VOCABULARY

prehistoric
artifact
natural resource
trade
barter

Vocabulary Strategy

prehistoric

The prefix **pre-** in **prehistoric** means "before." Prehistoric means the time before people began to write.

READING SKILL

Sequence As you read, use an organizer to put important events in the correct order.

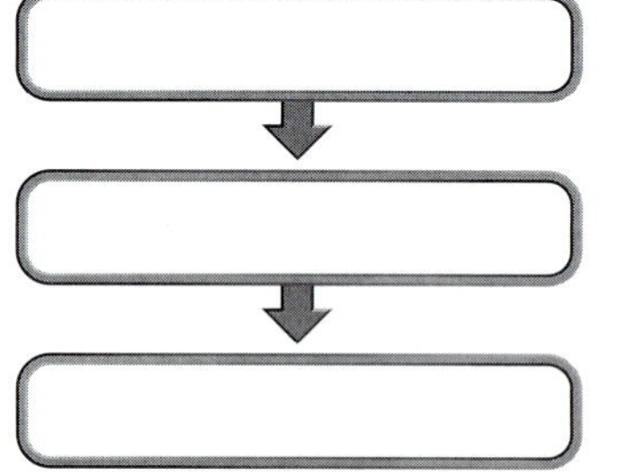

Build on What You Know Where does the food you eat come from? The earliest people of Maryland had no stores or gardens. How do you think they got their food?

People Come to Maryland

Main Idea Scientists believe that people first came to Maryland thousands of years ago when land was very different.

The land around you has changed over time. Long ago, during the Ice Age, much of the land was covered with ice.

Many scientists believe that an area of dry land, called a land bridge, connected Asia and North America. Animals from Asia may have crossed this land bridge to North America. People who hunted those animals may have followed them. Other scientists think that people might have used boats to travel from Asia to North America. Slowly, these early people spread across the continent.

Early Hunting During the Ice Age, huge animals such as these woolly mammoths provided food for the first North Americans.

Prehistoric Indian Tools

Spear Prehistoric Indians living in present-day Maryland used spears to hunt for food.

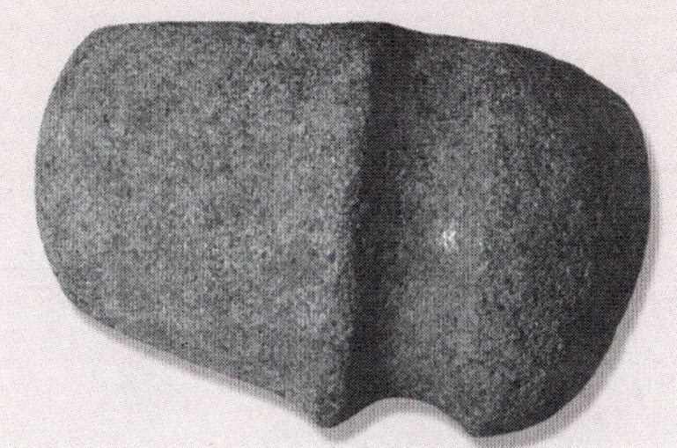

Axe A stone axe head would have been used to cut down trees and to hollow logs.

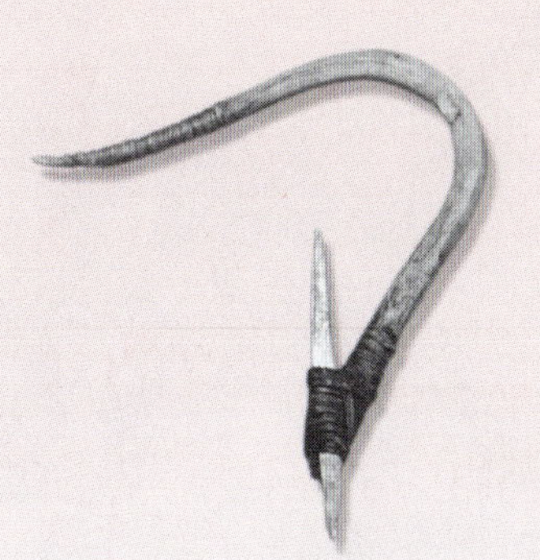

Fish Hooks Fish hooks were used by early American Indians living near the Chesapeake Bay to catch fish for food.

Early People

The first people to come to what is now Maryland are called Paleo-Indians. Many scientists believe that Paleo-Indians were living in Maryland about 11,000 years ago. Little is known about Paleo-Indians because they arrived during prehistoric times. The word **prehistoric** describes people and things that existed before writing was invented. To learn how prehistoric people lived, scientists study artifacts. An **artifact** is an object made by humans. Spear points, fishing hooks, and cooking pots are kinds of artifacts.

The scientists who study artifacts ask questions about them: When were they made? What were they made of? How were they used? By answering such questions, scientists learn what life was like for prehistoric people.

As Paleo-Indians reached Maryland, the Ice Age was ending. The climate became warmer. Ice melted, and seawater flooded over the land, creating the Chesapeake Bay.

Because of these changes, people had to change the way they lived. Early Americans changed their way of life so much that scientists gave them a new name. Scientists call the people who lived in Maryland about 10,000 years ago Archaic (ar KA ik) Indians. Archaic Indians gathered food like the Paleo-Indians had, but they also began to hunt smaller animals because the larger animals were dying out. Archaic Indians invented new types of tools, such as fishhooks and spear-throwers. They also began to depend more on fishing to survive.

REVIEW How did climate affect the lives of early people in present-day Maryland?

Ancient Farmlands The rich soil around Maryland's rivers attracted early farmers.

The Woodland Indians

Main Idea The Woodland Indians in Maryland began to settle in villages, grow crops, and trade.

Over time, the Archaic Indians also began to change their way of life. They began to settle in villages and to farm. These first settlers are known as the Woodland Indians because they lived in the thick forests of the East.

Scientists think that the first Woodland Indians in Maryland settled on the Atlantic Coastal Plain about 1,000 years ago. There were plenty of fish and shellfish for food on the coast and in the rivers. The Chesapeake Bay area provided many natural resources. A **natural resource** is something useful from nature.

Ancient Hoe Tools such as this one helped Maryland's early farmers to raise their crops.

In addition to using the natural resources provided by the Chesapeake Bay, Woodland Indians in Maryland learned how to grow their own food. They used the rich soil to grow corn, beans, and squash in the Piedmont and along the Atlantic Coastal Plain. Over time, farming became the main source of food for Woodland Indians in present-day Maryland. People on the Eastern Shore farmed but depended mostly on fishing for food.

As Woodland Indians depended more on farming, they needed to stay in one place so they could raise their crops. They settled in villages. Woodland Indians in Maryland found ways to share their food with other villages. They stored food at a central place that was easy for people from nearby villages to reach.

Trade

The Woodland Indians of Maryland did not have all of the natural resources they needed. To solve this problem, they set up trade with other American Indian groups in distant places. **Trade** is the exchange of goods and services. A good is a product that someone might need, such as furs or tools. A service is work done for someone, such as repairing a tool.

Woodland Indians did not use money. Instead, they bartered. To **barter** is to trade one item for another item. Woodland Indians in Maryland traded goods such as pottery for other goods such as beads.

REVIEW In what ways did the Woodland Indians differ from the Paleo-Indians?

Lesson Summary

Scientists believe people reached Maryland about 11,000 years ago. The Chesapeake Bay provided early settlers with many natural resources. By about 1,000 years ago, Woodland Indians in present-day Maryland settled in villages, farmed, and traded.

Why It Matters . . .

The first Marylanders depended on the area's water, plants, and animals to live. Today, Marylanders still depend on these natural resources.

Shellfish Early people found oysters and other shellfish in the Chesapeake Bay. Shellfish were an important source of food.

Lesson Review

1. **VOCABULARY** Use **barter** and **trade** to describe the life of the Woodland Indians.
2. **READING SKILL** Review your **sequence** chart. Who were the first people in Maryland?
3. **MAIN IDEA: History** What changes affected the Paleo-Indians as they reached Maryland? How did they change as a result?
4. **MAIN IDEA: Geography** Why did Woodland Indians settle on the coast or near rivers?
5. **TIMELINE SKILL** About how long ago did people first come to Maryland?
6. **CRITICAL THINKING: Infer** Why do you think that Woodland Indians on the Eastern Shore continued to get their food mostly through fishing, even after most others were farming?

WRITING ACTIVITY Write a short conversation between two Woodland Indians living in different parts of Maryland. Tell about where and how each one lived.

Core Lesson 3

Maryland Indians

VOCABULARY

culture
custom
longhouse

Vocabulary Strategy

longhouse

The compound word **longhouse** is made up of two words, **long** and **house.**

READING SKILL

Compare and Contrast
Note ways that American Indian groups in Maryland were alike and different.

Build on What You Know Have you ever been fishing? American Indians living near the Chesapeake Bay fished. They depended on the bay's many resources for their needs.

Eastern Woodland Indians

Main Idea The Nanticoke, the Piscataway, and the Susquehannock were three Eastern Woodland groups.

The American Indians who lived in Maryland about 400 years ago had a culture that was similar to many other Indian groups in eastern North America. A **culture** is a way of life shared by a certain group of people. People who share a culture often share ideas, languages, art, and customs. A **custom** is a way of doing something that is shared by a group, such as shaking hands when saying hello.

The American Indian groups who lived in the forests of much of eastern North America did not all share the same language. However, they are all called Eastern Woodland Indians.

An Eastern Woodland Village
This American Indian village in what is now Maryland included homes and storage buildings surrounded by a wall of pointed logs.

Nanticoke Basket This Nanticoke basket is made from pine needles. It contains pine nuts, which some American Indians gathered for food.

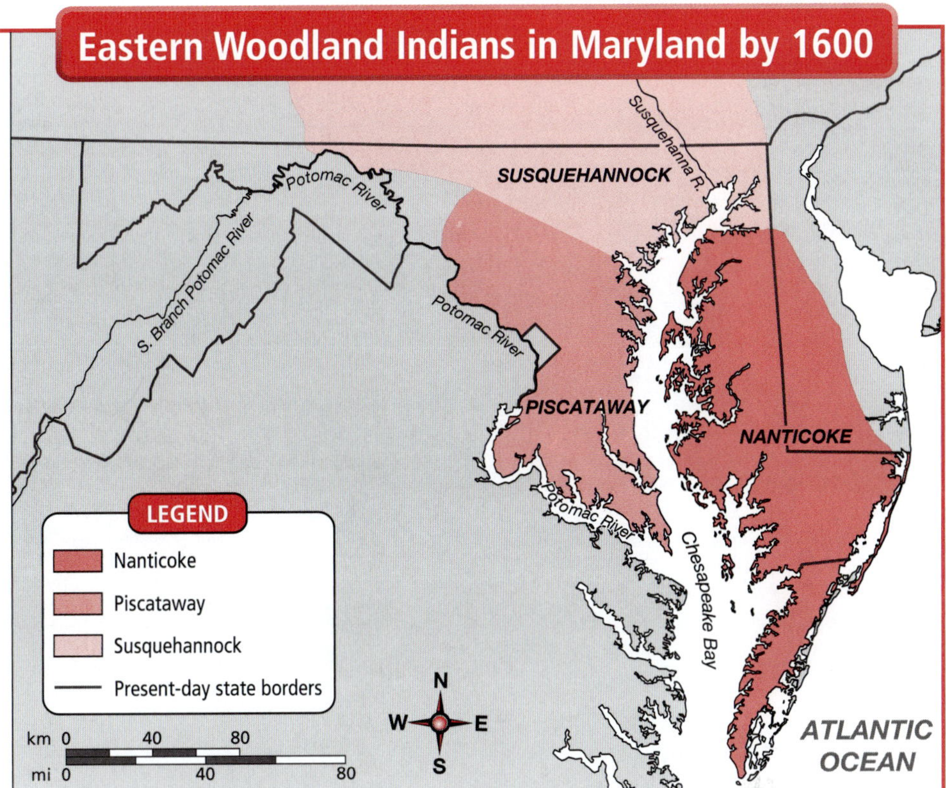

Living Around the Bay Many groups of American Indians lived near the Chesapeake Bay. **SKILL** **Reading Maps** What group of Maryland Indians lived along the Atlantic coast?

The Nanticoke and the Piscataway

By the 1600s, several Eastern Woodland groups had settled around the Chesapeake Bay. The largest Woodland group on the Eastern Shore was the Nanticoke (NAN tih kohk), which means "people of the tidewater." The Nanticoke grew corn, beans, and squash, but they mostly fished for their food. They lived in small round homes called wigwams and traveled in canoes they carved from wood.

The Piscataway (pis KAT uh way) was the largest group on the Western Shore. Their main village was near the mouth of the Piscataway Creek. The chief, or ruler of Piscataway, also ruled over many other Piscataway villages.

The Susquehannock

The Susquehannock (sus kwuh HAN ok) were members of a large and powerful Woodland Indian group. They lived in walled villages north of the Chesapeake Bay along the Susquehanna River in present-day Maryland, Pennsylvania, and New York.

They often fought wars against less powerful groups to the south, such as the Piscataway. Like other groups that lived on the Western Shore, the Susquehannock depended mostly on farming.

REVIEW Name three Eastern Woodland groups that lived near the Chesapeake Bay in the 1600s.

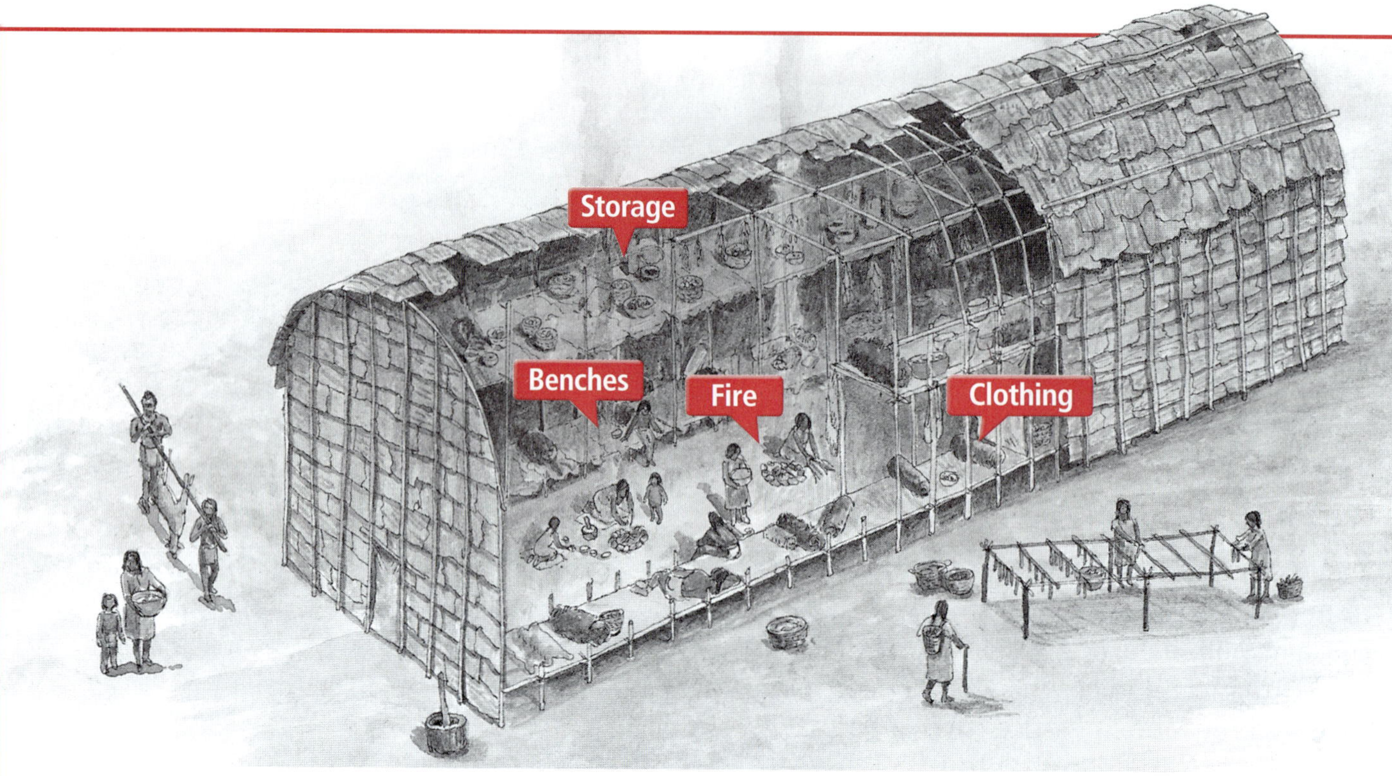

Longhouse The Eastern Woodland Indians built longhouses by pushing long poles into the ground, then bending them over to form a roof. They built walls of sharpened logs around their villages for protection.

Ways of Life

Main Idea Maryland Indians depended on the environment to meet their basic needs.

The forests and rivers of the woodlands provided most of what the Nanticoke, Piscataway, and Susquehannock needed to live. They fished, hunted, and raised crops. They also gathered berries, roots, nuts, and other wild foods. They made clothes from animal skins and grasses. Their clothing was decorated with shells, beads, and paint.

Like most Eastern Woodland Indians, Maryland Indians built longhouses for shelter. A **longhouse** was a large house with a frame of wood poles covered with sheets of bark. A number of families shared one longhouse.

Eastern Woodlands Society

Woodland Indian groups usually had two chiefs. One chief made decisions during times of peace and the other ruled during times of war. Important decisions needed to be approved by a council of wise men. A council is a group of people chosen to make important decisions or give advice.

Within each village, men and women divided the work. The men fished and hunted. They built houses and made tools and weapons. Men also traded and defended the village. The women gathered food, farmed, and cooked. They also took care of the children and made clothing.

Maryland Indians Today

Some American Indians live in Maryland today. They are proud of their connections to Maryland's past. Many of them gather at festivals and other celebrations. There, they celebrate their culture and share it with others. They perform traditional ceremonies, as well as dancing, singing, drumming, and storytelling.

People of all backgrounds can also learn about American Indian culture at these festivals and at the Piscataway Indian Museum and the Baltimore American Indian Center.

REVIEW Describe how the land and water provided what Maryland Indians needed to live.

Lesson Summary

- The Nanticoke, Piscataway, and Susquehannock lived in Maryland in the 1600s.
- American Indians in Maryland lived in villages with a common culture.

Why It Matters . . .

American Indians used many resources near the Chesapeake Bay long ago. Today, many Marylanders still depend on the natural resources there.

Science Class in Maryland Many Piscataway children, such as these students in St. Mary's county, live in Maryland today.

Lesson Review

1. **VOCABULARY** Use the words **culture** and **custom** to describe Woodland Indians in Maryland.
2. **READING SKILL Compare** What are two important ways in which Woodland Indian groups in Maryland were alike?
3. **MAIN IDEA: Geography** Why do you think the Nanticoke depended on fishing more than the Susquehannock?
4. **MAIN IDEA: Government** Describe how Maryland's Indian groups made important decisions.
5. **MAIN IDEA: Culture** How do Maryland's American Indians continue to celebrate their culture today?
6. **CRITICAL THINKING: Infer** How might one American Indian group learn about the culture of another group through trade, even if they spoke different languages?

WRITING ACTIVITY Use library resources to learn more about the Nanticoke, the Piscataway, or the Susquehannock. Write a one-page report telling something new that you learned about the group you chose.

Skillbuilder

Use Latitude and Longitude

VOCABULARY
lines of latitude
lines of longitude

Where in the world is Maryland? One way to answer that question is to use lines of latitude and longitude. These imaginary lines cross one another to form a grid over the earth's surface. Lines of latitude run east and west. Lines of longitude run north and south.

Learn the Skill

Step 1: Find the labels for the lines of latitude. Lines of latitude, or parallels, show a location's distance from the equator. The equator is located at 0° latitude. Maryland lies north of the equator, so its lines of latitude are labeled N.

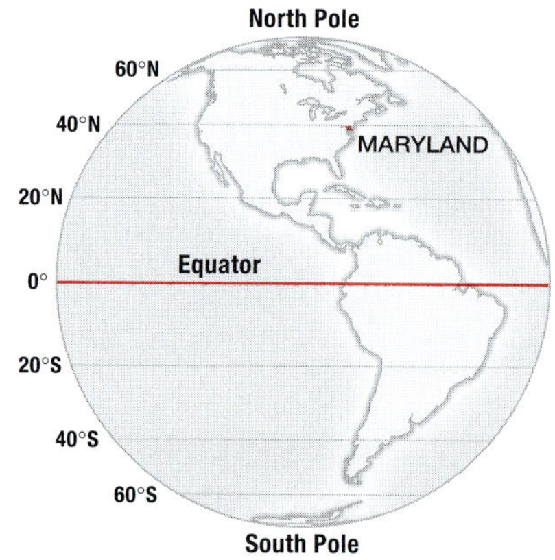

Step 2: Find the labels for the lines of longitude, also called meridians. The prime meridian is an imaginary line running north and south through England. Other lines of longitude show a location's distance east and west of the prime meridian. Maryland lies west of the prime meridian, so its lines of longitude are labeled W.

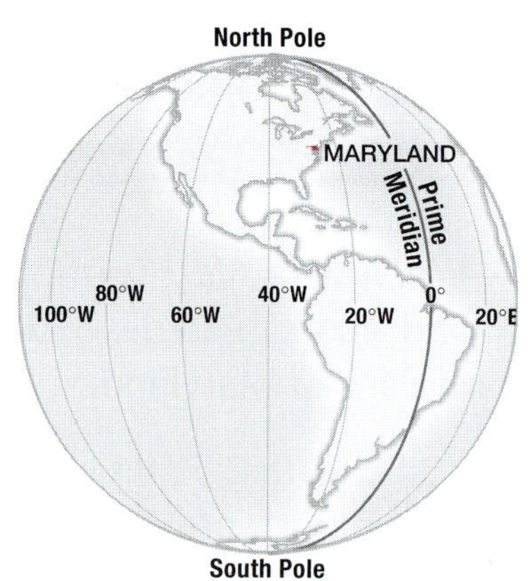

Step 3: Use the point at which lines of latitude and longitude meet to name the location of a place.

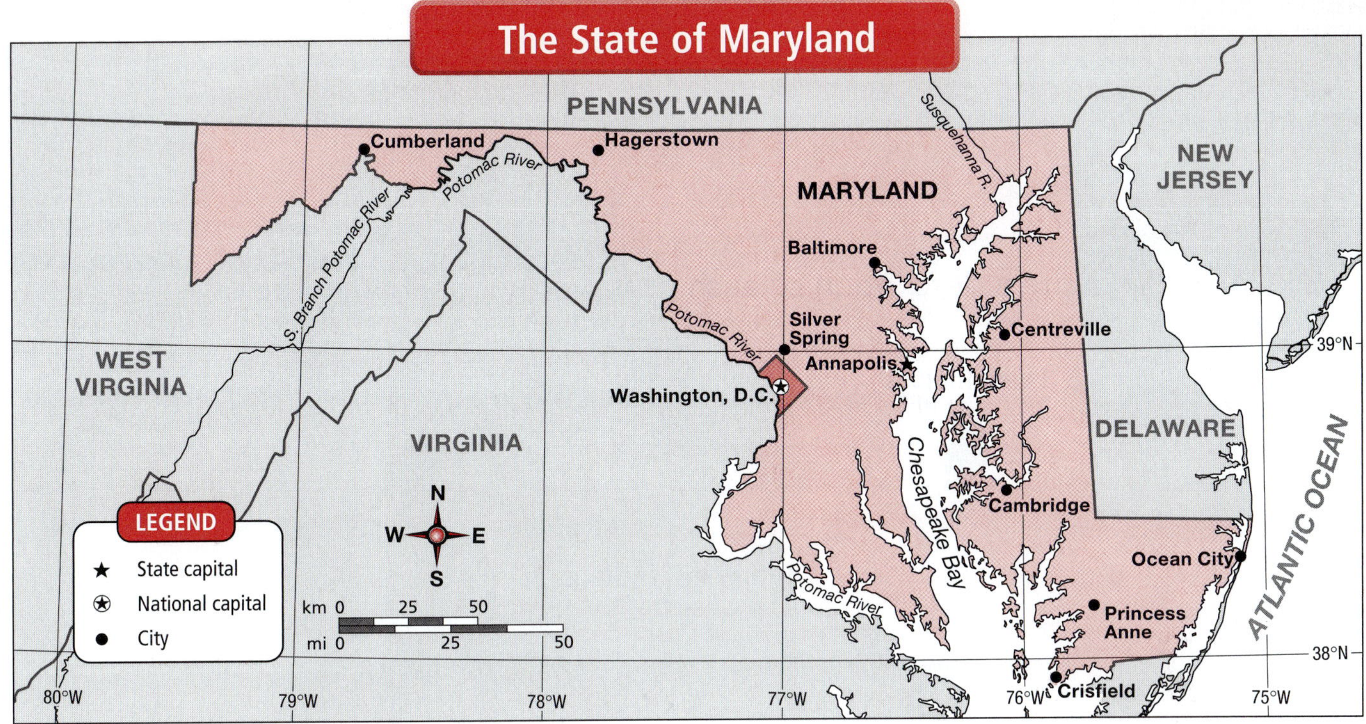

Practice the Skill

Use the map of Maryland to answer these questions.

1. What line of longitude is Silver Spring near?
2. Which city is located nearest to 38°N, 76°W?
3. Which cities on the map have almost the same latitude as Silver Spring?

Apply the Skill

Use the grid on this map of Maryland. List two points where a line of latitude crosses a line of longitude. Beside each point, name the nearest city or town. For example, the town nearest to 39°N, 76°W is Centreville.

Chapter 1 Review and Test Prep

Visual Summary

1 – 4. Write a description of each group of people named below.

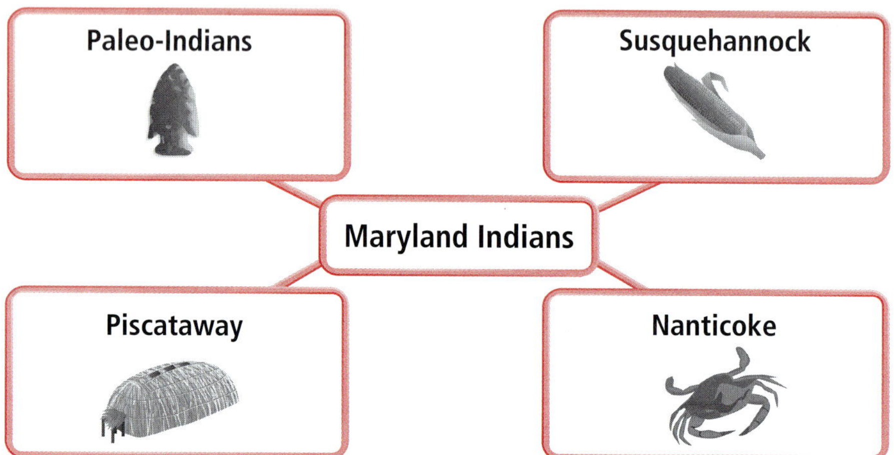

Facts and Main Ideas

TEST PREP Answer each question below.

5. **Geography** What are the three natural regions of Maryland?
6. **Geography** What body of water divides the Eastern Shore and the Western Shore?
7. **Economics** How did Woodland peoples get things they could not make?
8. **History** How was the environment changing as Paleo-Indians reached Maryland?
9. **Culture** How do Maryland Indians celebrate their culture today?

Vocabulary

TEST PREP Choose the correct word from the list below to complete each sentence.

landform, p. 4
artifact, p. 11
custom, p. 14

10. An object made by humans is an ______.
11. A ______ is a feature on the earth's surface, such as a mountain.
12. People who share the same culture might also share a ______ such as shaking hands when they meet.

CHAPTER SUMMARY TIMELINE

About 11,000 years ago
People living in Maryland

About 1,000 years ago
People begin farming in Maryland

12,000 years ago | 8,000 years ago | 4,000 years ago | Today

Apply Skills

TEST PREP **Map Skill** Study the map of Maryland below. Then use what you have learned about reading a map to answer each question.

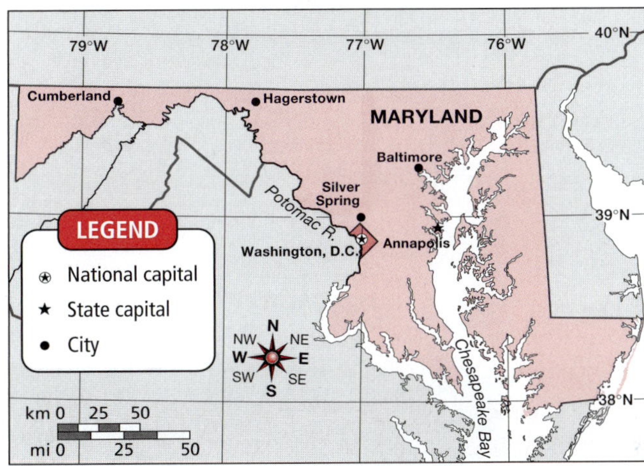

13. In which direction would you travel from Cumberland to the Chesapeake Bay?

A. northeast
B. south
C. southeast
D. north

14. Which of the following cities is located at about 39°N, 77°W?

A. Hagerstown
B. Annapolis
C. Baltimore
D. Silver Spring

Critical Thinking

TEST PREP Write a short paragraph to answer each question below.

15. Compare and Contrast Describe how Maryland's three natural regions are alike and different.

16. Infer What types of things might the Woodland Indians have traded with other groups?

Timeline

Use the Chapter Summary Timeline above to answer these questions.

17. About when did people start farming in Maryland?

Activities

Speaking Activity Prepare a guided tour of the landforms of Maryland as you might view them from an airplane.

Writing Activity Write a museum description of a prehistoric artifact that might be found in Maryland. Tell what it was used for and what it tells about prehistoric life.

Technology
Writing Process Tips
Get help with your description at **www.eduplace.com/kids/hmss/**

Chapter 2 Colonial Maryland

Technology

e • **glossary**
e • **word games**
www.eduplace.com/kids/hmss/

Vocabulary Preview

colony

The **colony** of Maryland was one of the first English settlements in North America. Most people who settled there hoped to make money by raising crops. **page 24**

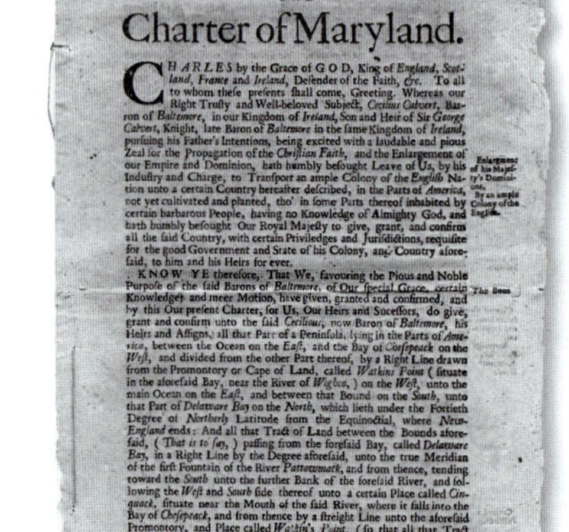

THE

Charter of Maryland.

CHARLES by the Grace of GOD, King of *England*, *Scotland*, *France* and *Ireland*, Defender of the Faith, *&c.* To all to whom theſe preſents ſhall come, Greeting. Whereas our Right Truſty and Well-beloved Subject, *Cecilius Calvert*, Baron of *Baltemore*, in our Kingdom of *Ireland*, Son and Heir of Sir *George Calvert*, Knight, late Baron of *Baltemore* in the ſame Kingdom of *Ireland*, purſuing his Father's Intentions, being excited with a laudable and pious Zeal for the Propagation of the *Christian Faith*, and the Enlargement of our Empire and Dominion, hath humbly beſought Leave of Us, by his Induſtry and Charge, to Tranſport an ample Colony of the *English* Nation unto a certain Country hereafter deſcribed, in the Parts of *America*, not yet cultivated and planted, tho' in ſome Parts thereof inhabited by certain barbarous People, having no Knowledge of Almighty God, and hath humbly beſought Our Royal Majeſty to give, grant, and confirm all the ſaid Country, with certain Priviledges and Juriſdictions, requiſite for the good Government and State of his Colony, and Country aforeſaid, to him and his Heirs for ever.

Enlargement of his Majesty's Dominions.
By an ample Colony of the English.

KNOW YE therefore, That We, favouring the Pious and Noble Purpoſe of the ſaid Barons of *Baltemore*, of Our ſpecial Grace, certain Knowledge, and meer Motion, have given, granted and confirmed, and by this Our preſent Charter, for Us, Our Heirs and Sucefſors, do give, grant and confirm unto the ſaid *Cecilious*, now Baron of *Baltemore*, his Heirs and Aſſigns, all that Part of a Peninſula, lying in the Parts of *America*, between the Ocean on the *East*, and the Bay of *Chesepeack* on the *West*, and divided from the other Part thereof, by a Right Line drawn from the Promontory or Cape of Land, called *Watkins Point* (ſituate in the aforeſaid Bay, near the River of *Wigheo*,) on the *West*, unto the main Ocean on the *East*, and between that Bound on the *South*, unto that Part of *Delaware Bay* on the *North*, which lieth under the Fortieth Degree of *Northerly* Latitude from the Equinoctial, where *New-England* ends: And all that Tract of Land between the Bounds aforeſaid, (*That is to ſay*,) paſſing from the foreſaid Bay, called *Delaware Bay*, in a Right Line by the Degree aforeſaid, unto the true Meridian of the firſt Fountain of the River *Pattowmack*, and from thence, tending toward the *South* unto the further Bank of the foreſaid River, and following the *West* and *South* ſide thereof unto a certain Place called *Cinquack*, ſituate near the Mouth of the ſaid River, where it falls into the Bay of *Chesepeack*, and from thence by a ſtreight Line unto the aforeſaid Promontory, and Place called *Watkin's Point*, (ſo that all that Tract of Land divided by the Line aforeſaid, drawn between the Main Ocean and *Watkin's Point*, unto the Promontory called *Cape Charles*, and all its Apurtenances, do remain entirely excepted to Us, our Heirs and Succeſſors for ever.)

The Bou

WE do alſo grant and confirm unto the ſaid now *Lord Baltemore*, his Heirs and Aſſigns, all Iſlands and Ilets within the Limits aforeſaid, and all and ſingular the Iſlands and Ilets, which are, or ſhall be in the Ocean, within Ten Leagues from the *Eastern* Shore of the ſaid Coun-

b try

charter

The king of England signed a **charter** in 1632. This document gave Cecil Calvert permission to start a colony in Maryland. **page 25**

Chapter Timeline

1524
Verrazano explores Atlantic Coast

1500 — 1550 — 1600

Reading Strategy

Monitor and Clarify Use this strategy to improve your understanding of events in this chapter.

If you are confused about events in a lesson, reread or read ahead.

plantation

A **plantation** in colonial Maryland often depended on a single crop such as tobacco and could be hundreds of acres in size.
page 31

port

Maryland farmers often settled near a **port** because they needed to ship their harvest to customers in other colonies.
page 36

1634
Maryland Colony founded

1694
Anne Arundel becomes capital

1650 | 1700

Core Lesson 1

The Founding of Maryland

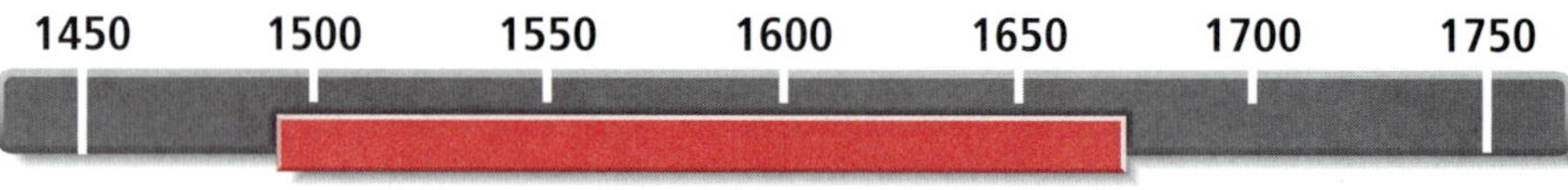

VOCABULARY

colony
tolerance
charter
proprietor

Vocabulary Strategy

proprietor

Proprietor comes from the word **property.** A proprietor owns and controls an area of land.

READING SKILL

Sequence As you read, list in order the events that led to Maryland becoming a colony.

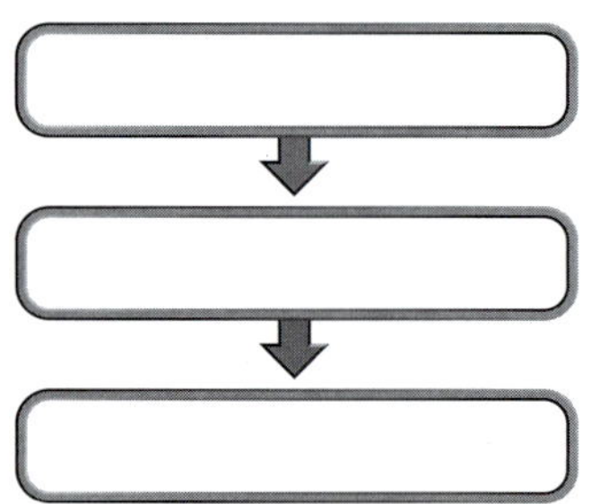

Build on What You Know Have you ever moved to a new place? In the 1600s, people were leaving Europe and moving to North America to start new lives.

Europeans Come to North America

Main Idea Europeans began exploring and settling in North America during the late 1400s and early 1500s.

In the 1500s, people from many different countries began to explore North and South America. These explorers came from countries such as France, Spain, England, Holland, and Italy. They wanted to find riches and claim lands. The explorer **Christopher Columbus** reached the Americas in 1492. His success led other Europeans to explore North America.

The first European to see the Chesapeake Bay was probably **Giovanni da Verrazano** (VEHR uh ZAH noh). He was an Italian explorer who sailed a French ship to North America in about 1524. Soon, European countries were sending settlers to North America to start colonies. A **colony** is a settlement ruled by another country. The first successful English colony was founded, or started, at Jamestown, Virginia, in 1607. Soon, other leaders from England began to plan colonies in North America.

Coat of Arms This symbol of the Calvert family is still used on the state flag of Maryland today.

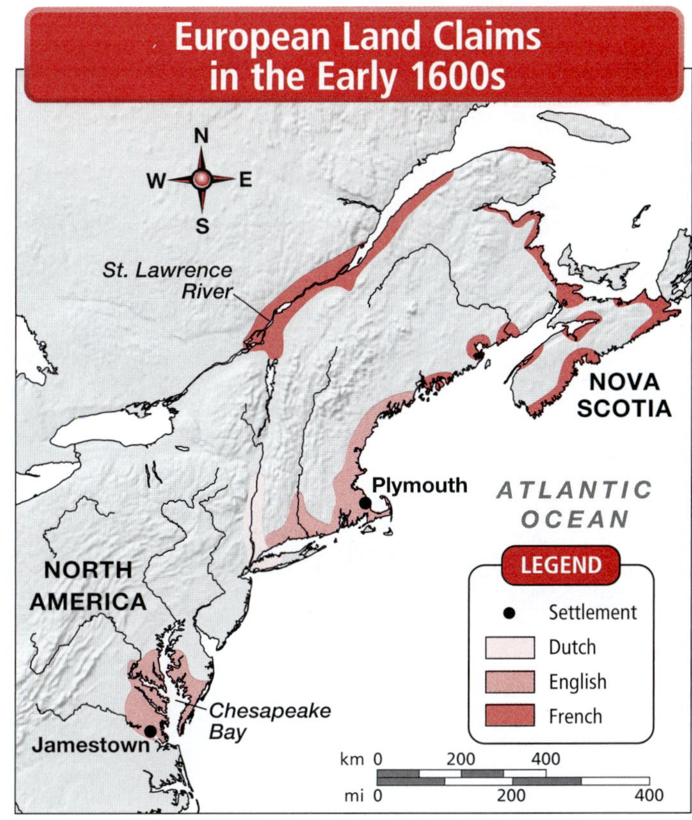

A Rush for Land In the 1600s, England and other countries claimed land in North America.

The Calverts Plan a Colony

One English leader who wanted to start a colony was **George Calvert.** George Calvert was a government official who was also known as **Lord Baltimore.** Calvert asked the king of England for land near Virginia to start a colony.

Before George Calvert could receive the land, however, he died. His son **Cecil Calvert** became the second Lord Baltimore. Like his father, he wanted to start a colony. He hoped that he could earn money by running a colony. He also hoped that his colony would be a place where people could practice their religion freely.

During this time, religious differences were causing problems in England. By law, everyone was supposed to belong to the Church of England. This made life hard for other religious groups, including Catholics. Cecil Calvert had many Catholic friends. He wanted his colony to have religious tolerance. **Tolerance** means allowing people to have differing beliefs.

In 1632, **King Charles I** of England signed a charter allowing Calvert to start a colony. A **charter** is a plan for a business or an organization. The colony was named Maryland, after the English queen, **Henrietta Maria.**

The charter explained where the colony would be located and how it would be ruled. It also made Cecil Calvert the proprietor of the colony. A **proprietor** is a person who owns and controls the land of a colony.

REVIEW What were the two main reasons for the founding of the Maryland Colony?

Cecil Calvert
The second Lord Baltimore received a charter to found the Maryland Colony.

St. Mary's City The illustration above shows Maryland's first settlement. The land was good for farming, and there were many places to anchor ships and boats.

Maryland's First Colonists

Main Idea In 1634, English settlers founded a colony at Chesapeake Bay.

Cecil Calvert did not go to North America. Instead, he sent his brother, **Leonard Calvert.** Leonard would act as governor, or leader, of Maryland, but Cecil still made many decisions.

In November 1633, Leonard Calvert sailed from England. About 200 people also went, including some Protestants, some Catholics, and two Catholic priests. They traveled in two ships, the *Ark* and the *Dove.* After many months of travel, the ships reached the Chesapeake Bay.

On March 25, 1634, they landed on an island they named St. Clement's Island. Soon, the settlers met a group of American Indians known as the Yaocomaco (yuh KAH muh ko). The settlers traded axes, hoes, and cloth with the Indians for land on St. Clement's. The Yaocomaco showed the settlers the best way to plant corn. The settlers named their settlement St. Mary's City.

One challenge for the new colony came from other English people who had settled on nearby Kent Island in 1631. They did not want to follow Cecil Calvert's rules. After some disagreements, the Kent Island settlers agreed to obey the rules of the Maryland Colony.

Governing the New Colony

As proprietor of a colony, Cecil Calvert was allowed to run the colony as he wished. However, the Maryland Charter of 1632 said that laws in Maryland had to be made by and approved by the colonists themselves.

The Maryland colonists formed a group called the General Assembly. The General Assembly then made a set of laws. Cecil Calvert liked the laws and agreed that the General Assembly could make Maryland's laws. From the very beginning, Marylanders participated in their own government.

REVIEW In what way did Maryland colonists participate in the colony's government?

Lesson Summary

- The English king gave Cecil Calvert a charter to start the Maryland Colony.
- Cecil Calvert tried to make the colony safe for Catholics.
- Maryland colonists traded with the Yaocomaco Indians for land.
- Maryland colonists were allowed to make their own laws through the General Assembly.

Why It Matters . . .

Since the beginning of the Maryland Colony, people have lived by the rule of law in Maryland and have had an active part in its government.

English Pottery This jar was brought to Maryland by early colonists.

Lesson Review

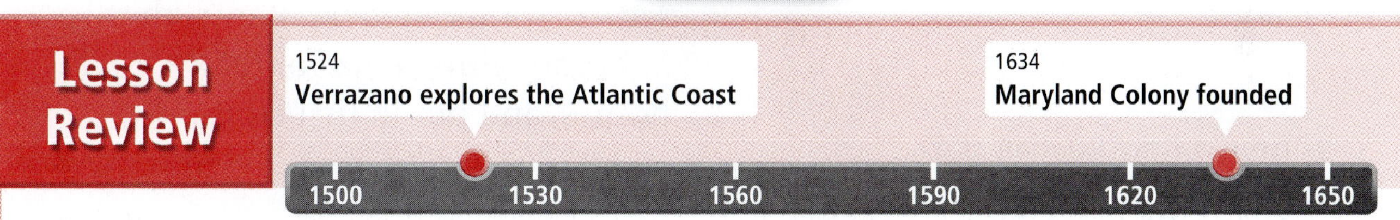

1. **VOCABULARY** Use the words **proprietor** and **colony** to explain Cecil Calvert's control over Maryland.
2. **READING SKILL** Write three sentences describing events in your **sequence** chart. Use the words "first," "second," and "third" to start your sentences.
3. **MAIN IDEA: Economics** Why did European countries explore North America?
4. **MAIN IDEA: History** Describe the Calverts' reasons for starting a colony.
5. **MAIN IDEA: Government** Why was the General Assembly important in the colony?
6. **CRITICAL THINKING: Cause and Effect** Why was trading with the Yaocomaco Indians helpful to settlers on St. Clement's?

WRITING ACTIVITY Write a letter from a Maryland colonist to a friend in England explaining why he or she should move to Maryland.

Skillbuilder

Identify Primary and Secondary Sources

VOCABULARY
primary source
secondary source

A **primary source** is a firsthand account of an event. It is firsthand information recorded by a person who was there. Diaries, speeches, photographs, and letters are primary sources.

A **secondary source** is created by someone who was not there when an event took place. History books, encyclopedias, and museum Web sites are secondary sources. They often include information that someone at the scene would not have been able to include. The sources below tell about St. Mary's City.

... we bought the space of thirtie miles of ground of them, for axes, hoes, cloth and hatchets,... some few Indians are here to stay by us till next yeare, and then the land is wholy to be ours alone.

—from *A Brief Relation of the Voyage Unto Maryland* by Father Andrew White

... he traded English-made axes, hoes, hatchets, and cloth for about thirty miles of land.... The settlers could hardly have hoped for such a welcome.... Around the spot the settlers soon called St. Mary's, they ... began felling trees for their homes, and put in first crops.

—from the book *Maryland* by Robert J. Brugger

Learn the Skill

Step 1: Identify the subject of both sources.

Step 2: Read both passages. Look for clue words such as *I, my, we, us* and *ours.* These words are often used in primary sources.

Step 3: Identify each passage as being a primary or secondary source. To help you figure this out, ask yourself questions such as these: *Who wrote the passage? Was the writer at the event?*

Practice the Skill

Answer these questions about the primary and secondary sources on page 28.

1. Which passage is a primary source? How do you know?
2. Which passage is a secondary source? How do you know?
3. What pieces of information are in both sources?
4. What is an important difference between the secondary source and the primary source?

Apply the Skill

Find an example of a primary source in a book, newspaper, or magazine article. Then find an article that is an example of a secondary source. In a paragraph, explain how you identified each source.

Core Lesson 2

Colonial Life

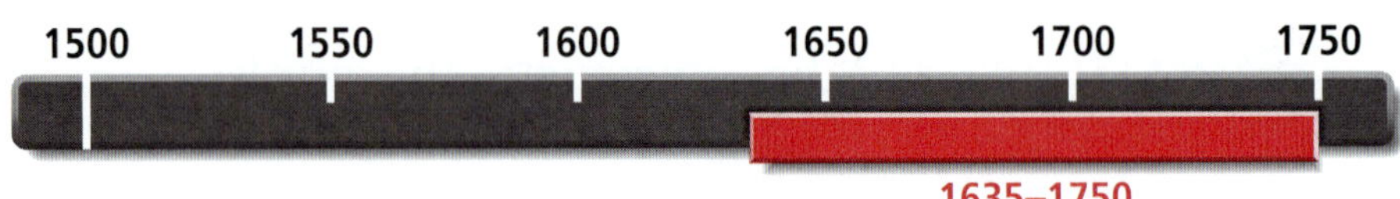

VOCABULARY

economy
plantation
indentured servant
slavery

Vocabulary Strategy

plantation

Look for the word **plant** in **plantation**. A plantation is a huge farm where plants, or crops, are grown.

READING SKILL

Main Idea and Details

Note details that support the first main idea.

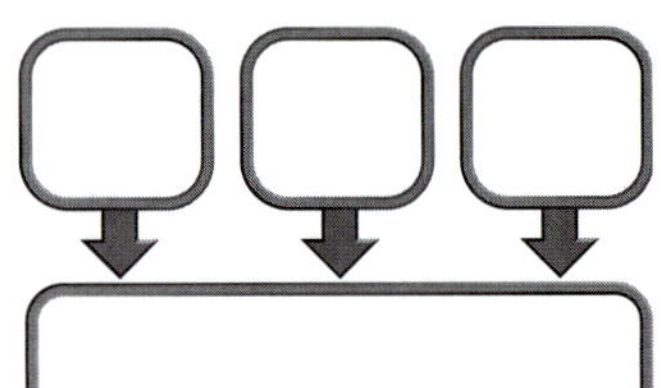

Build on What You Know What are some ways in which people make a living in Maryland today? In the Maryland Colony, many people took advantage of the mild climate and worked as farmers.

Maryland's Early Economy

Main Idea Maryland colonists grew tobacco and other crops, using indentured servants and enslaved people to help them.

For the Maryland Colony to make money, people were needed to farm the land. Cecil Calvert, the second Lord Baltimore, encouraged colonists to come to Maryland by providing them with land to farm. The colonists had to pay Lord Baltimore a fee for the land each year. Lord Baltimore gave more land to people who brought other colonists to Maryland. For example, people who brought five or more colonists received 2,000 acres of land. As more people came to Maryland, the economy of the colony grew. An **economy** is the way people run businesses and make money in an area.

Father Andrew White was a Catholic priest who was one of the first settlers in Maryland. He wrote a description of the colony that made many people become interested in moving there. In 1635, Lord Baltimore used Father White's description in a booklet called *A Relation of Maryland.*

A Settler's Violin This handmade violin and bow were used by colonists at St. Mary's City.

Tobacco Plantation Maryland colonists and their workers tended tobacco plants on plantations like this one.

Farming the New Land

Soon after colonists arrived in Maryland, they realized the climate was perfect for growing tobacco. They could make money by selling tobacco in Europe. Tobacco became so valuable that colonists bartered with it and used it as money. Many tobacco planters soon owned plantations. A **plantation** is a large farm where people both live and work.

At first, many Europeans wanted to come to Maryland but could not afford to do so. These people were able to pay for their transportation by coming to Maryland as indentured servants. **Indentured servants** are people who agree to work for a certain time without pay in order to pay money they owe. Many indentured servants in Maryland worked on tobacco plantations until they paid off the cost of their trip to North America.

One of the first Africans to come to Maryland was an indentured servant named **Mathias DeSousa.** He later became a fur trader. In 1641, DeSousa served as a member of Maryland's General Assembly.

Slavery in Maryland

Because each indentured servant only worked for a few years, plantation owners were constantly losing workers.

Many plantation owners switched from using indentured servants to slavery. **Slavery** is a cruel system in which people can be bought and sold and forced to work with no pay. Enslaved people could be forced to work for their entire lives. Maryland allowed slavery starting in 1664. Some people in Maryland also made money through buying and selling enslaved people.

In the early 1700s, almost 4,000 enslaved people were brought to Maryland. Many came from Africa. Some came from the Caribbean Islands. They soon became a large part of Maryland's population. Slowly, Maryland's farming economy grew to depend on slavery.

REVIEW How did becoming an indentured servant help people come to Maryland?

The Maryland Colony Grows

Main Idea In the 1600s and 1700s, the population of Maryland changed.

By 1650, the population of Maryland had begun to grow steadily. Many people wanted to come to the colony. They realized that they could become wealthy by growing tobacco. The freedom to practice different religions also drew Presbyterians and Quakers from England and from other colonies.

In 1650, Maryland's population was about 1,000 people. By 1670, it was 10,000, and by 1750, it was just over 100,000.

Many colonists settled near the Chesapeake Bay so that they could easily ship their tobacco to other places. Later, other farm products, such as wheat and corn, also became important to the economy.

Anne Arundel Early settlers named the town of Anne Arundel after the wife of Cecil Calvert.

Changes for American Indians

At first, the American Indians near the Chesapeake Bay lived peacefully with the English settlers. However, they could not fight against the illnesses that the settlers had brought from Europe. By 1650, many of them had died.

The Susquehannock wanted the land that the other American Indian groups had controlled. This caused conflict with the settlers until a treaty, or written agreement, was signed in 1652. Then many of the Susquehannock became ill as well. In 1673, the few remaining Susquehannock settled along the Potomac River.

Changes for Cities

Along the Chesapeake Bay, a town called Anne Arundel grew rapidly. Later, the capital of the colony was moved to Anne Arundel from St. Mary's City. In 1695, Anne Arundel was renamed Annapolis and continued to grow. When many of the colony's leaders moved away from St. Mary's City, that town became much smaller. So many people had moved away that by the early 1700s, no one lived in St. Mary's City at all.

St. Mary's City Modern Marylanders make history come alive at the site of St. Mary's City and show what life was like for colonists.

Free African Americans

While the number of enslaved people in Maryland continued to grow, Maryland was also home to many free African Americans. Many supported themselves by learning trades. A trade is a kind of work that requires special knowledge. Free African American trade workers in Maryland included blacksmiths, carpenters, and oyster harvesters. Many African American men also became sailors on large ships.

In parts of Maryland, African Americans lived in communities. In these communities, free men and women ran businesses and participated in local government.

REVIEW How was the growth of Anne Arundel different from that of St. Mary's?

Lesson Summary

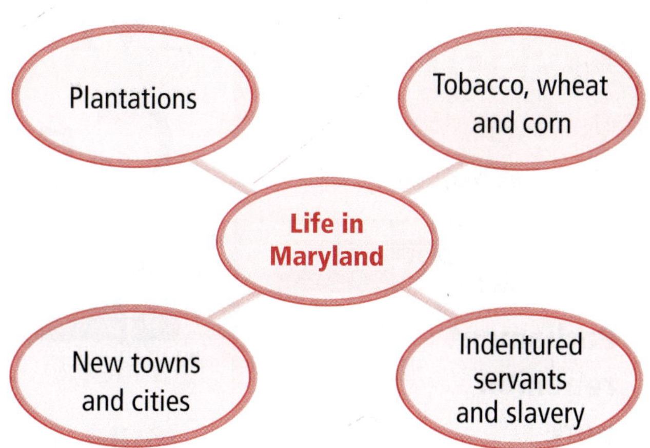

Why It Matters . . .

Maryland's economy grew during the 1600s and 1700s. New towns and cities were started as people moved to new places to farm. Most of those cities are still important in Maryland today.

Lesson Review

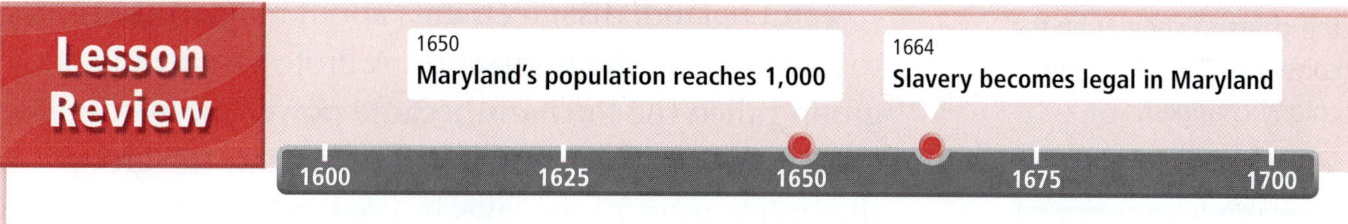

1. **VOCABULARY** Explain how **plantations** used **indentured servants** and **slavery.**
2. **READING SKILL** Name a **detail** that explains why people in Maryland began growing tobacco.
3. **MAIN IDEA: History** Name at least two reasons why people moved to Maryland.
4. **MAIN IDEA: Government** What were some of the different religious groups that came to Maryland? Why did they come?
5. **TIMELINE SKILL** When did slavery become legal in Maryland?
6. **CRITICAL THINKING: Draw Conclusions** Why do you think certain places in Maryland, such as Anne Arundel, grew so quickly?

WRITING ACTIVITY Write a letter from an early colonist in Maryland. Explain how he or she traveled to the colony and now makes a living.

Core Lesson 3

Maryland Grows Stronger

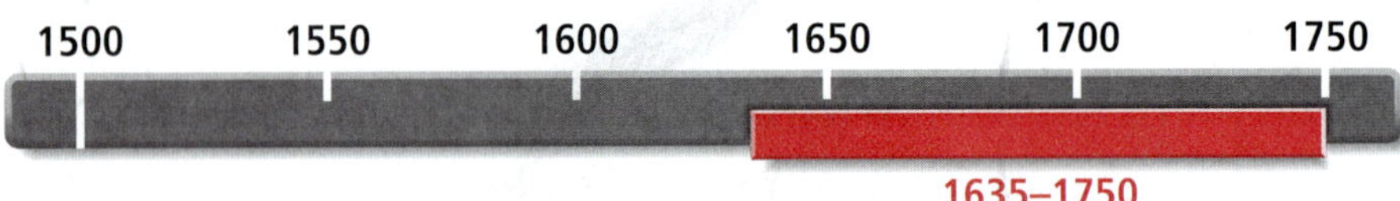

VOCABULARY

Parliament
rebellion
port

Vocabulary Strategy

rebellion

Rebellion includes the word **rebel. Rebel** is a verb that means to oppose one's leaders. **Rebellion** is a noun that means an attempt to get rid of the leaders in power.

READING SKILL

Cause and Effect Fill in the chart to show why the control of the Maryland colony changed.

Cause	Effect

Build on What You Know Have you seen changes in your neighborhood during the time you have lived there? The colony of Maryland went through many changes in its first 150 years.

Struggles for Control

Main Idea Religious disagreements in England caused conflicts in Maryland and led to government changes.

Maryland's colonists kept close ties with England. For that reason, political problems in England often led to problems in the colonies.

In England, disagreements about religion continued to grow during the mid-1600s. A Protestant religious group called the Puritans became powerful. By the 1640s, the Puritans controlled **Parliament,** the group that made most of the laws in England. Soon Parliament challenged the king's power there.

The second Lord Baltimore, Cecil Calvert, was living in England. To keep control over Maryland, Calvert had to remain friendly with both the king and with Parliament. This was very difficult.

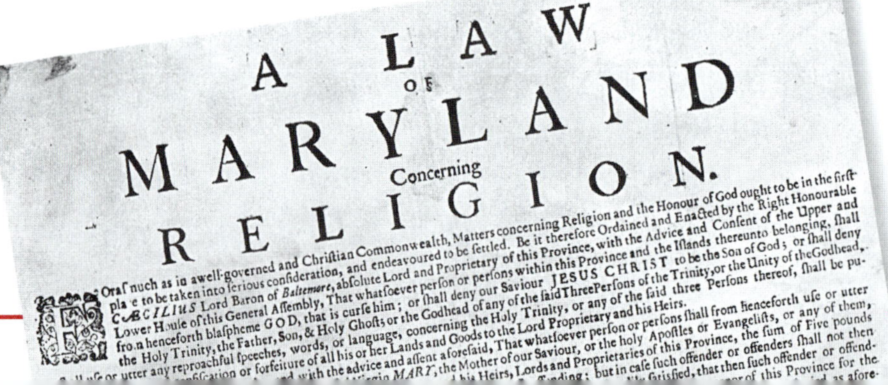

A LAW OF MARYLAND Concerning RELIGION.

Foraſmuch as in a well-governed and Chriſtian Commonwealth, Matters concerning Religion and the Honour of God ought to be in the firſt
place to be taken into ſerious conſideration, and endeavoured to be ſettled. Be it therefore Ordained and Enacted by the Right Honourable
CÆCILIUS Lord Baron of *Baltemore*, abſolute Lord and Proprietary of this Province, with the Advice and Conſent of the Upper and
Lower Houſe of this General Aſſembly, That whatſoever perſon or perſons within this Province and the Iſlands thereunto belonging, ſhall
from henceforth blaſpheme GOD, that is curſe him; or ſhall deny our Saviour JESUS CHRIST to be the Son of God; or ſhall deny
the Holy Trinity, the Father, Son, & Holy Ghoſt, or the Godhead of any of the ſaid Three Perſons of the Trinity, or the Unity of the Godhead,
or uſe or utter any reproachful ſpeeches, words, or language, concerning the Holy Trinity, or any of the ſaid three Perſons thereof, ſhall be pu-
niſhed with death and confiſcation or forfeiture of all his or her Lands and Goods to the Lord Proprietary and his Heirs.
... That whatſoever perſon or perſons ſhall from henceforth uſe or utter
... the Mother of our Saviour, or the holy Apoſtles or Evangeliſts, or any of them,
... Lords and Proprietaries of this Province, the ſum of Five pounds
... but in caſe ſuch offender or offenders ſhall not then
... ſatisfied, that then ſuch offender or offend-
... of this Province for the

Tolerance Acts of 1649 This law made it illegal to criticize other people's religions.

Margaret Brent Because Brent was making important decisions about money in the colony, she felt she should have a say in the government.

Rebellion in the Colony

In 1645, Puritans in Maryland rebelled against Calvert's government. A **rebellion** is an attempt to overthrow a government or change it by force. They were successful in gaining control of the government for a short time.

In 1646, Leonard Calvert regained control of Maryland but he died soon after. Before his death, Leonard Calvert named **Margaret Brent** to take care of his money matters. By handling the Calverts' money well, Brent helped keep the colony's government running. Brent asked the General Assembly for the right to vote on important decisions. Although the General Assembly did not grant her request, Brent is known as the first woman in North America to ask for the right to vote.

The Maryland Colony had begun as a place of religious tolerance. To make sure that this tolerance would be guaranteed, the Maryland government created the Tolerance Acts of 1649. The Tolerance Acts said that people who criticized others' religions would be punished. Maryland was the only colony with such a law.

In 1652, the English Parliament took control of the colony away from Cecil Calvert. They banned anyone from practicing the Catholic religion. The Calverts regained control of the colony in 1657. However, political and religious disagreements continued.

REVIEW What did the Tolerance Acts do to change the lives of Marylanders?

Changes in Maryland

Main Idea Maryland's government and economy continued to change.

In 1688, a new Protestant king began to rule England. The next year, Protestant settlers in Maryland rebelled against the Calvert government, which was tolerant of Catholics. They were upset with some of the decisions of the third Lord Baltimore, Charles Calvert. They asked the king of England to take control of Maryland, and in 1692 Maryland became a royal colony. It was ruled by a royal governor, someone appointed by the English king.

In 1715, the king gave control of Maryland to the fourth Lord Baltimore, **Benedict Leonard Calvert.** However, religious freedom was not allowed again in Maryland until 1776.

The Maryland government had changed many times since its beginning. During all this time, though, the General Assembly continued to pass laws and Marylanders lived by the rule of law.

New Farmland, New Towns

During the late 1600s and early 1700s, many people moved to the west and north of earlier settlements such as Anne Arundel. Some families were moving away from farmland that had been overused. Other families were new to Maryland. These settlers needed to send their farm products to people in other places. So, new ports were built. A **port** is a place where ships and boats can dock, load, and unload products.

Farm products from Maryland, such as flour and corn, were shipped out for sale. Other products such as tea, tools, and cloth for clothing were brought in. As these new ports became more important to the economy, more towns and cities grew up around them.

The Fourth Lord Baltimore Benedict Leonard Calvert (right) died soon after asking the king to return Maryland to his family. In 1729, a town named after Lord Baltimore was founded as a port city (below).

The Founding of Baltimore

One important new port city was Baltimore. Founded in 1729, the city of Baltimore grew quickly. At first, most of the city's economy depended on its port. However, other businesses grew along with the city.

There was much iron in the ground nearby. Business leaders began a company to build an iron mill. By 1734, the company was selling iron to customers in England.

The iron mills brought other businesses to Baltimore. As people began coming to Baltimore to look for jobs, the city grew even faster.

REVIEW How did Maryland's government change in 1692?

Lesson Summary

- Disagreements in England affected Maryland in the 1600s.
- The Maryland government created the Tolerance Acts of 1649.
- Between 1645 and 1715 control of Maryland changed several times.
- In the early 1700s, Maryland and its economy continued to grow.
- In 1729, Baltimore was founded.

Why It Matters . . .

The challenges that early Marylanders faced affected Maryland's economy and government for the next century.

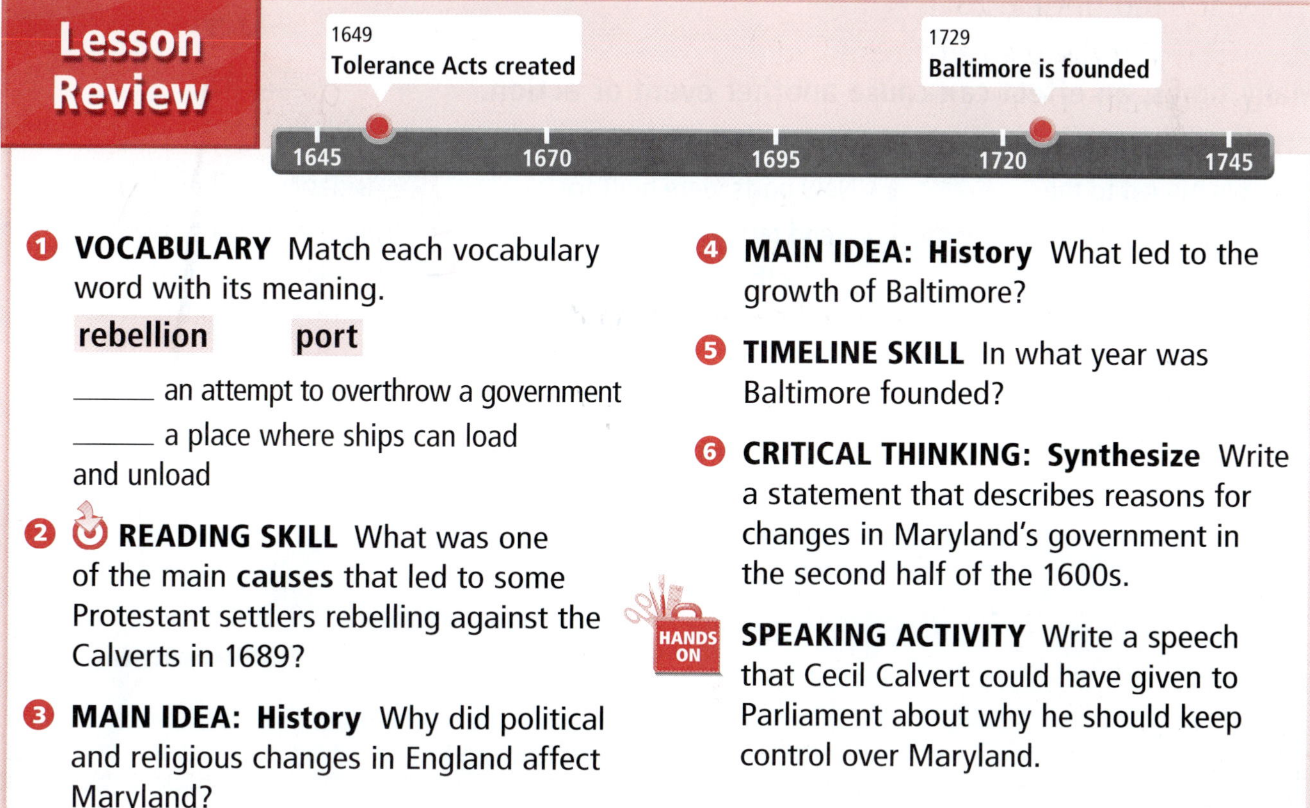

Lesson Review

1. **VOCABULARY** Match each vocabulary word with its meaning.

   rebellion **port**

   ______ an attempt to overthrow a government

   ______ a place where ships can load and unload

2. **READING SKILL** What was one of the main **causes** that led to some Protestant settlers rebelling against the Calverts in 1689?

3. **MAIN IDEA: History** Why did political and religious changes in England affect Maryland?

4. **MAIN IDEA: History** What led to the growth of Baltimore?

5. **TIMELINE SKILL** In what year was Baltimore founded?

6. **CRITICAL THINKING: Synthesize** Write a statement that describes reasons for changes in Maryland's government in the second half of the 1600s.

HANDS ON **SPEAKING ACTIVITY** Write a speech that Cecil Calvert could have given to Parliament about why he should keep control over Maryland.

Skillbuilder

Identify Cause and Effect

VOCABULARY
cause
effect

Studying causes and effects helps us to understand not only what happened but why it happened. A cause is an event or action that makes something else happen. An effect is the event or action that is the result of the cause.

Some events have more than one effect.

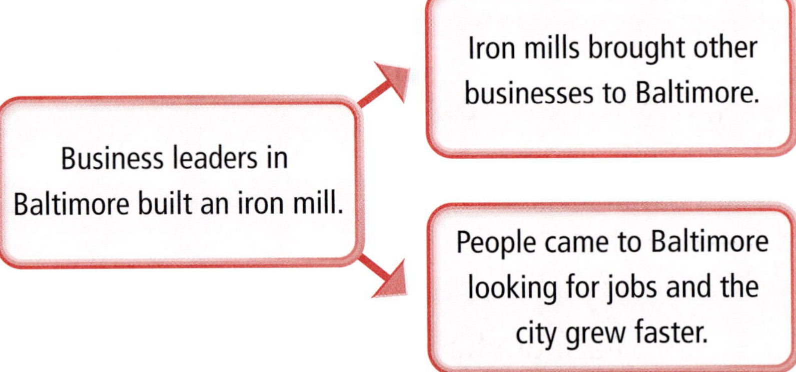

Many times, an effect can cause another event or action.

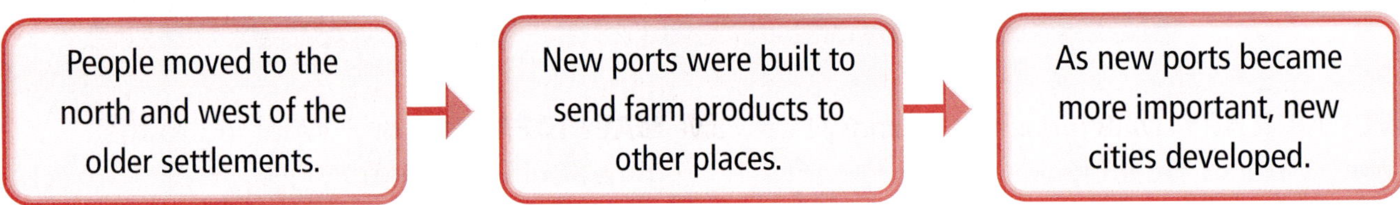

Learn the Skill

Step 1: Look for words that are clues to causes and effects. Words or phrases such as *because, since, led to,* and *why* are clues to causes. Words or phrases such as *after, then, so,* and *as a result* signal effects.

Step 2: Identify the cause of an event. Check to see if there is more than one cause.

Step 3: Identify the effect. Ask yourself what happened as a result of the cause. Check to see if there is more than one effect. Think about whether any of the effects then become causes.

Practice the Skill

Reread page 36 of Lesson 3 about changes in Maryland's government. Then answer the following questions, and fill out a diagram like the one below.

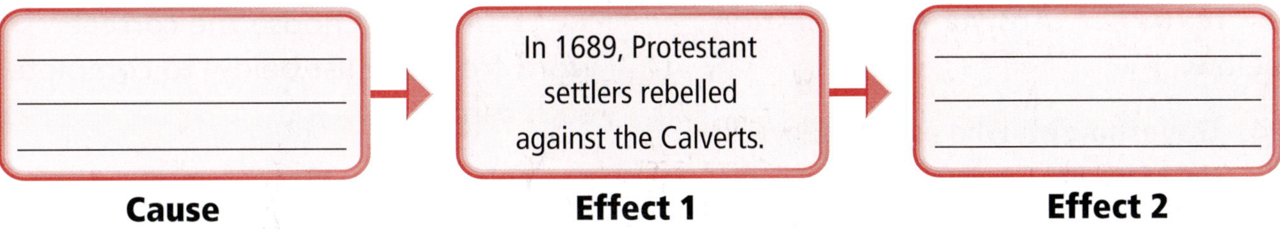

1. What caused the Protestant settlers to rebel against the Calverts?
2. What was the effect when Protestant settlers rebelled against the Calverts?

Apply the Skill

Reread pages 34–36. Then make a chart to show causes and effects of government changes between 1640 and 1689. Name some of the clue words that helped you to find the causes and effects.

Chapter 2 Review and Test Prep

Visual Summary

1 – 3. Write a description of each item named below.

Maryland Charter

____
____
____

Tolerance Acts of 1649

____
____
____

Baltimore's Port

____
____
____

Facts and Main Ideas

TEST PREP Answer each question below.

4. **Government** Who made the laws in the Maryland Colony?
5. **Geography** In what ways did the Chesapeake Bay affect the growth of the Maryland Colony?
6. **Economics** What resource was found near Baltimore that helped the economy of the city?
7. **Government** When Maryland was a royal colony, who ruled the colony?

Vocabulary

TEST PREP Choose the correct word from the list below to complete each sentence.

tolerance, p. 25
charter, p. 25
slavery, p. 31

8. Some Catholics came to Maryland looking for religious _____.
9. Many plantation owners in Maryland chose to depend on _____.
10. The king of England granted Lord Baltimore a _____ for the Maryland Colony.

CHAPTER SUMMARY TIMELINE

1524	Verrazano explores Atlantic Coast
1634	Maryland Colony founded
1694	Anne Arundel becomes capital

1500 1550 1600 1650 1700

Apply Skills

✔ TEST PREP **Identify Cause and Effect** Read the passage below. Then use what you have learned about cause and effect to answer each question.

In November 1688, a new Protestant king began to rule England. In 1689, Protestant colonists in Maryland rebelled against Lord Baltimore's government. They asked the king to take direct control of Maryland's government. As a result of the rebellion, Maryland became a royal colony.

11. Which of the following is the effect of the events described in the passage?

A. Settlers rebelled against the Calverts.
B. A new king and queen were crowned in England.
C. Maryland became a royal colony.
D. Maryland's economy struggled.

12. Which of the following is NOT a cause of Maryland becoming a royal colony?

A. Margaret Brent handled Leonard Calvert's money.
B. Settlers rebelled against the Calverts.
C. The new king and queen were Protestant.
D. The Calverts had controlled Maryland.

Critical Thinking

✔ TEST PREP Write a short paragraph to answer each question below.

13. Draw Conclusions Do you think the fact that Marylanders made their own laws affected Lord Baltimore's control of the colony? Explain your answer.

14. Infer Why did religious disagreements in England affect Maryland so much?

Timeline

Use the chapter summary timeline above to answer the following question.

15. How many years after the Maryland Colony was founded did Anne Arundel become the capital?

Activities

Research Activity The city of Baltimore developed in the 1700s. Find out what helped the city to grow.

Writing Activity Write a newspaper announcement for Marylanders, informing them that Maryland has become a royal colony.

Technology
Writing Process Tips
Get help with your announcement at **www.eduplace.com/kids/hmss/**

UNIT 1 Review and Test Prep

Vocabulary and Main Ideas

TEST PREP **Write a sentence to answer each question.**

1. What **landform** in Maryland has the highest **elevation?**
2. Name an **artifact** scientists might study to learn about **prehistoric** Maryland.
3. What kinds of houses did people of the Woodland **culture** build?
4. Who was the first **proprietor** of the Maryland **colony?**
5. Why did many Maryland **plantation** owners switch from using **indentured servants** to **slavery?**
6. Why was **tolerance** important in Maryland?

Critical Thinking

TEST PREP **Write a short paragraph to answer each question.**

7. **Synthesize** In what way did the Chesapeake Bay affect both American Indians and early European settlement in Maryland?
8. **Compare** How was the life of an indentured servant different from the life of an enslaved person?

Apply Skills

TEST PREP **Identify Primary and Secondary Sources** **Use the passage below and what you have learned about primary and secondary sources to answer each question.**

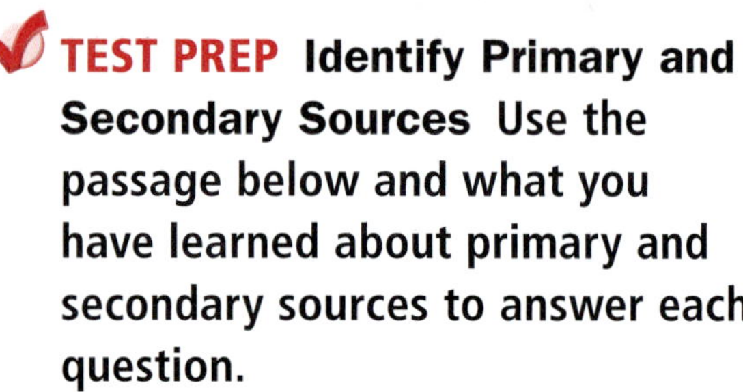

During the first hundred years of European settlement in Maryland, most towns were built close to the Chesapeake Bay and to rivers that flowed into the bay. The first settlement in Maryland was established at St. Mary's City, near the southern end of the Chesapeake Bay.

Soon, other towns such as Anne Arundel were established. Settlers in these towns needed to be close to the Chesapeake Bay in order to ship products, such as tobacco, to Europe and other colonies.

9. This passage is an example of
   - **A.** a secondary source.
   - **B.** a primary source.
   - **C.** a charter.
   - **D.** a journal entry.
10. Which one is a secondary source?
    - **A.** a letter
    - **B.** an original map
    - **C.** a charter
    - **D.** a museum Web site

Unit Activity

Prepare a "What Makes Maryland Special?" News Report

- Choose one thing about Maryland that you think makes it a good place to live.
- Identify or create pictures, photographs, or objects that show your idea.
- Prepare a "What Makes Maryland Special?" report for a television news program, using the images you found or created.

At the Library

You may find these books at your school or public library.

Waterman's Boy by Susan Sharpe

A boy learns to protect the Chesapeake Bay.

Leonard Calvert and the Maryland Adventure by Ann Jensen and Marcy Dunn Ramsey

A son of the first Lord Baltimore experiences life in the Maryland Colony.

CURRENT EVENTS WEEKLY WR READER

Connect to Today

Create a display about a place in colonial Maryland.

- Look for information about a historic place from Maryland's colonial past.
- Write a description of the place and its importance in Maryland history.
- Find or draw pictures of the place.
- Create a display with the information and pictures.

Technology

Weekly Reader online offers social studies articles. Go to: **www.eduplace.com/kids/hmss/**

UNIT 2

Independence and Growth

What brings people together as a nation?

"America is a growing country: in time [it] must and will be independent."

Charles Carroll, Maryland signer of the Declaration of Independence, 1763

Charles Carroll

1737–1832

Charles Carroll wrote newspaper articles to protest unfair British rules. After fighting started, he signed the Declaration of Independence. **page 51**

The MARYLAND GAZETTE

History Makers

Samuel Chase

1741–1811

Samuel Chase helped organize the Sons of Liberty in Maryland and led protests against British laws.

page 55

Dolley Madison

1768–1849

Dolley Madison saved important papers before the British set the White House on fire during the War of 1812.

page 70

Chapter 3 Revolution and Independence

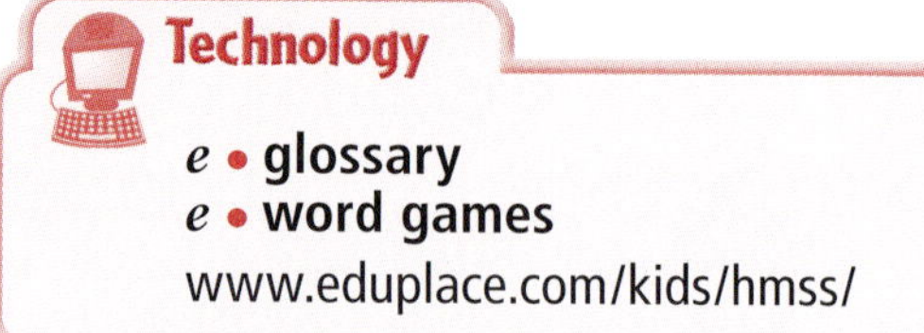

Vocabulary Preview

tax

Britain made the colonists pay a **tax** on items such as tea and newspapers. Stamps such as this one showed that the tax was paid. **page 49**

boycott

Colonists decided to hold a **boycott** against British goods. They refused to buy or use goods from Britain. **page 50**

Chapter Timeline

1763 French and Indian War ends

1776 Declaration of Independence signed

1781 Battle of Yorktown

1760 — 1770 — 1780

Reading Strategy

Summarize Use this strategy to focus on important ideas.

Quick Tip Review the main ideas. Then look for important details that support the main idea.

independence

Colonists wanted **independence** from Britain. They wanted to be free of British rule.
page 55

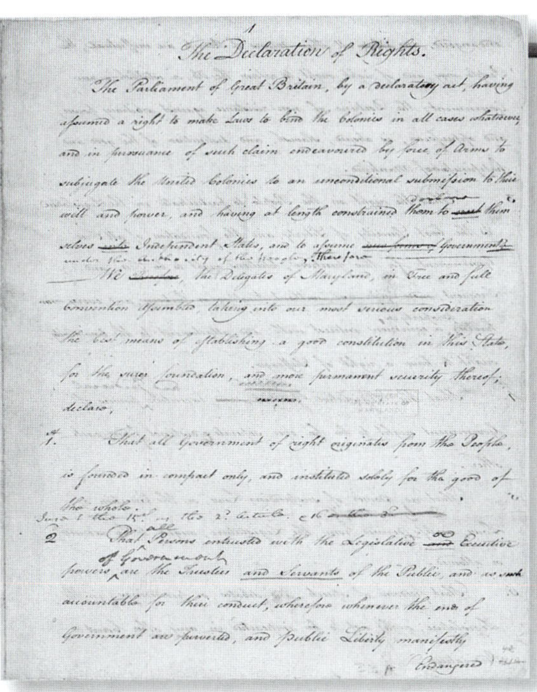

The Declaration of Rights.

The Parliament of Great Britain, by a declaratory act, having assumed a right to make Laws to bind the Colonies in all cases whatsoever, and in pursuance of such claim endeavoured by force of Arms to subjugate the United Colonies to an unconditional submission to their will and power, and having at length constrained them to declare themselves Independent States, and to assume Government under the authority of the people, Therefore

We the Delegates of Maryland, in free and full Convention assembled, taking into our most serious consideration the best means of establishing a good constitution in this State, for the surer foundation, and more permanent security thereof, declare,

1. That all Government of right originates from the People, is founded in compact only, and instituted solely for the good of the whole.

2. That all Persons entrusted with the Legislative and Executive powers of Government are the Trustees and Servants of the Public, and as such accountable for their conduct, wherefore whenever the ends of Government are perverted, and Public Liberty manifestly Endangered

constitution

Maryland wrote a **constitution** at the beginning of the American Revolution. It was a plan for how the state would be governed. **page 58**

1791
Maryland donates land for Washington, D.C.

1790 — 1800

Core Lesson 1

Conflicts in the Colonies

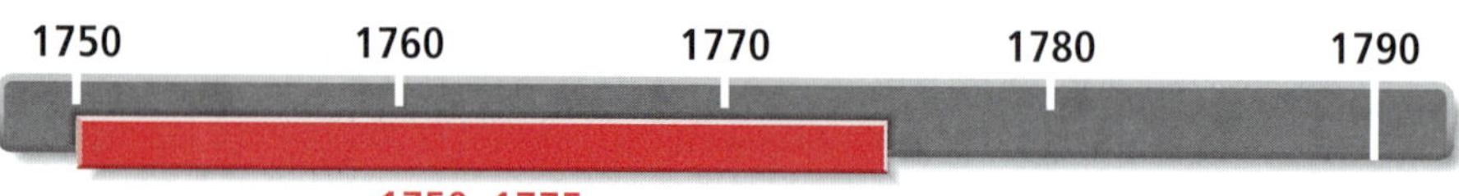

VOCABULARY

allies
tax
boycott

Vocabulary Strategy

allies

The word **allies** comes from an old word meaning "to unite." **Allies** are people or groups that join with another group to work for something.

READING SKILL

Cause and Effect List two effects of the raid on the *Peggy Stewart.*

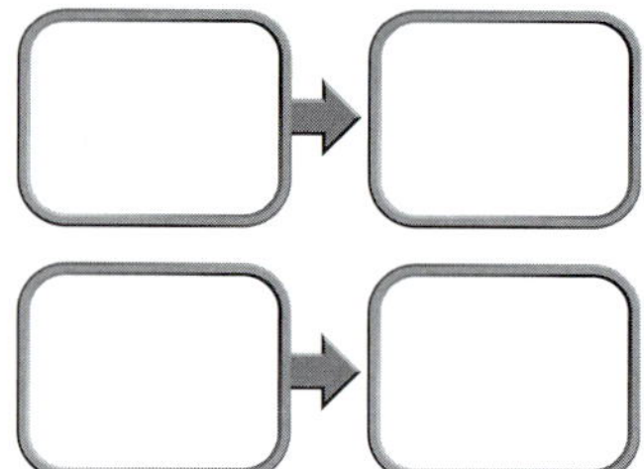

Build on What You Know Have you ever needed help doing something? When Britain went to war with France, Britain wanted the colonies to help.

The French and Indian War

Main Idea In the French and Indian War, Britain and France fought for control of the Ohio River valley in North America.

During the 1600s, Britain and France founded colonies in North America. In the 1700s, the two countries disagreed over which country should control the Ohio River valley.

In 1754, war broke out between the British and French in North America. French forces in North America convinced many American Indians to become their allies against the British. **Allies** are people or groups that join with another person or group to work toward a goal. The war became known as the French and Indian War.

Fort Frederick This fort was built to help defend western Maryland during the French and Indian War.

Maryland Defends Itself

Early in the French and Indian War, many Marylanders were afraid that American Indians might attack western Maryland. Colonists formed a militia to protect western Maryland. A militia is a group of ordinary people who train for battle. Colonists also built Fort Frederick near present-day Hagerstown. The fort was an important supply center for British and colonial troops during the war.

The British defeated the French in 1763. Because France lost the war, it had to give up control of its land in North America.

Effects of the War on Maryland

Sending soldiers and equipment to North America cost Britain a great deal of money. After the war was over, Britain expected the American colonies to help pay for those costs. However, many colonists did not believe that they should have to pay for the war.

The colonists in Maryland were divided. Some people felt that Lord Baltimore should pay Maryland's share of the costs since he was the proprietor of the colony.

The British government passed several laws to collect taxes from the colonists. A **tax** is money that people pay to their government in return for services. The new taxes affected merchants and farmers in Maryland. Taxes on items that they produced and shipped cost them money.

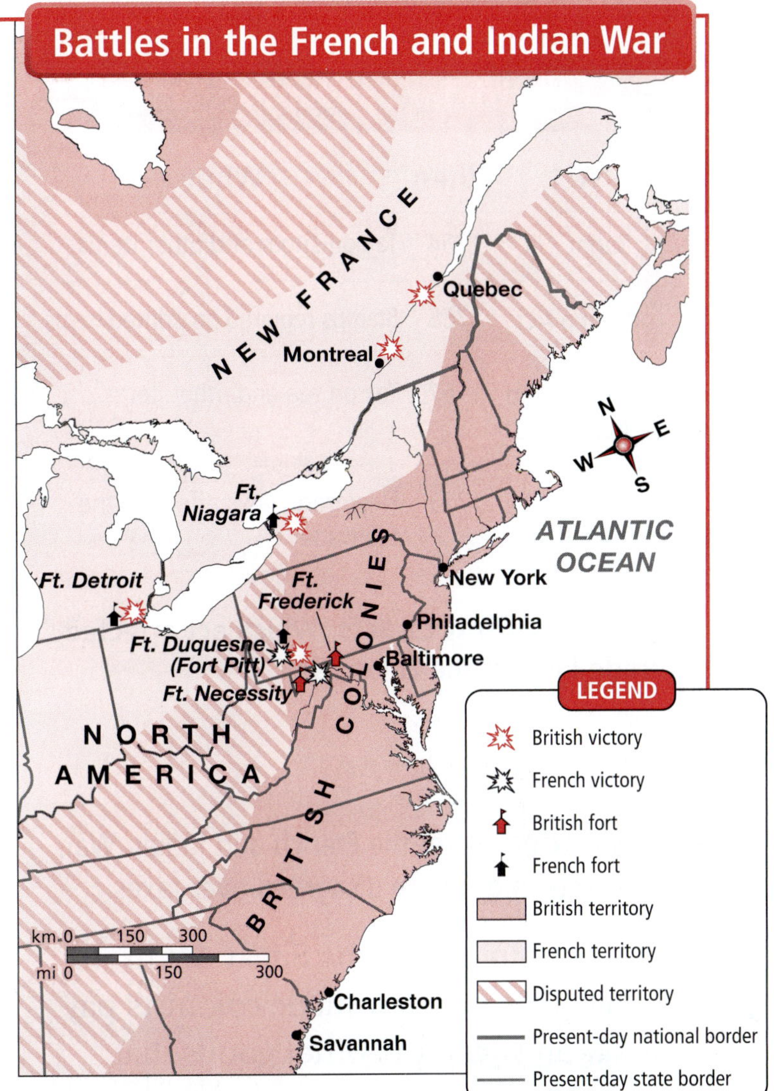

Battle for North America Fort Frederick helped to defend the British colonies from the French. **SKILL Reading Maps** Which French fort was closest to Fort Frederick?

In addition to the new taxes, Britain started making other laws that affected the colonists. British soldiers remained in some cities after the war. Colonists in those cities had to give the soldiers food and a place to stay. This made the colonists in those areas even more upset.

REVIEW What effect did the French and Indian War have on Maryland?

British Tax and Business Laws

Act	When	What
Sugar Act	1764	Tax on sugar and other items
Stamp Act	1765	Stamps required on printed items
Townshend Acts	1767	Tax on tea and other items
Tea Act	1773	New trade laws affecting the tea trade

SKILL **Reading Charts** **Which act affected trade laws in the colonies?**

Tea and Taxes

Main Idea After the French and Indian War, colonists and Britain disagreed over taxes.

Britain passed the Sugar Act in 1764. This new law made colonists pay a tax on sugar and other goods that were brought to the colonies.

Then, in 1765, Britain passed the Stamp Act. This law forced colonists to buy special stamps and put them on most printed items such as contracts and newspapers.

The Sugar Act and the Stamp Act angered the colonists. Many believed that Britain should not tax them because no one was speaking for the colonists in British government. To show that they opposed the new taxes, some colonists held a boycott of British goods. In a **boycott,** people refuse to buy certain goods. The boycott made it harder for the British to sell goods or to collect taxes.

Maryland Colonists React

In 1766, Britain canceled the Stamp Act. But in 1767, they passed the Townshend (TOWN zuhnd) Acts. These acts put taxes on many items. The colonists protested, or spoke out against, the Townshend Acts. Britain then canceled most of the Townshend Acts.

In 1773, Britain passed the Tea Act. It changed the way colonists sold and bought tea.

In Boston, colonists protested the Tea Act by going onto ships and throwing the tea they were carrying into Boston Harbor.

In May 1774, Marylanders went onto a ship loaded with tea and threw the tea into the Chester River. This became known as the Chestertown Tea Party.

Later that year, a ship called the *Peggy Stewart* brought tea to Annapolis. Marylanders were angry that the ship's owner had paid the tax, and they forced him to set the ship on fire.

The *Peggy Stewart* **Anthony Stewart, the owner of the *Peggy Stewart,* burned his own ship and the tea it carried.**

Maryland Leaders

Marylanders began saying that they should have more control over their own government. One Marylander who felt strongly about this issue was **Charles Carroll.** He wrote many newspaper articles that encouraged Marylanders to demand more control over the laws that affected them.

A lawyer from Maryland, **William Paca,** protested what he considered unfair laws and taxes. With another Maryland lawyer, **Samuel Chase,** Paca helped other leaders fight unfair taxes in court.

REVIEW In what way did Charles Carroll encourage Marylanders to demand change?

Lesson Summary

Britain taxes colonists to pay for French and Indian War

Colonists protest taxes and boycott British goods

Marylanders protest the tea tax

Why It Matters . . .

Marylanders began to work together to gain greater control of their own government.

Tax Stamps **The Stamp Act put a tax on almost everything that was printed.**

Lesson Review

1. **VOCABULARY** Use the words **tax** and **boycott** in a paragraph to describe how colonists reacted when Britain passed new taxes that affected the colonies.
2. **READING SKILL** What **cause** led Maryland colonists to force the burning of the *Peggy Stewart?*
3. **MAIN IDEA: History** What was the main reason for the French and Indian War?
4. **MAIN IDEA: History** Why were Marylanders and other colonists angry at Britain for the Tea Act?
5. **TIMELINE SKILL** How long after the Stamp Act did Marylanders burn the *Peggy Stewart?*
6. **CRITICAL THINKING: Compare and Contrast** How were protests against the Tea Act in Boston and in Annapolis alike and different?

WRITING ACTIVITY Write a letter to the editor of a 1700s newspaper. Explain why you believe it is unfair to pay taxes to a government that does not listen to the people in Maryland.

Skillbuilder

Use Reference Materials

Where would you look if you wanted to find information on a topic? One place to look is the library. The Internet is another place where you can find information. This lesson will help you use atlases, encyclopedias, and websites to find information.

VOCABULARY
- atlas
- encyclopedia
- index
- website
- search engine

Learn the Skill

Step 1: Write the question you want to answer. For example: *What were the effects on Maryland of the French and Indian War?*

Step 2: Name the topic in your question. The topic in the question is "French and Indian War."

Step 3: Choose reference materials that contain the information you need.

Step 4: Use the topic "French and Indian War" as a search term in the reference materials you have chosen.

Reference Material	How to Find Information
An **atlas** contains many different kinds of maps. 	Look in the **index** for the location you want to find. The index is in the back of the atlas. It is an alphabetized list of topics included in the book.
An **encyclopedia** has information about people, places, and events. 	Find the volume that includes the first letter of the topic. If your topic isn't listed, think of a bigger idea that your topic might be a part of.
An Internet **website** is a source of information that can be found online by using a computer. 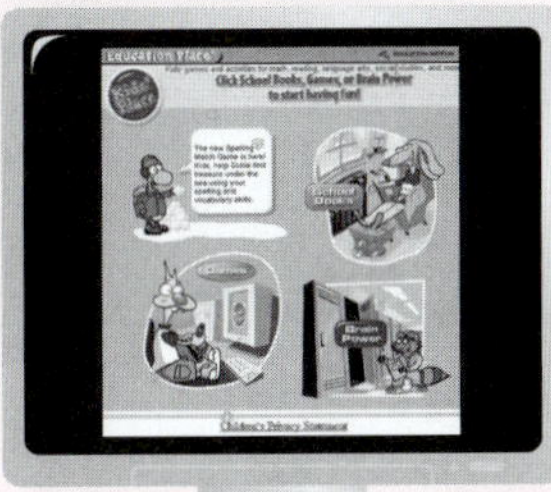	Type your topic into a search engine. A **search engine** is a website that helps you find other websites. A search engine will show you a list of websites related to the topic.

Practice the Skill

Look at the reference materials on this page. Identify those that are most likely to have the answer to each of these questions.

1. Fort Frederick was built near present-day Hagerstown. Where is Hagerstown, Maryland?
2. What effects did the French and Indian War have on Marylanders?

Apply the Skill

Review the information in Lesson 1, pages 48–51. Write a question about something you would like to know more about. Use one or more of the reference materials listed on this page to answer your question.

Core Lesson 2

The American Revolution

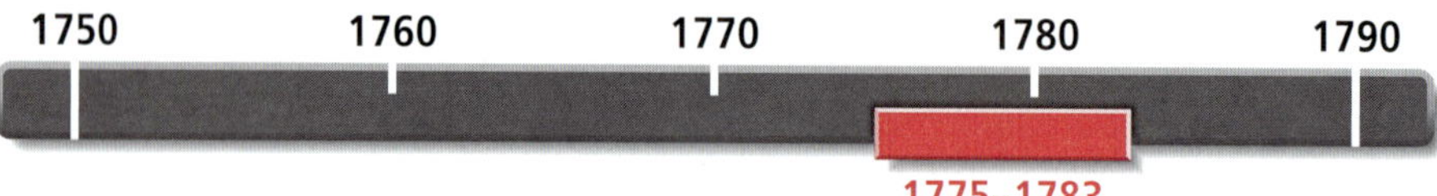

Build on What You Know Have you ever had to choose sides on an issue? In 1776, Marylanders had to choose between supporting Britain or fighting for freedom from British rule.

VOCABULARY

Loyalist
Patriot
independence
rights
privateer

Vocabulary Strategy

Loyalist

Look for the base word **loyal** in **Loyalist.** The **-ist** suffix means "someone who." Loyalists were people who were loyal to the British.

READING SKILL

Sequence As you read, list the sequence of those major events of the American Revolution that are related to Maryland.

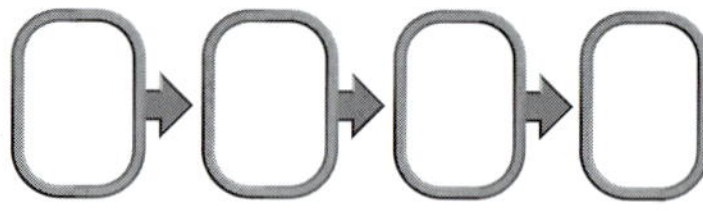

War Breaks Out

Main Idea In 1775, disagreements between the colonists and Britain led to the Revolutionary War.

As disagreements between the colonists and Britain grew worse, Marylanders had a hard time deciding which side to take. Some people were called Loyalists. A **Loyalist** stayed loyal to the British king. Other people were called Patriots. A **Patriot** was against British rule and wanted the colonies to be free from Britain.

The Sons of Liberty was a group of Patriots who protested British taxes. The group held meetings under a tree in Annapolis. The tree came to be called the Liberty Tree.

The Battle of Lexington American colonists first fought British soldiers near the town of Lexington, Massachusetts.

The Declaration of Independence **Colonial leaders met in Philadelphia to declare their independence from Britain.**

Declaration of Independence

On April 19, 1775, a small group of colonists battled against British soldiers in Lexington, Massachusetts. The British then marched to Concord, where the colonists fought back strongly. When the British soldiers returned to Boston, the colonists trapped them in the city.

The colonists realized they would soon be at war with Britain. They created an army called the Continental Army. **George Washington** became the army's commander.

In July 1776, the colonists decided to declare independence from Britain. **Independence** means freedom from being ruled by someone else. A Patriot named **Thomas Jefferson** was asked to write a document saying why the colonies should be independent.

The document that Jefferson wrote became known as the Declaration of Independence. The Declaration of Independence states that people have rights that cannot be taken away. **Rights** are freedoms protected by a government. Jefferson wrote that Britain failed to protect colonists' rights because they had no voice in British government.

Although not all Marylanders supported the idea of independence, the Maryland government agreed to support the Declaration of Independence. Four Maryland Patriots signed the document. They were Samuel Chase, Charles Carroll, **Thomas Stone**, and William Paca.

REVIEW What was the difference between the Sons of Liberty and the Loyalists?

Maryland and the War

Main Idea Marylanders helped with the war effort.

Marylanders fought in many of the battles of the Revolutionary War. The Maryland Continental Army fought with George Washington in New York, New Jersey, and Pennsylvania. Marylanders also fought in the southern states.

Maryland sent supplies such as flour and corn to the Continental Army. Colonists in Maryland also made supplies that the army needed, such as shovels and cannons. In fact, several businesses in Maryland grew during the war.

Baltimore served as the capital of the American colonies during the winter of 1776–1777. The British were near the capital city of Philadelphia, so government leaders moved to nearby Baltimore.

Shipbuilding Shipyards, such as this one at Gray's Harbor, built many ships during the war.

Battles of the Revolutionary War

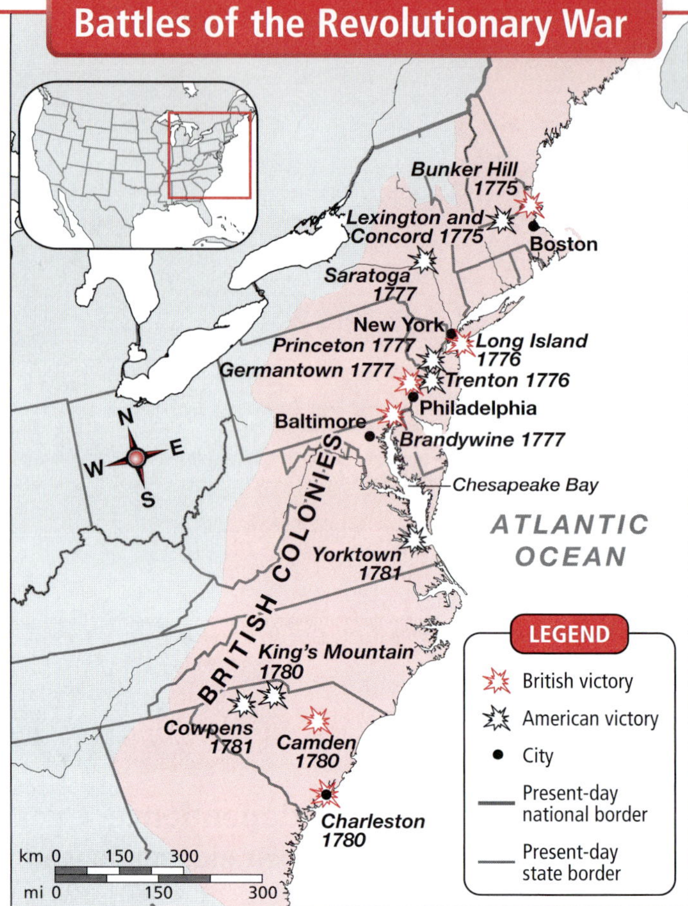

Battle Sites Several important battles were fought near Maryland.

SKILL Reading Maps Which battle shown on the map was closest to Baltimore?

The War at Sea

Britain had a powerful navy that could move soldiers quickly. At first, the colonists had few war ships to defend the shores of the colonies.

The ships that did the most damage to Britain's navy were privateers. A **privateer** was a privately owned ship that attacked British ships.

Baltimore became home to many privateers because of its location on the Chesapeake Bay. Maryland's shipbuilders also made many ships during the war.

Patriots Win the War

In 1781, George Washington and his army fought the British at Yorktown, Virginia. The British were trapped and forced to give up.

The battle at Yorktown was the last major battle of the war. The colonies had won their independence from Britain and become the United States.

REVIEW Under what American general did some Marylanders serve?

Yorktown British General Cornwallis makes peace with General Washington.

Lesson Summary

- Patriots and Loyalists took different sides over British rule.
- In 1776, the colonies declared independence from Britain.
- Maryland sent soldiers and produced war supplies.
- Baltimore served as the colonial capital and a home port to many privateers.
- After winning the battle of Yorktown, the Americans won the war.

Why It Matters . . .

By winning the Revolutionary War, the colonies gained independence and formed a new country.

Lesson Review

1776 Declaration of Independence

1781 Battle of Yorktown

1775 — 1780 — 1785

1. **VOCABULARY** Use the words **Patriot** and **Loyalist** to describe what was happening in Maryland before and during the Revolutionary War.
2. **READING SKILL** What sequence of events led to the signing of the Declaration of Independence?
3. **MAIN IDEA: History** What did Marylanders do to show their support for the Declaration of Independence?
4. **MAIN IDEA: Economics** In what way did the Revolutionary War affect the economy in Maryland?
5. **TIMELINE SKILL** How many years after the Declaration of Independence did the battle of Yorktown take place?
6. **CRITICAL THINKING: Draw Conclusions** Why do you think the Chesapeake Bay was a good place for privateers?

SPEAKING ACTIVITY Write a short speech that a Loyalist or Patriot might give to other colonists about independence from Britain.

Core Lesson 3

A New Nation, a New State

VOCABULARY

constitution
ratify
representative

Vocabulary Strategy

ratify

A synonym for **ratify** is accept. When state or government leaders accept an agreement, they ratify it.

READING SKILL
Problem and Solution
As you read, list some of the problems people had after the war and how these problems were solved.

Problem	Solution

Build on What You Know Have you ever planned how a group would work together on something? Maryland leaders had to plan how the people in Maryland would work together as a new state in a new nation.

A New Government

Main Idea Maryland and the country planned new governments.

When the United States declared independence in 1776, Marylanders knew that they needed a new government. Leaders gathered in Annapolis to decide how Maryland should be governed. They wrote a constitution and signed it on November 11, 1776. A **constitution** is a written plan for government. The new constitution described Maryland's new government and explained how it would provide fairness and order. It also explained the rights of Marylanders and how the law would protect those rights.

Thomas Johnson
This Patriot from Calvert County was the state's first governor.

Freedom of Religion

Since it first became a colony, freedom to choose their own way of worship was important to the people of Maryland. However, as a royal colony, Maryland did not have this freedom. Maryland leaders made sure the new state constitution guaranteed freedom of religion. This led to the growth of many different churches.

In Baltimore, the number of Catholics increased. The number of Baptists, Quakers, and Presbyterians increased as well.

A New National Government

In 1781, the states began to use the Articles of Confederation, a plan for the new national government. But the states had a difficult time working together under this plan. So in 1787, representatives began to write a new plan for government. A **representative** is a person who speaks for other people. The representatives from Maryland were **Daniel Carroll, St. Thomas Jenifer, Luther Martin, James McHenry,** and **John Francis Mercer.**

The new plan became the Constitution of the United States. The states needed to ratify the Constitution before it could be used. To **ratify** means to officially accept. The Constitution was ratified in 1788. It added a section called the Bill of Rights, which protects basic rights and freedoms, such as freedom of religion and freedom of speech.

Now, a location for the new government was needed. In 1791, Maryland and Virginia gave land to the United States for the nation's capital. The area was named Washington, District of Columbia.

REVIEW What did Maryland do to help the new United States government?

Writing the Constitution Representatives from all the states met in Philadelphia to fix the Articles of Confederation. In the end, they wrote a new plan for the American government.

Maryland's Economy Grows

Main Idea Baltimore's growth led to more growth in Maryland.

In the 1790s, Baltimore grew very quickly. It was a shipbuilding center that soon became famous for its speedy clipper ships. Ships carried goods from Baltimore to other states and to Europe.

As Baltimore grew, people built more roads to the city. People in western Maryland used the roads to take their farm products to Baltimore. They sent goods such as flour and tobacco in covered wagons there. Items made in Baltimore, such as iron products, were shipped to the newer settlements in western Maryland.

Learning in Maryland

Soon after the Revolutionary War ended, Marylanders began making plans to help their children learn to become good workers and citizens. By 1800, Maryland had several public schools and many schools run by churches.

In 1809 in Emmitsburg, **Elizabeth Seton** started the first free Roman Catholic school for girls in the United States.

A Growing City As Baltimore businesses grew, many new roads connected Baltimore to other cities. The Baltimore Clipper ship (right) carried goods to other states and countries.

Benjamin Banneker

One Marylander who loved to study math as a child grew to become a mathematician. **Benjamin Banneker** was a free African American. When he grew up, Banneker invented a wooden clock and studied the stars. He also published a series of books that listed information about the movement of the earth, moon, and planets.

REVIEW In what ways did Maryland benefit from changes in transportation after the war?

Lesson Summary

Maryland wrote a state constitution during the Revolutionary War. After the war, the United States also wrote a national constitution. During the 1790s, Maryland's economy and cities grew.

Why It Matters . . .

The type of government described in the Maryland and United States constitutions is still used today.

Benjamin Banneker He was one of several people who helped measure the land for the construction of Washington, D.C.

Lesson Review

- 1776 Maryland constitution signed
- 1781 Articles of Confederation
- 1788 U.S. Constitution ratified

1770 — 1780 — 1790

1. **VOCABULARY** Complete the sentence using one of the following vocabulary words: **constitution** and **ratify.**

   The states needed to _____ the _____ of the United States after it was written.

2. **READING SKILL** How did the country solve the problem of finding a place for the national capital?

3. **MAIN IDEA: Government** What is the Bill of Rights?

4. **MAIN IDEA: History** What was the result of having religious freedom protected in the Maryland constitution?

5. **TIMELINE SKILL** In what year was Maryland's constitution signed?

6. **CRITICAL THINKING: Analyze** Why do you think that Marylanders wrote a constitution before the United States Constitution was ratified?

WRITING ACTIVITY Write a paragraph describing your opinion about Maryland giving some of its land for the nation's capital.

Skillbuilder

Make a Timeline

A timeline shows events in the order in which they happened. You can organize and remember information by making a timeline of important events and dates.

Learn the Skill

Step 1: List the important events and their dates. This list shows three events from Lesson 3.

1776—Maryland state constitution is written.
1781—Articles of Confederation are adopted.
1787—United States Constitution is written.

Step 2: Decide how many years you will show on the timeline. The listed events cover a time period of eleven years, from 1776 to 1787. Draw the line so that each section stands for the same number of years.

Step 3: Write each event above its listed year. Add a title.

New Forms of Government

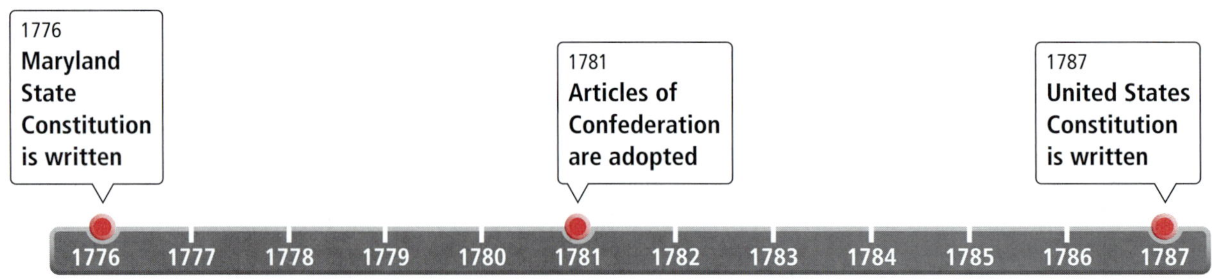

Practice the Skill

Read the paragraph below. It tells about events during and after the Revolutionary War in Maryland. Answer the questions. Then make a timeline of the events.

In 1777, after Maryland leaders wrote the state constitution, Thomas Johnson became the state's first governor. Maryland was the last state to sign the Articles of Confederation, in 1781. In 1786, leaders of the new nation met in Annapolis to talk about changes to the Articles of Confederation. The representatives decided that the Articles of Confederation would not solve their economic problems. They wrote a new plan for the United States government, the United States Constitution. In 1788, Maryland became the seventh state to ratify the U.S. Constitution.

1. What events and dates would you show on your timeline?
2. How many years would be covered on your timeline?
3. What title would you give your timeline?

Apply the Skill

Reread the section about British taxes on the colonies on page 50. Make a timeline to show when at least four important events occurred.

Chapter 3 Review and Test Prep

Visual Summary

1 – 4. Write a description for each item or event named below.

Declaration of Independence	Maryland Constitution	Freedom of Religion	Representative

______	______	______	______
______	______	______	______
______	______	______	______

Facts and Main Ideas

TEST PREP Answer each question below.

5. **Geography** What part of Maryland was in danger of attack during the French and Indian War?
6. **History** In what ways did Marylanders show their anger about British taxes?
7. **History** What group supported the British government during the Revolutionary War?
8. **Economics** Why did Baltimore grow after the Revolutionary War?
9. **Government** What was described and explained in Maryland's constitution?

Vocabulary

TEST PREP Choose the correct word from the list below to complete each sentence.

allies, p. 48
constitution, p. 58
representative, p. 59

10. A person who speaks for many people in the government is a _____.
11. American Indian groups were _____ of France during the French and Indian War.
12. Maryland wrote its _____ shortly after the Declaration of Independence was signed.

CHAPTER SUMMARY TIMELINE

1763 French and Indian War ends	1776 Declaration of Independence	1787 U.S. Constitution written

1760 — 1770 — 1780 — 1790 — 1800

Apply Skills

TEST PREP **Timeline Skill** Apply what you have learned about making a timeline. Use the information about Baltimore's history to answer each question.

1729: Baltimore is founded.
1776: Baltimore serves as U.S. capital.
1779: U.S. Navy's first ship built in Baltimore.

13. If you marked your timeline to show every tenth year, where would Baltimore's serving as the U.S. capital be found?

A. between 1780 and 1790
B. between 1770 and 1780
C. between 1720 and 1730
D. between 1760 and 1770

14. Baltimore and Fells Point were joined in 1773. Where would you place this information on the timeline?

A. to the right of 1780
B. to the left of 1729
C. to the left of 1776
D. between 1776 and 1780

Critical Thinking

TEST PREP Write a short paragraph to answer each question below. Use details from the chapter to support your response.

15. Predict What might have happened to the state economy if roads had not been built from Baltimore to other areas?

16. Cause and Effect What effect did the French and Indian War have on U.S. history?

Timeline

Use the Chapter Summary Timeline above to answer the question.

17. In what year was the Constitution of the United States written?

Activities

Art Activity Create a poster supporting either the Loyalists or the Patriots in the Revolutionary War.

Writing Activity Write a list of events that led up to the Revolutionary War. For each event, write one sentence that describes the colonists' actions.

Technology
Writing Process Tips
Get help with your list at **www.eduplace.com/kids/hmss/**

Chapter 4 Maryland and the Nation

Technology

e • glossary
e • word games
www.eduplace.com/kids/hmss/

Vocabulary Preview

blockade

The British set up a **blockade** in the Chesapeake Bay. The blockade kept ships from entering or leaving Baltimore harbor. **page 70**

anthem

Francis Scott Key watched the Battle of Baltimore and wrote a poem about it. The poem was later set to music. It became our national **anthem.** **page 72**

Chapter Timeline

1812	War with Britain
1814	Battle of Baltimore
1818	National Road reaches Ohio River

1810 — 1815 — 1820

Reading Strategy

Question As you read the lessons in this chapter, ask yourself questions to check your understanding.

List questions you have. When you finish reading, go back to find the answers.

turnpike

An important **turnpike** in Maryland was built in the early 1800s. Travelers paid to use this road.
page 77

canal

A **canal** is a waterway that links separate bodies of water. Boats on the Chesapeake and Ohio Canal carried goods and people across Maryland. **page 78**

1828
Work on Baltimore and Ohio Railroad begins

1825 1830 1835

Core Lesson 1

The War of 1812

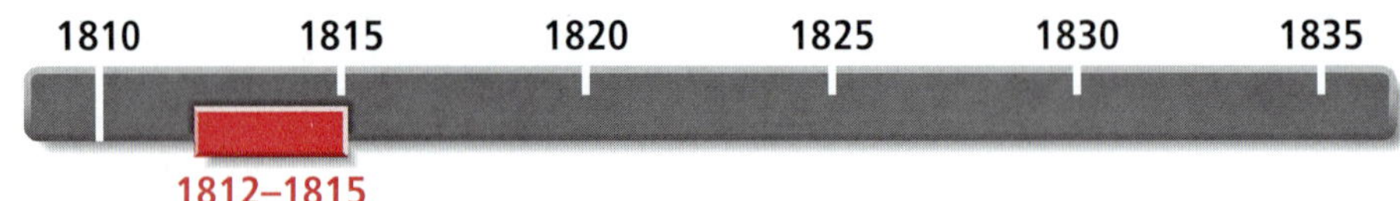

VOCABULARY

blockade
surrender
anthem

Vocabulary Strategy

blockade

Look at the verb **block** in **blockade.** Block means to stop movement. In a **blockade,** ships block people and supplies from getting into an area.

READING SKILL

Cause and Effect Show causes of the War of 1812.

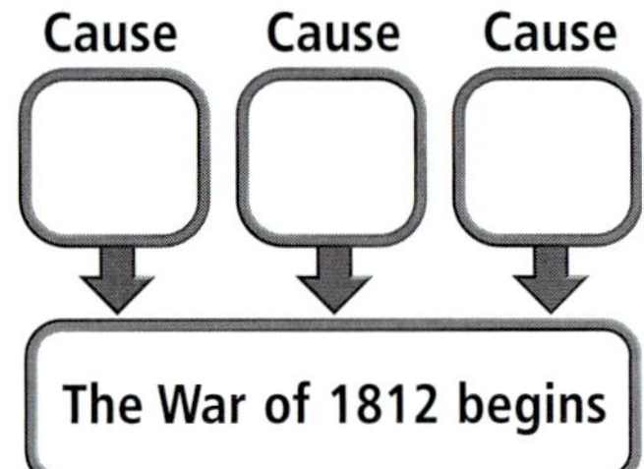

Build on What You Know What do you feel or think of when you hear "The Star-Spangled Banner"? The words of our nation's official song were written near Baltimore during the War of 1812.

Troubles with the British

Main Idea Conflict developed again between the United States and Britain in the early 1800s.

The United States and Britain became enemies again in the early 1800s. Britain was at war with France. The United States did not want to take sides, but disagreements developed between the United States and Britain.

The British had a powerful navy. Yet, British sailors often went to work on U.S. ships because they could earn more money. The British navy would make raids on U.S. ships to look for these sailors. Sometimes the British captured U.S. sailors and made them serve in the British navy.

The British navy also tried to keep U.S. ships from carrying goods to France. These actions made Americans angry.

British Buckle This was part of the uniform worn by the British navy in the early 1800s.

Call for War

At the same time, U.S. settlers were moving west of the original 13 states. The American Indians living in the west did not want to give up their land. A Shawnee leader named **Tecumseh** (tih CUHM suh) urged American Indians to join together and fight. He also asked the British for help.

Soon some members of Congress became angry at Britain. They believed that the British were helping the American Indians fight the settlers. They were also upset about the actions of the British navy. In 1811, United States troops defeated American Indians in the Battle of Tippecanoe in present-day Indiana. After the battle, Tecumseh traveled to Canada to join British allies fighting there.

Tecumseh
This Shawnee leader traveled thousands of miles to convince other American Indians to fight for their land.

The War of 1812 Begins

After the Battle of Tippecanoe, Americans knew that the British and the American Indians were working together. Most Marylanders believed that the United States should show Britain that the United States was fully independent. President **James Madison** asked Congress to declare war on Britain. Congress declared war on June 18, 1812.

Many early battles of the war took place near the Great Lakes. In 1813, Captain **Oliver Hazard Perry** defeated the British in the Battle of Lake Erie. Then, the United States won other battles in Canada.

REVIEW Why did most Marylanders think the United States should go to war with Britain?

The *Constitution*
This U.S. ship is shown defeating the British ship *Java*.

The War in Maryland

Main Idea Maryland's location made it an important battleground in the war.

Early in 1813, British ships sailed into the Chesapeake Bay. They set up a blockade there. In a **blockade,** ships or soldiers are used to keep people and goods from entering or leaving an area. The British blockade stopped ships from entering or leaving the port of Baltimore. The blockade caused serious trade problems for both Baltimore and the United States.

The British also made raids from their ships in the Chesapeake Bay. They attacked communities on the eastern and western shores of Maryland. In May 1813, the British entered the town of Havre de Grace. They wrecked and burned many homes there.

In 1814, Britain's war with France ended. Now the British could send more soldiers to North America. With new soldiers, the British planned to attack Washington, D.C.

On August 19, the British set out for Washington, D.C. They had to cross the bridge at Bladensburg to get there. On August 24, United States soldiers met the British at Bladensburg. The soldiers fought hard but had to retreat, or move back. Now the British had a clear path to Washington, D.C.

Outside the nation's capital, President James Madison was with other leaders who were trying to prepare the city for attack. British ships were sailing quickly up the Chesapeake Bay. At the same time, many British soldiers were moving toward the city.

President James Madison Madison believed that the United States needed to stand up against Great Britain.

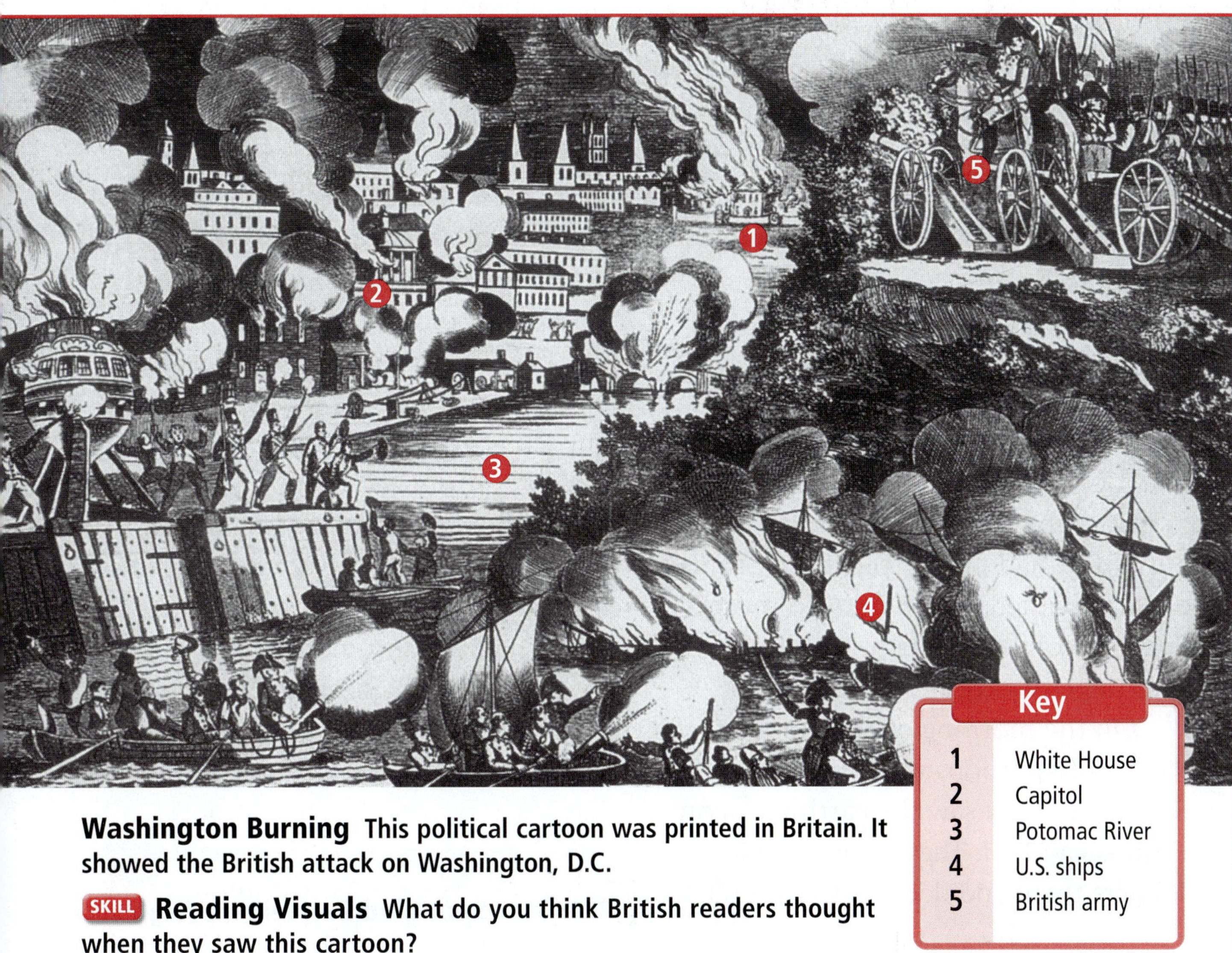

Key	
1	White House
2	Capitol
3	Potomac River
4	U.S. ships
5	British army

Washington Burning **This political cartoon was printed in Britain. It showed the British attack on Washington, D.C.**

SKILL **Reading Visuals** **What do you think British readers thought when they saw this cartoon?**

The Burning of Washington, D.C.

Although the President was outside Washington, D.C., the president's wife, **Dolley Madison,** escaped the city just before the British arrived. She left behind most of her belongings. She did, however, take important government papers with her. She also saved a famous painting of George Washington that hung in the White House.

The British entered Washington, D.C., with little fighting. They set fire to many government buildings, including the Capitol and the White House.

The streets were crowded with people leaving the city. One person described seeing

> **"soldiers and senators, men, women and children, horses, carriages, and carts loaded with household furniture, all hastening [hurrying] toward a wooden bridge which crosses the Potomac."**

The red glow of the burning capital could be seen as far away as Baltimore.

REVIEW Why did British and American soldiers fight at Bladensburg?

The Battle of Baltimore

Main Idea The British attacked Baltimore, but U.S. forces did not give up the city.

The people of Baltimore heard about the British victories in Bladensburg and Washington, D.C. They began to prepare their city for an attack by the British. They chose **Samuel Smith,** a businessman who had fought in the Revolutionary War, to organize the preparations.

Smith had people pile up mounds of earth, called earthworks, to protect the city from the British. People all over the city gave supplies.

On the morning of September 13, 1814, British troops were east of Baltimore. They saw the earthworks on Hampstead Hill. They also saw U.S. soldiers there and decided to turn back.

Fort McHenry Defends Baltimore

The same morning, British ships attacked Fort McHenry in Baltimore harbor. For almost 24 hours the British fired on the fort. They did much damage to Fort McHenry, but the U.S. soldiers would not **surrender,** or give up. The British finally had to retreat.

Francis Scott Key, a Maryland lawyer, watched the attack on Fort McHenry from a ship several miles away. The next morning he saw the United States flag still flying above the fort. Key felt proud that the United States had not surrendered. He wrote a poem that later became our national anthem, "The Star-Spangled Banner." An **anthem** is a song of praise or loyalty.

The Star-Spangled Banner The flag that Francis Scott Key saw over Fort McHenry was sewn by Marylander Mary Pickersgill.

The Star-Spangled Banner

O say, can you see, by the dawn's early light,
What so proudly we hailed at the twilight's last gleaming,
Whose broad stripes and bright stars, through the perilous fight,
O'er the ramparts we watched were so gallantly streaming?
And the rockets' red glare, the bombs bursting in air,
Gave proof through the night that our flag was still there
O say, does that Star-Spangled Banner yet wave
O'er the land of the free and the home of the brave?

The War Ends

In 1814, the United States and Britain had been fighting each other for two years. Neither side seemed to be winning. The two nations agreed to meet in Ghent, Belgium, to discuss peace. On December 24, 1814, the United States and Britain finally signed a peace treaty. The Treaty of Ghent ended the war.

Because news traveled slowly, one of the United States' greatest victories occurred two weeks after the treaty had already been signed. In January 1815, U.S. soldiers defeated the British in a large battle near New Orleans.

After the war, the British stopped raiding United States ships. They also stopped helping the American Indians fight the U.S. settlers.

REVIEW Why was a battle fought near New Orleans after the Treaty of Ghent was signed?

Lesson Summary

- The British captured U.S. sailors, and tried to control U.S. trade.
- The United States declared war against Britain in 1812.
- The British burned parts of Washington, D.C., but couldn't capture Baltimore.
- The United States and Britain signed a treaty ending the war on December 24, 1814.

Why It Matters . . .

After the War of 1812, Britain and other nations began to treat the United States more as an independent nation.

Lesson Review

1. **VOCABULARY** Explain what the Battle of Baltimore has to do with the national **anthem.**
2. **READING SKILL** What was one **effect** of the Battle of Tippecanoe?
3. **MAIN IDEA: History** Why did the United States declare war on Britain?
4. **MAIN IDEA: History** How did the people of Baltimore keep the British from entering their city?
5. **TIMELINE SKILL** When was war on Britain declared?
6. **CRITICAL THINKING: Evaluate** Why do you think "The Star-Spangled Banner" was chosen to be the national anthem?

WRITING ACTIVITY Write a newspaper article describing the British attack on Washington, D.C. Make sure your article answers the questions *Who?, What?, Where?, When?,* and *Why?*

Skillbuilder

Summarize

VOCABULARY
summary

If you wanted to tell someone about something that you read, you would give a summary of it. A summary is a short way of telling what something is about. It includes only the most important ideas.

Learn the Skill

Step 1: Find the main idea of the passage you are reading. The main idea is what the passage is mostly about.

Step 2: Find important details that tell more about the main idea.

Step 3: Use your own words to tell about the main idea and the important ideas you identified.

After burning Washington, D.C., the British commanders could not agree on what to do next. Some thought they should attack Baltimore right away. Others thought it was too hot and humid for a battle at Baltimore. They suggested going north for a while. Then they could return to Baltimore when the weather was cooler. In the end, the British decided to stay and attack Baltimore. They did not make a decision until September 7, however. That gave the people of Baltimore almost two weeks to get ready.

Main Idea

The British disagreed about what to do after burning Washington, D.C. Some wanted to attack Baltimore right away. Others wanted to go north and come back later. They finally decided to attack Baltimore right away. While the British were deciding, the people of Baltimore had time to prepare for an attack.

Practice the Skill

Read the passage below. Then answer the questions that follow.

> Everyone agreed that Samuel Smith was the right person to take charge of preparing Baltimore for attack. There were many reasons why Smith was chosen. He had been a United States senator. He was head of the Maryland soldiers that protected Baltimore. He was also very organized.

1. What is the main idea of the passage?
2. Name two details that support the main idea.
3. Summarize the passage in your own words.

Apply the Skill

Reread page 72. Use what you learned to summarize the Battle of Baltimore.

Core Lesson 2

Maryland Looks West

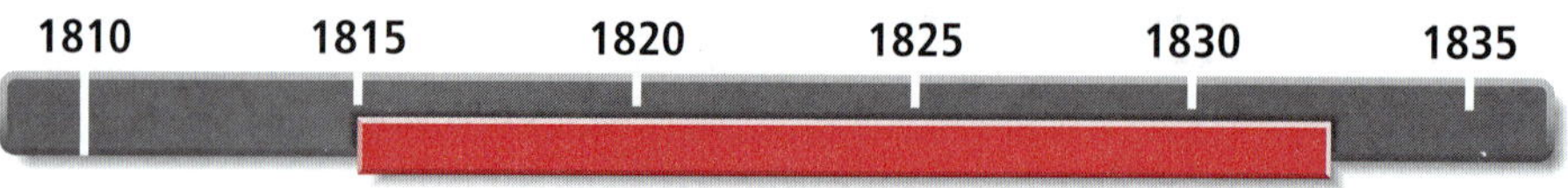

VOCABULARY

frontier
turnpike
canal

Vocabulary Strategy

canal

Canal comes from a word meaning passageway. Canals allow boats to pass from one body of water to another.

READING SKILL

Main Idea and Details

Provide details that support the main idea that transportation west helped Maryland grow.

Build on What You Know How do you travel to a place that is far away? Before trains, cars, or airplanes, many people in Maryland traveled by boat or horse-drawn wagon.

Better Travel by Land

Main Idea New and better roads connected Maryland with other states and the west in the early 1800s.

After the War of 1812, Marylanders continued to move toward the western frontier. A **frontier** is the edge of a country or settled region. Many settlers already lived west of the Appalachian Mountains. More people moved west after the war.

Land travel in the early 1800s was slow and difficult. Roads were rough and narrow and became muddy when it rained. In order for Maryland and the nation to grow, better transportation for goods and people was needed.

Frontier Travel Wagons such as this one were used to move people and goods over the rough frontier roads.

Wagon Travel **It took 16 to 18 days for a loaded wagon pulled by six horses to travel from Wheeling to Baltimore.**

The National Road

The United States government saw the need for a better road to the west. In 1811, it began building the National Road to connect Ohio with the East. The National Road started in Cumberland, Maryland and went west. In 1818, the road reached the Ohio River at what is now Wheeling, West Virginia. By about 1833, the road reached all the way to Columbus, Ohio.

People and goods traveled faster on the wide National Road. Goods from Baltimore, such as clothing and iron tools, traveled to new customers in the west. Businesses such as inns and blacksmiths sprang up along the road to serve travelers. As a result, the towns of Frederick, Hagerstown, and Cumberland grew quickly.

New Maryland Roads

Maryland also needed better state roads. According to one writer, travelers on roads west from Baltimore were in danger of "being upset [knocked over] at any moment on sharp stones or of being thrown into mudholes."

Soon, companies began building other turnpikes. A toll, or payment, for travel is collected on a **turnpike.** In 1821, a turnpike was completed that linked Baltimore to Cumberland. Other turnpikes connected Baltimore to Washington, D.C., and Frederick to Georgetown. As cities and towns became better connected, Marylanders could buy and sell their goods in new places. This helped the state economy to grow.

REVIEW How did new roads help businesses grow in Maryland?

Canals and Railroads

Main Idea Canals and railroads built in the early 1800s helped Maryland's economy grow.

Marylanders continued to look for better ways to move people and goods. They planned to build a canal to the west. A **canal** is a waterway built by people for travel and shipping.

In 1828, work began on the Chesapeake and Ohio Canal. The canal started near Georgetown. It was built all the way to Cumberland. By the time it reached the Appalachian Mountains, however, other forms of transportation had become more important, so construction stopped.

Traveling in Maryland, 1840s

Cumberland
Potomac River
Frederick
Baltimore
Georgetown
Washington, D.C.
MARYLAND
VIRGINIA
NEW JERSEY
DELAWARE
Delaware River
Chesapeake Bay
Potomac River
ATLANTIC OCEAN
N
S
E
W

LEGEND
National Road
Baltimore & Ohio Railroad
Chesapeake & Ohio Canal
Chesapeake & Delaware Canal

km 0 25 50
mi 0 25 50

Travel Routes The Chesapeake and Ohio Canal followed the Potomac River.

SKILL **Reading Maps** What Maryland cities did the Baltimore and Ohio Railroads connect?

The Baltimore and Ohio Railroad

By the 1820s, people were also talking about another form of transportation—railroads. New steam-powered engines were already pulling trains of people and goods in Britain. Many believed that railroads would one day replace canals.

A group of Baltimore business leaders decided to build a railroad west. Work began on the Baltimore and Ohio Railroad the same year that work began on the Chesapeake and Ohio Canal. However, the railroad grew more quickly because it was easier to construct a railroad over hilly regions.

The Baltimore and Ohio Railroad Charles Carroll helped lay the first stone of the Baltimore and Ohio Railroad on July 4, 1828.

Effects of the Railroad

The Baltimore and Ohio Railroad helped Maryland's economy grow. Products such as grain, cloth, and iron pipes traveled from Maryland to customers in other states. Products could be shipped between Wheeling and Baltimore in only a few days. The same journey took as long as 18 days before the railroad. The railroad could ship Chesapeake Bay oysters quickly so that they stayed fresh. The railroad also brought products such as lumber from the west to Maryland.

REVIEW Why did Marylanders want to build a canal and a railroad west?

Lesson Summary

- New roads improved the economy and helped cities and towns grow.
- The Chesapeake and Ohio Canal went as far as Cumberland.
- The Baltimore and Ohio Railroad carried goods and people faster.

Why It Matters . . .

Many transportation routes developed in the early 1800s are still used by Marylanders today.

Steam Engine The first steam locomotive on the Baltimore and Ohio Railroad was called the *Tom Thumb*. This picture shows the *Tom Thumb* winning a race with a horse.

Lesson Review

1815	1818	1820	1825	1828	1830	1835
	National Road reaches Ohio River			B & O Railroad started		

1. **VOCABULARY** Use the words **turnpike** and **canal** to explain how transportation in Maryland changed in the early 1800s.
2. **READING SKILL** Name some **details** that support this **main idea:** The Baltimore and Ohio Railroad helped Maryland's economy grow.
3. **MAIN IDEA: History** Why were new roads needed in the early 1800s?
4. **MAIN IDEA: Economics** In what ways did new forms of transportation help Maryland's economy?
5. **TIMELINE SKILL** How long did it take to build the National Road from the Ohio River to Columbus, Ohio?
6. **CRITICAL THINKING: Draw Conclusions** Many people believed that railroads would one day be more important than canals. Were they correct? Why or why not?

HANDS ON **ART ACTIVITY** Make a transportation collage. Label one half "Maryland in the Early 1800s" and the other half "Maryland Today."

Skillbuilder

Make a Map

VOCABULARY
route

You have read about transportation in Maryland in the early 1800s. A map helps you understand the routes of roads, canals, and railroads. A route is a way of going from one place to another. You can also make a map showing the route you take on your way to school.

Learn the Skill

Step 1: List the starting point, stops, along the way, and the ending point of the route you take to school.

1. My house
2. Lara's house
3. Peter's house
4. School

Step 2: Make an outline map of your community. Label each point from Step 1.

Step 3: Choose a color for the line you will draw to show the route on the map. Label a line with that color in a legend.

Step 4: Draw the route.

Step 5: Add a map title.

My Route to School

Practice the Skill

Read the paragraph below about the route of the Baltimore and Ohio Railroad. Use an outline map of the United States to mark its route.

By 1830, the Baltimore and Ohio Railroad ran from Baltimore to Ellicott's Mills (now Ellicott City). By 1852, it went as far as Wheeling, in present-day West Virginia. It reached Chicago, Illinois, in the 1860s. In the 1870s, it stopped in the middle of the country, at St. Louis, Missouri.

Apply the Skill

Make a map of your own travels in Maryland. You might show a route you have really taken, or one you would like to take.

Chapter 4 Review and Test Prep

Visual Summary

1 – 4. Write a description of each item named below.

War of 1812

Battle of Baltimore

Baltimore and Ohio Railroad

National Road

Facts and Main Ideas

TEST PREP Answer each question below.

5. **History** List three causes of the War of 1812.
6. **Geography** Why did the British set up a blockade of the Chesapeake Bay?
7. **Citizenship** Who wrote "The Star-Spangled Banner" and why?
8. **Economics** How did the National Road change western Maryland?
9. **Geography** Why did the Chesapeake and Ohio Canal stop at Cumberland?

Vocabulary

TEST PREP Choose the correct word from the list below to complete each sentence.

frontier, p. 76
turnpike, p. 77
canal, p. 78

10. Travelers paid a toll to use a _____.
11. Many people moved to the western _____ after the War of 1812.
12. Marylanders wanted to build a _____ linking the Potomac and Ohio Rivers.

1812	War on Britain declared
1814	Battle of Baltimore
1828	B & O Railroad started

1805 1810 1815 1820 1825 1830

Apply Skills

TEST PREP Map Skill Study the Maryland map below. Then use your map skills to answer each question.

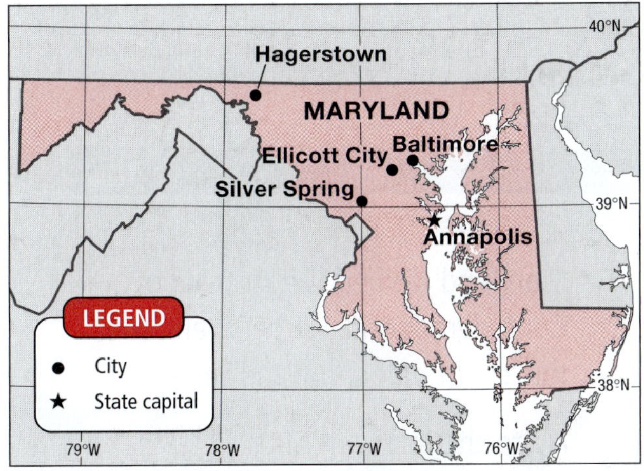

13. To show the route of the Baltimore and Ohio Railroad in Maryland, which of the following should you add to the legend?

A. a compass rose with names of directions
B. a box with the railroad's name
C. a track symbol with the railroad's name
D. a train symbol

14. To add Maryland cities to the map, which symbol would you use?

A. —
B. ★
C. ┼┼┼┼
D. ●

Critical Thinking

TEST PREP Write a short paragraph to answer each question below.

15. Contrast The battles at Washington, D.C., and at Baltimore had different outcomes. How were the battles different?

16. Cause and Effect What were some effects of changes in transportation in Maryland in the early 1800s?

Timeline

Use the Chapter Summary Timeline above to answer the question.

17. In what year was the B & O Railroad started?

Activities

Music Activity Learn the words of "The Star-Spangled Banner." Then speak or sing them along with a recording of the song.

Writing Activity Write a description of travel in Maryland before and after new roads were built.

Technology
Writing Process Tips
Get help with your description at **www.eduplace.com/kids/hmss/**

UNIT 2

Review and Test Prep

Vocabulary and Main Ideas

TEST PREP Write a sentence to answer each question.

1. Why did colonists not want to pay **taxes** to the British?
2. What was the main difference between the Sons of Liberty and **Loyalists?**
3. How did the Maryland **Constitution** support people of different religions?
4. Why was it important for the states to **ratify** the United States Constitution?
5. During which battle was the national **anthem** of the United States written?
6. What changes in **transportation** led more people to move further west?

Critical Thinking

TEST PREP Write a short paragraph to answer each question.

7. **Cause and Effect** Explain why Britain's taxes on the colonies led to the Revolutionary War.
8. **Synthesize** Based on your reading, how do you think your life in Maryland would be different today if transportation had not changed in the early 1800s?

Apply Skills

TEST PREP Use what you have learned about making a timeline to answer each question.

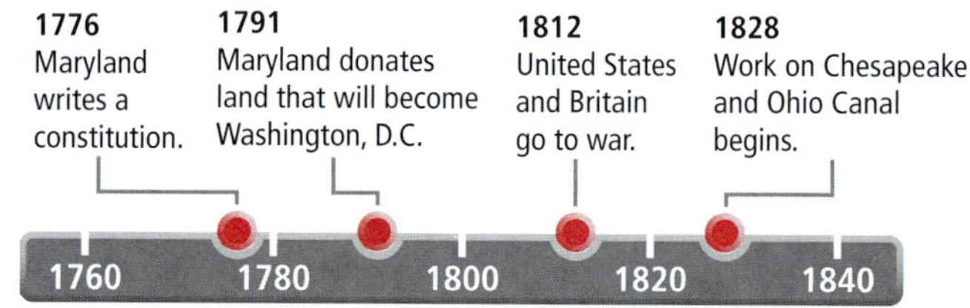

9. Maryland ratified the Articles of Confederation in 1781. Where does this event belong on the timeline?
   A. to the left of 1760
   B. between 1780 and 1800
   C. between 1760 and 1780
   D. to the right of 1820

10. Which of the following events would be placed between 1800 and 1820?
   A. Baltimore is founded in 1729.
   B. In 1787, the U.S. Constitution was written.
   C. The Battle of Tippecanoe was fought in 1811.
   D. Work on the Chesapeake and Ohio Canal begins in 1828.

Unit Activity

Make a "Now-and-Then Mural"

- Think about how transportation changed in Maryland during the 1800s.
- Make a sketch that shows Maryland before these changes. Make another sketch to show Maryland in the mid-1800s and also today.
- Plan a mural that will combine your three sketches.

At the Library

Go to your school or public library to find these books.

The Declaration of Independence (History of the World) by Don Nardo
Find out more about the writing of the Declaration of Independence.

The Flag Maker by Susan Campbell Bartoletti
Learn about Mary Pickersgill, the woman who made the flag that flew above Fort McHenry during the Battle of Baltimore.

CURRENT EVENTS
WEEKLY WR READER

Current Events Project

Create a bulletin board about independence around the world today.

- Find information that tells about nations that are trying to achieve greater independence and freedom today.
- Write a summary of each article. Draw a picture or map to illustrate each summary.
- Post your illustrated summaries on a bulletin board.

Technology

Weekly Reader online offers social studies articles. Go to: **www.eduplace.com/kids/hmss/**

UNIT 3

A Changing State

In what way do changes affect people?

"If there is no struggle, there is no progress."

Frederick Douglass

Harriet Tubman

1820–1913

Harriet Tubman was born into slavery in Maryland. She escaped and then returned to help others reach freedom. **page 93**

History Makers

Frederick Douglass

1818–1895

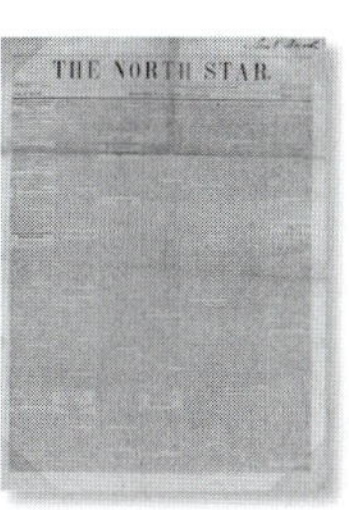
THE NORTH STAR.

After escaping from slavery in Maryland, Douglass became an important speaker and writer and worked to end slavery in the United States. **page 93**

Franklin Delano Roosevelt

1882–1945

During the Great Depression, President Roosevelt started many government programs to help people get jobs. **page 115**

Chapter 5

The Civil War

Technology
e • glossary
e • word games
www.eduplace.com/kids/hmss/

Vocabulary Preview

abolitionist

An **abolitionist** was someone who worked to end slavery in the United States. William Lloyd Garrison and others wrote about why slavery was wrong. **page 93**

civil war

In a **civil war,** people who live in the same country fight against one another. The U.S. Civil War divided the country into the North against the South. **page 98**

Chapter Timeline

1860

1861 Civil War starts

1862 Battle of Antietam

1865 Civil War ends

1865

Reading Strategy

Predict and Infer Use this strategy as you read this chapter.

Look at the pictures in the lesson to predict what it will be about.

Reconstruction

During the **Reconstruction** period, plans were made to help southern states rejoin the nation and recover from the Civil War. **page 102**

Freedmen's Bureau

After the Civil War, the United States set up the **Freedmen's Bureau.** It helped newly-freed African Americans get jobs and an education. **page 103**

1870
15th Amendment passes

1870

Core Lesson 1

A Growing Conflict

VOCABULARY

abolitionist
secede
Union

Vocabulary Strategy

abolitionist

Abolitionist comes from the verb **abolish,** which means "to end." Abolitionists wanted to end slavery.

READING SKILL

Compare and Contrast List the differences between the North and South in the early 1800s.

North	South

Build on What You Know Have you ever had a disagreement with someone? How did you find a solution to the problem? In the 1800s, people in the northern and southern states disagreed about slavery.

Two Different Economies

Main Idea Maryland was caught in the middle of a growing disagreement between the North and the South.

Maryland is located in the middle of the United States Atlantic Coast. The states north of Maryland are often grouped as the North. The states south of Maryland are often grouped as the South.

After the Revolutionary War, many northern states passed laws to end slavery in their states. Southern states, including Maryland, did not.

As new states were added to the United States in the 1800s, the North and the South disagreed about whether the new states should allow slavery.

Plantations Enslaved people did the difficult work on southern plantations.

SKILL **Reading Maps** According to the map, was Maryland a free state or a slave state?

Maryland's Divided Economy

By the mid-1800s, the North and South had developed very different economies. In the South, the economy depended mostly on farming crops such as cotton and tobacco. In the North, however, the economy was based on industry. Industry is the making of many goods by a group of businesses or factories.

Maryland's economy depended on both farming and industry. Western Maryland had more industry, while eastern and southern Maryland had more agriculture, or farming. Because farms used more enslaved workers than factories did, Marylanders were divided about the issue of slavery.

The shipbuilding and iron industries did not depend on enslaved workers. Neither did transportation industries, such as the Baltimore and Ohio Railroad.

In Maryland cities where industries were important, there were few enslaved people. Factory owners paid people to work in the factories. Machines were able to do factory work instead of people.

Tobacco was an important crop in Maryland in the 1800s. Many of the tobacco plantations were found in southern Maryland and on the Eastern Shore.

Tobacco plantation owners had grown to depend on enslaved people. Tobacco crops required a lot of care. For example, hornworms had to be picked from tobacco plants by hand. Plantation owners could make the most money by using enslaved workers.

REVIEW Why were enslaved people used to work on tobacco plantations, and not in factories?

African American Churches Free African Americans in Baltimore founded several churches including the First Baptist Church (above), founded in 1836 by Moses Clayton (right).

African Americans in Maryland

Main Idea There were almost as many free African Americans in Maryland as there were enslaved African Americans in the mid-1800s.

Not all African Americans in Maryland were enslaved. In 1860, there were more than 80,000 free African Americans in the state. These free African Americans most often had either been freed from slavery or had been born to parents who were free.

Life for some free African Americans was still very hard. This was especially true on the Eastern Shore. There, free African Americans did the same work as enslaved African Americans. Men and women worked in the fields. Some women worked in homes as maids. These African Americans were often paid in food and clothing. Although they were freed from slavery, they had few opportunities for better lives.

Free African-Americans in Baltimore

Free African Americans in cities such as Baltimore were more successful. Some of them worked in skilled jobs as blacksmiths, barbers, and shoemakers. Others worked as shopkeepers and shipbuilders.

The 25,000 free African Americans in Baltimore formed a community. They built churches and schools and established two banks. They lived together in neighborhoods with names such as Happy Alley and Welcome Alley.

In the 1830s and 1840s, free African Americans faced greater challenges in Maryland as white immigrants came to the state. These immigrants took the jobs that many free African Americans had been doing. Some Marylanders did not like that free African Americans lived in a state where slavery was allowed. They worried that free African Americans were helping enslaved people escape.

Abolitionists in Maryland

Slavery became an important issue in Maryland in the mid-1800s. People were divided on whether it should be allowed. Some people became abolitionists. An **abolitionist** was someone who worked to end slavery. Abolitionists often spoke and wrote articles about why slavery should end.

One Maryland abolitionist was **Frederick Douglass.** Douglass was born into slavery in Talbot County, but escaped as a young man. Douglass began speaking and writing against slavery. Douglass was soon mentioned in the *Liberator,* an anti-slavery newspaper published by Marylander **William Lloyd Garrison.**

In 1845 Douglass published a book about his life as an enslaved person. He traveled through the North and to Great Britain telling people about the evils of slavery.

Finding Freedom **This drawing shows enslaved people traveling through Maryland with the help of the Underground Railroad.**

The Underground Railroad

Some abolitionists helped enslaved people escape from slavery. They formed a system known as the Underground Railroad. This was a series of secret escape routes and hiding places to bring southern slaves to freedom in the North. Many routes went through Maryland.

Free African Americans gave money and support to the Underground Railroad. The high number of free African Americans in Maryland and its location between the South and the North helped the Underground Railroad to grow in the state.

Members of the Underground Railroad gave food and clothing to runaways. They also hid them until it was safe to move on. The hiding places were known as stations. The people who guided runaways from one station to the next were known as conductors.

One famous conductor on the Underground Railroad was **Harriet Tubman.** She escaped from slavery in Maryland. She returned to the South several times to help about 300 people escape slavery. She risked being caught and enslaved again. She spoke about helping enslaved people escape, saying,

> **"I have heard their groans and sighs, and seen their tears, and I would give every drop of blood in my veins to free them."**

REVIEW Why was the Underground Railroad able to grow in Maryland?

Division Grows

Main Idea Disagreements led to the breakup of the United States.

The differences between the economies of the North and South led to disagreements about tariffs. A tariff is a tax on goods made outside the United States. Tariffs raised the price of goods made outside of the United States. The United States government passed tariffs to help American industries. Tariffs helped industries in the North, but the South had few industries.

Some southerners felt the federal government did not have the power to create tariffs. They argued in favor of states' rights. This is the idea that the states, not the federal government, should make the final decisions about issues that affect them such as slavery and tariffs. States' rights became a popular idea in the South. These disagreements led to greater division between the North and South.

The Election of 1860

In 1860, the country held an election for President. The Democratic Party was divided and could not agree on only one candidate. Democrats in the North chose **Stephen Douglas** of Illinois. Democrats in the South chose **John Breckenridge** of Kentucky. Breckenridge wanted to allow slavery in all the new United States territories.

The Republican Party chose **Abraham Lincoln** as its candidate. Lincoln was against slavery. He had support in the North, but very little in the South. Lincoln won the close election, but he did not win in a single southern state.

Conflicts between the North and the South continued to grow. Southern states talked about whether to secede from the United States. **Secede** means to leave or break off from a country. With Lincoln as President, the southern states feared that he would try to end slavery.

Lincoln Speaks In several public debates about slavery, Lincoln became known as a great speaker.

A Divided Maryland

In 1860, southern states began seceding. Eleven southern states seceded and formed a new country called the Confederate States of America, or the Confederacy. President Lincoln wanted to keep the Union together. The **Union** was the name for the United States.

Maryland's citizens and leaders were divided about whether they should also secede. Eastern and southern Marylanders who depended on slavery for their farms and plantations often sided with the South. Western Marylanders who depended more on industry often sided with the North.

REVIEW Why did some Marylanders side with the North while others did not?

Lesson Summary

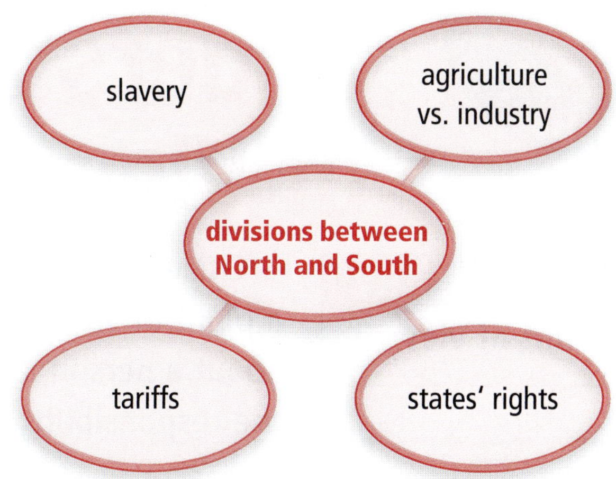

Why It Matters . . .

Disagreements between the South and North led southern states to secede from the Union.

Lesson Review

1845
Frederick Douglass writes against slavery

1860
Abraham Lincoln elected president

1830 1840 1850 1860 1870

1. **VOCABULARY** Use the words **secede** and **Union** to describe what Marylanders thought about leaving the United States.
2. **READING SKILL** In what ways were the economies of the North and the South different? Use your notes to **compare** and **contrast.**
3. **MAIN IDEA: Economics** Describe Maryland's economy in the mid-1800s. How was it similar to and different from the northern and southern economies?
4. **MAIN IDEA: History** How did abolitionists such as Frederick Douglass work to end slavery?
5. **TIMELINE SKILL** When was Abraham Lincoln elected president?
6. **CRITICAL THINKING: Draw Conclusions** In what way would the growth of the Underground Railroad have been different in Maryland if there had been fewer free African Americans in the state?

SPEAKING ACTIVITY Write what you think an abolitionist would say to Marylanders who believed slavery was necessary.

Skillbuilder

Understand Point of View

VOCABULARY
point of view

Citizens who live in the United States have a right to express a point of view. A **point of view** is the way someone thinks about a person, a situation, or an event. Citizens also have the responsibility, or duty, to listen to the views of others.

Andrea's Point of View

"Our city has just opened a beautiful new park. I think that there aren't enough parking spaces for people who come to the park from other neighborhoods. In my opinion, a new parking lot would make it much easier for everyone to visit the park."

Carlos' Point of View

"I live near the new park, and I believe there is already too much traffic on the streets. More parking spaces would make the problem worse. Visitors should walk or take a bus to the park. The noise and pollution of more cars would spoil the park."

Learn the Skill

Step 1: Read the statements carefully. Figure out what the subject is.

Step 2: Identify the point of view of the author or speaker. Look for phrases such as *I think, in my opinion,* or *I believe.* These phrases help show a person's ideas about an issue.

Step 3: Think about the person who is speaking or writing. What experiences have helped shape the person's point of view? What facts does the person give?

Step 4: Tell the person's point of view in your own words. How is it similar to or different from the way you feel about this issue?

Practice the Skill

1. What is the subject of both of the statements on page 96?
2. Describe each person's point of view on the subject.
3. What facts does each person present? Do those facts support their points of view?

Apply the Skill

What is your point of view about providing more parking spaces? Write a paragraph that states your point of view. Be sure to provide good reasons for your opinion.

Core Lesson 2

Fighting the War

VOCABULARY

civil war
border state
casualty

Vocabulary Strategy

civil war

Civil refers to what happens within a society. A **civil war** is a war between two groups or regions within a nation.

READING SKILL

Sequence As you read, list the sequence of major events of the Civil War.

1	
2	
3	
4	

Build on What You Know Have you ever felt strongly about an issue? Were you willing to struggle for your beliefs? Abraham Lincoln believed that the Union was worth preserving, or keeping together.

Civil War Begins

Main Idea Disagreements between the North and the South finally led to a civil war.

In 1861, fighting broke out at Fort Sumter, South Carolina. Fort Sumter was a fort that belonged to the United States government. Confederate soldiers surrounded Fort Sumter, attempting to take control of it. President Lincoln would not surrender the fort. Instead, he sent supplies to the soldiers there.

The Confederate leaders did not want the supplies to reach the fort. On April 12, 1861, the Confederates fired cannons at the fort, and Union soldiers were forced to surrender. This was the beginning of the Civil War. A **civil war** is a war between two groups or regions within a nation.

Fort Sumter After two days of attacks from Confederate soldiers, Union soldiers left the fort on April 14, 1861.

The Baltimore Riots Violence broke out when Marylanders loyal to the Confederacy tried to stop Union troops from passing through Baltimore.

Riots in Baltimore

After the surrender of Fort Sumter, President Lincoln called on the states to gather troops, or soldiers, to fight the South to keep the Union together. Marylanders were divided about whether they should support the Union or the Confederacy.

Maryland was first affected by the war's violence on April 19, 1861. Riots, or street fighting, broke out as Union troops traveling through Maryland had to switch trains in Baltimore. A group of people who supported the Confederacy shouted and threw stones at the troops. Eventually, shots were fired. Police officers prevented the rioters from attacking the troops. As a result, the Union troops were able to get through Baltimore to their train.

Maryland Chooses Sides

After the Baltimore riots, the governor called the Maryland government together to discuss whether to secede and join the Confederacy or to stay in the Union.

The United States government wanted Maryland to stay in the Union. If Maryland seceded, then Washington, D.C., would be surrounded by Confederate states.

The Maryland government decided to stay in the Union. Maryland became a border state. A **border state** was a state that allowed slavery but chose not to secede from the Union.

Although Maryland stayed in the Union throughout the war, many Marylanders fought on the side of the Confederacy.

REVIEW Why did the Union need Maryland to stay in the Union?

The War in Maryland

Main Idea One of the worst battles in the Civil War took place in Maryland.

In September 1862, General **Robert E. Lee** and the Confederate army entered Maryland. Lee was in charge of the Confederate army. He wanted to win a victory in the North, close to Washington, D.C. On September 17, Union and Confederate soldiers fought near Sharpsburg, Maryland. This is known as the Battle of Antietam.

The Union army almost pushed the Confederate troops back into the South. Then more Confederate troops arrived. By the end of the day, there were over 23,000 casualties, more than in any of the previous battles. A **casualty** is a soldier who is killed or wounded.

The Union forces stopped General Lee's attempt to invade the North for a time.

Soon after the battle, President Lincoln issued the Emancipation Proclamation. To emancipate means "to free." This gave freedom to enslaved people in the states that were rebelling against the Union. Since Maryland did not rebel, slaves in Maryland were not set free at that time.

As the war continued over the next few years, troops from both sides traveled through Maryland. In addition to the Battle of Antietam, several smaller battles were also fought in Maryland.

Maryland Women During the War

Family life for many Marylanders changed during the war. While men were fighting the war, women were running farms and businesses.

Women performed many jobs during the Civil War. They organized groups to make bandages for injured troops and to get supplies to army hospitals. They also served as nurses on the battlefield and in hospitals.

One Civil War nurse was **Clara Barton.** Barton brought medical supplies to Antietam and other battle sites. Then she stayed to help take care of wounded soldiers, even though she was in danger herself. Her experiences later led Barton to found the American Red Cross, an organization that helps people who are suffering from great hardships.

Antietam **Union troops, led by General George McClellan, prevented Confederate troops from pushing north near Washington, D.C.**

Effects of the War on Maryland

The Civil War had more casualties than any other war in United States history. When Confederate and Union troops entered Maryland, they destroyed homes and stole supplies. The war also affected the government of Maryland. In 1864, Maryland wrote a new constitution, which ended slavery in the state.

Finally, after four years, the Civil War ended. On April 9, 1865, General Robert E. Lee surrendered to General **Ulysses S. Grant,** the leader of the Union army. The United States would remain one country. With the end of the Civil War, the long and difficult process of bringing the Confederate states back into the Union began.

REVIEW Describe an effect of the Civil War on families in Maryland.

The War Ends Lee surrendered to Grant at Appomattox Court House in Virginia.

Lesson Summary

- Maryland was considered a border state during the Civil War.
- The Battle of Antietam took place in Maryland.
- The Union won the Civil War in 1865.

Why It Matters . . .

The new constitution that Maryland wrote during the war guaranteed freedoms that Marylanders still hold.

Lesson Review

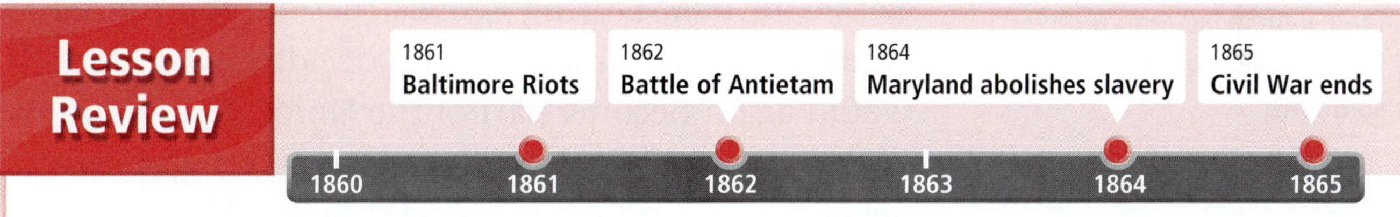

1. **VOCABULARY** Explain why Maryland was a **border state** during the **Civil War.**
2. **READING SKILL** Look at the **sequence** of the major events of the Civil War that you listed. What event do you think affected Maryland the most?
3. **MAIN IDEA: History** Why did riots break out in Baltimore at the beginning of the Civil War?
4. **MAIN IDEA: Government** In what way was slavery officially ended in Maryland?
5. **TIMELINE SKILL** About how much time passed between the Battle of Antietam and the end of the Civil War?
6. **CRITICAL THINKING: Synthesize** Make a statement about life for Marylanders during the Civil War based on what you have read.

WRITING ACTIVITY Write a short newspaper article announcing that slavery has ended in Maryland. Include a headline for your article.

Core Lesson 3

Recovery and Growth

VOCABULARY

Reconstruction
Freedmen's Bureau
segregation

Vocabulary Strategy

Reconstruction

The prefix **re-** means "again." After the Civil War, the southern states had to construct themselves again.

READING SKILL

Problem and Solution

Take notes to identify the problems facing the United States and Maryland after the Civil War and their solutions.

Problem	Solution

Build on What You Know Have you ever been working on a project and then had to start over because something went wrong? In many ways, the United States had to start over after the Civil War.

The Nation Rebuilds

Main Idea Following the Civil War, the United States had to work to bring the North and the South back together.

After the Civil War, people disagreed about how to bring the South back into the Union. The period during which the South rejoined the Union is called **Reconstruction.** During Reconstruction, the United States had to rebuild cities and decide how the South would again become part of the Union. President Lincoln wanted the southern states to set up new governments and rejoin the Union quickly. However, on April 14, 1865, President Lincoln was shot by **John Wilkes Booth,** an actor from Maryland.

Lincoln's Funeral Train
The train left Washington, D.C., and stopped in Baltimore for two hours.

New Schools The Freedmen's Bureau helped build schools for African Americans in Maryland and across the South. The photo on the left shows a teacher with students at the school shown above.

Maryland and Reconstruction

After Lincoln died, Vice President **Andrew Johnson** became president. He tried to put Lincoln's plan for Reconstruction into action. The southern states had to write new constitutions and set up new governments. In 1865, Congress passed the 13th Amendment, which officially ended slavery. As a result, all states had to abolish slavery.

Southern states, including Maryland, passed Black Codes after the Civil War. These were unfair laws that limited the rights of newly freed African Americans. In Maryland, newly freed people were required by law to have jobs even though there were few available to them. They were not allowed to travel wherever they wished or to meet in large groups. The Black Codes made life difficult for African Americans in Maryland.

The Freedmen's Bureau

As a result of the Black Codes, the United States Congress established the Freedmen's Bureau. The **Freedmen's Bureau** was an organization that provided food, clothing, and advice to poor African Americans.

The Black Codes in southern states angered some members of Congress. In 1866, Congress passed the 14th Amendment, which gave all African Americans the rights of U.S. citizens. This law forced Maryland and other southern states to end the Black Codes.

After the Black Codes ended, life improved somewhat for African Americans in Maryland. With help from different organizations, many African Americans were able to go to school. They also began to find better jobs and to hold elected government offices.

REVIEW What did the Black Codes require of African Americans?

The Oyster Industry After oysters were caught (above), they were taken to factories. The picture (right) shows how oysters were canned to ship to places throughout the United States.

Rebuilding Maryland

Main Idea Marylanders faced many challenges during Reconstruction.

In 1870, the 15th Amendment to the United States Constitution was passed. It gave African American men the right to vote. Although African American men could now vote, many politicians in Maryland opposed this change.

When African Americans tried to vote, some Marylanders tried to keep them from voting. Being able to vote was difficult for African Americans in Maryland and throughout much of the South for nearly the next 100 years.

African Americans faced segregation in Maryland and elsewhere after the war ended. **Segregation** is keeping people of different races apart, especially in public places such as schools.

Economic Recovery

After the war, Maryland's economy was struggling. Railroads and canals had been destroyed during the war. This made shipping goods and products more difficult. Some factories and businesses closed during the war because they could not ship their products. Others closed because they could not get the supplies they needed.

Other industries, however, had been successful during the war. Industries that provided the Union troops with supplies such as flour and corn did well.

As transportation routes improved after the war, some new industries started in the state. Growth in both the farming and oyster-harvesting industries helped the canning industry grow. In the canning process, food is preserved by boiling it before putting it into sealed jars or cans.

Newly Freed African Americans

Following the end of slavery in the South, newly freed African Americans began moving north. Some of them settled in Maryland. In Baltimore, they established their own churches. By 1867, there were more than 100 schools for African Americans located in Baltimore and on the Eastern Shore.

African Americans in Maryland also started their own businesses. **Isaac Myers** established the Chesapeake Marine Railway and Dry Dock Company in Baltimore to provide jobs for African Americans. Myers also worked to improve economic conditions for African Americans in Maryland and throughout the United States.

REVIEW In what ways did the condition of railroads and canals after the Civil War affect some Maryland industries?

Lesson Summary

After the Civil War ended, the nation struggled to come back together, and Maryland struggled to rebuild its economy. For a time new laws kept African Americans in Maryland from having the same freedoms as everyone else. Then the 13th, 14th, and 15th amendments protected African Americans' rights as U.S. citizens. As more African Americans settled in Maryland, they started their own schools, churches, and businesses.

Why It Matters . . .

After living through the Civil War, Marylanders began rebuilding their state and looking toward the future.

Lesson Review

1. **VOCABULARY** Write a short paragraph explaining how **Reconstruction** affected life in Maryland.
2. **READING SKILL** What **solution** did the Freedmen's Bureau provide for African Americans after the Civil War?
3. **MAIN IDEA: History** What challenges did African Americans in Maryland face after the Civil War?
4. **TIMELINE SKILL** In what year did President Lincoln die?
5. **CRITICAL THINKING: Infer** Why do you think it was important for Maryland's economy after the Civil War to rebuild railroads and canals?

HANDS ON

RESEARCH ACTIVITY Use library resources to learn more about the changes in Maryland during Reconstruction. Write a three-paragraph summary of your findings. Include two photos or illustrations and write captions for them.

Skillbuilder

Distinguish Fact from Opinion

VOCABULARY
opinion
fact

A writer may express opinions about a topic. An **opinion** is a belief or a feeling. An opinion is neither true nor false. A writer supports his or her opinion with facts. A **fact** is information that can be proved true. Good readers understand the difference between a fact and an opinion.

Learn the Skill

Step 1: Read what the writer wrote.

Step 2: Find words that signal an opinion. Examples include *I think, I believe,* and *We should.* Other examples are words that suggest feelings or beliefs, such as *terrible, wonderful, proud, worst,* and *best.*

Step 3: Decide what the writer's opinion about the topic seems to be.

Step 4: Find facts, such as names or dates, that the writer used. Think about how you could check each fact.

Passage A

After the Second Battle of Bull Run, Confederate soldiers marched into Maryland. Their goal was to win a major victory in the North. On September 17, 1862, Confederate soldiers and Union soldiers fought at Antietam. The Union troops stopped the Confederate troops and forced them back to Virginia.

Passage B

I think that the Battle of Antietam was the most important battle during the Civil War. If the Confederate army had won a major battle close to Washington, D.C., I believe the Confederate states may have won the war. However, the Union army was able to push them back. As a result, the Union went on to win the Civil War.

Practice the Skill

Read the two passages above. Then answer the questions.

1. Which passage includes opinions? How do you know?
2. Which passage includes only facts? How do you know?
3. What clue words are used in the opinion?

Apply the Skill

Use facts from Lesson 1 of this chapter to write an opinion about the Underground Railroad. Support your opinion with at least two facts.

Chapter 5 Review and Test Prep

Visual Summary

1 – 3. Write a description for each item or event named below.

Underground Railroad

Battle of Antietam

Reconstruction

Facts and Main Ideas

TEST PREP Answer each question below.

4. **Geography** Why was Maryland's location so important to the Union?
5. **Citizenship** What different viewpoints did Marylanders have about the Civil War?
6. **History** Why is the Battle of Antietam considered one of the worst battles in United States history?
7. **Economics** What effects did the Civil War have on Maryland's economy?
8. **Government** Why did Congress create the Freedmen's Bureau?

Vocabulary

TEST PREP Choose the correct word from the list below to complete each sentence.

abolitionist, p. 93
casualty, p. 100
segregation, p. 104

9. Someone who fought against slavery was an _____.
10. African Americans experienced _____ after the Civil War.
11. A person who died or was injured in a battle is a _____.

CHAPTER SUMMARY TIMELINE

1860 | 1865 | 1870

- 1861 Civil War starts
- 1862 Battle of Antietam
- 1865 Civil War ends
- 1870 15th Amendment passes

Apply Skills

TEST PREP Fact and Opinion Read the paragraph below. Use what you have learned about fact and opinion to answer each question.

The Battle of Antietam was a major battle of the Civil War. Thousands of people on both sides died or were injured. It took place on September 17, 1862, near Sharpsburg, Maryland. The Union was winning until the South brought more troops. The Union should have sent more troops. I think they could have won the Civil War that day. People can visit the Antietam National Battlefield. It is a beautiful memorial.

12. Which sentence is an opinion?

A. The Battle of Antietam was a major battle of the Civil War.
B. It took place on September 17, 1862, near Sharpsburg, Maryland.
C. The Union was winning until the South brought more troops.
D. I think the Union should have sent more troops and ended the Civil War that day.

13. Which sentence is a fact?

A. It took place on September 17, 1862, near Sharpsburg, Maryland.
B. I think they could have won the Civil War that day.
C. I think the Union should have sent more troops
D. It is a beautiful memorial.

Critical Thinking

TEST PREP Write a short paragraph to answer each question.

14. Synthesize In what ways do you think that industries in the North helped the Union win the Civil War?

15. Categorize What two categories might you use to group the following?
agricultural economy, industrial economy, supports tariffs, against tariffs, anti-slavery, supports slavery

Timeline

Use the Chapter Summary Timeline above to answer the question.

16. Did the 15th Amendment pass before or after the Civil War ended?

Activities

Music Activity During the Civil War, many songs were written and sung about victory, missing home, and other topics. Find a song about one of these topics and share it with the class.

Writing Activity Write a short story about a girl or boy living in Maryland during or after the Civil War.

Technology
Writing Process Tips
Get help with your story at:
www.eduplace.com/kids/hmss/

Chapter 6

The Twentieth Century

Technology

e • glossary
e • word games
www.eduplace.com/kids/hmss/

Vocabulary Preview

dredge

Maryland oyster boats used to **dredge** in the Chesapeake Bay. They scooped oysters up in big baskets.
page 113

immigrant

An **immigrant** is a person who comes from another country to live in a new place. Many European immigrants settled in Maryland in the 1800s and early 1900s. **page 114**

Chapter Timeline

1877
Railroad strike

1917
United States enters World War I

1941
Japan attacks Pearl Harbor

1875 — 1900 — 1925

Reading Strategy

Monitor and Clarify As you read, use this strategy to check your understanding.

Stop and ask yourself whether what you are reading makes sense. Reread if you need to.

suburb

A **suburb** is a community outside of a city. Such areas grew quickly in the second half of the 20th century.
page 119

civil rights

The rights that every citizen has by law are called **civil rights.** During the 1950s and 1960s, African Americans worked together to gain civil rights. **page 122**

954
Schools integrate

1964
Civil Rights Act

1950 1975 2000

Core Lesson 1

Immigration and Industry

Build on What You Know Have you ever worked to make something better? In the late 1800s, many Marylanders worked to improve their pay and working conditions.

VOCABULARY

dredge
immigrant
reform

Vocabulary Strategy

reform

Look for the prefix **re-** in **reform.** *Re-* means "again." Reform means trying to fix something by making it over again.

READING SKILL

Problem and Solution

As you read, write down problems Marylanders faced and the solutions they found.

Problem	Solution

Challenges for Industries

Main Idea The continued growth of industries in Maryland after the Civil War brought new challenges.

During the late 1800s, industries in Maryland grew quickly. Cities were growing, and more people were coming to Maryland. The new growth was not good for everyone, though. Many people worked long hours for little pay, often in dangerous conditions. Workers began speaking out about unfair treatment. Two Maryland industries in which the working conditions changed in the late 1800s are the oyster industry and the railroad industry.

Port in Baltimore A grain elevator, the tall building in the photo, stored grain brought to Baltimore by trains. It was then loaded onto ships and shipped to other ports.

The Chesapeake Oyster Wars

During the late 1800s, railroads made it easier to send oysters to distant cities. As a result, more oysters could be sold. This changed life on the Chesapeake Bay in several ways.

Oyster harvesters looked for ways to gather more oysters faster. For many years, Marylanders had gathered oysters a few at a time, using long scissor-like tongs. But in the late 1800s, oyster boats began to **dredge,** or to drag large baskets along the bottom of the bay to get more oysters. This method meant that many more oysters could be collected quickly. As this industry grew, working on oyster boats became harder. Harvesters worked long hours in bad weather.

Dredging caused another problem. It hurt oyster beds, or the places where the oysters lived, so that later harvests were poor. Soon, oyster ships were fighting over the good oyster beds. Some captains became known as oyster pirates. They found many ways to take more than their fair share of oysters. For example, they dredged oysters at night, which was against the law.

Finally, Maryland's government created a special police force to protect the Chesapeake Bay from the fighting and the illegal dredging. A few years later, working conditions improved for oyster workers.

Oyster Tonging Some Marylanders used scissor-like tongs to scoop up oysters. This method was replaced with dredging, which allowed Marylanders to collect many more oysters at a time.

Railroad Troubles

In the 1870s, railroad companies such as the Baltimore and Ohio were not making as much money as they had earlier. To save money, they started paying their workers less. This made it difficult for workers to earn enough money to survive.

On July 16, 1877, some workers on the Baltimore and Ohio Railroad stopped doing their jobs. They were protesting unfair treatment. During the following week, railroad workers protested across Maryland. Later, many of the working conditions for the railroad workers improved.

REVIEW Why did people change the way they harvested oysters in the late 1800s?

A New Life Many immigrants entered the United States through Baltimore, Maryland.

Immigration and Reform

Main Idea In the late 1800s many immigrants came to Maryland.

Throughout the 1800s, people from Europe had been coming to Maryland to live. Many of these immigrants settled in Baltimore. An **immigrant** is someone who moves to a new country.

Before the Civil War, many immigrants came to Maryland from Ireland and Germany. Later, they came from several other countries, including Russia, Poland, and other Eastern European countries.

Many immigrants took jobs in the railroad industry, clothing production, and other industries. Many immigrant children took jobs in factories. Some of the jobs were dangerous and required the workers to work long hours.

The Need for Reforms

So many people had come to Maryland that there weren't enough good jobs for everyone. Some workers, often immigrants, had to take jobs in sweatshops. A sweatshop is a small factory in which people work very hard in poor conditions for very little money.

Immigrants also had a difficult time finding a place to live. Many lived in crowded, unsafe apartments.

In the 1890s, people worked hard to improve life for Marylanders. They wanted Maryland's government to pass important reforms. A **reform** is a change that makes something better.

Soon, the state passed laws to make life safer for Marylanders. In 1894, the Maryland government passed a law limiting the time that children could work in factories. In 1902, new laws made coal mines in Maryland safer for miners.

Working Families Children sometimes worked beside their parents in factories.

More Reforms

New medical schools and hospitals also opened. Johns Hopkins medical school opened in 1889 in Baltimore. There, doctors researched diseases. They found ways to stop the spread of disease. They also worked to improve conditions for the poor, such as cleaner water.

Some reforms improved people's lives in other ways. For example, more public schools opened and most Maryland children began going to public school instead of going to work in factories.

Women from Maryland and other states demanded more rights, including the right to vote. Women throughout the country won this right in 1920.

REVIEW In what ways did reforms affect the number of children in factories?

Lesson Summary

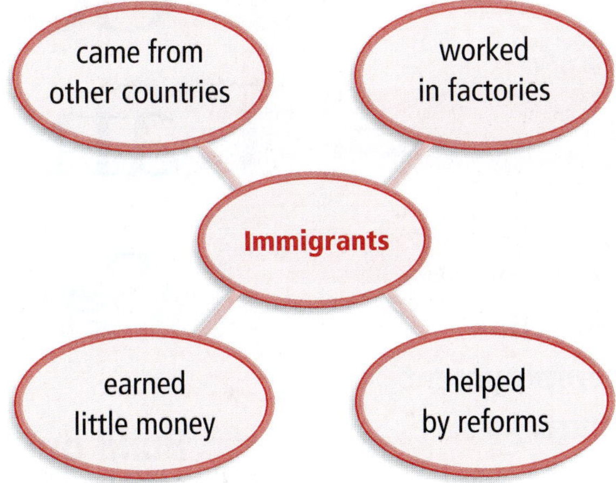

Why It Matters . . .

Because of reforms, health care and working conditions are better for Marylanders today.

Lesson Review

1. **VOCABULARY** Use the words **immigrant** and **reform** in a paragraph about Maryland in the late 1800s.
2. **READING SKILL** What **solution** did Marylanders find to the **problem** of poor working conditions?
3. **MAIN IDEA: Economics** What caused people to start harvesting many more oysters in Chesapeake Bay?
4. **MAIN IDEA: History** Why did some Marylanders work in sweatshops in the late 1800s?
5. **TIMELINE SKILL** When did railroad protests take place in Maryland?
6. **CRITICAL THINKING: Infer** Why do you think that Maryland's government believed it needed a special police force to stop oyster pirates from harvesting oysters in the Chesapeake Bay?

WRITING ACTIVITY Write an editorial for an 1800s newspaper calling for public schools in Maryland. Explain that children need to learn reading, writing, and math to get better jobs as they grow up.

Core Lesson 2

Conflict at Home and Abroad

VOCABULARY

depression
unemployment
suburb

Vocabulary Strategy

depression

Look for the word **depress** in **depression**. Depress can mean "to go down." During an economic depression, the values of many things go down.

READING SKILL

Main Idea and Details

As you read, write down details that tell about the main idea in this lesson.

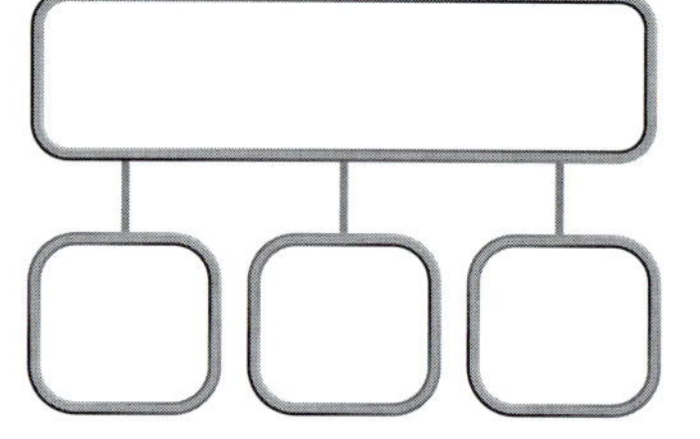

Build on What You Know What do you do when you need help? During the early 20th century, Marylanders worked together to help both their state and their country.

Maryland in a Changing World

Main Idea Worldwide events in the early 20th century affected the lives of Marylanders.

While Maryland's population and economy were growing, several countries in Europe were having disagreements and taking sides. In 1914, a war began in Europe. On one side were France, Britain, and their allies. The other side included Germany and its allies. This war was later called World War I because so many countries were involved in it.

In 1917, the United States joined the war by declaring war on Germany and its allies. More than 60,000 Marylanders signed up to fight. As men left jobs in Maryland, many women entered the work force to take their place. Many worked in office jobs or became nurses.

The Country Prepares for War Many sailors trained at the U.S. Naval Academy in Annapolis.

Maryland During World War I

During World War I, Maryland factories produced ships, guns, and uniforms. In addition, army and navy hospitals and training centers opened in Maryland. The U.S. Naval Academy in Annapolis trained many sailors.

Marylanders also contributed to the war effort at home. When food supplies began running low because of the need to supply food for the soldiers, they planted their own fruits and vegetables.

World War I ended in 1918. Germany and its allies surrendered.

The Great Depression in Maryland

Maryland's economy grew quickly during the 1920s. In 1929, however, the nation's economy suddenly stopped growing. The country went into a depression. An economic **depression** is a period when businesses fail, prices drop, and jobs are hard to find. The economy became so bad that this period became known as the Great Depression.

Many banks in Maryland closed, so many people lost their life savings. Unemployment in Maryland and throughout the country increased greatly. **Unemployment** is the condition of being without a job.

In 1933, President **Franklin Delano Roosevelt** started programs, called the New Deal, to give people jobs. In some of these programs, people built bridges and school buildings or worked to protect natural resources.

The New Deal Programs such as the Civilian Conservation Corps provided jobs. This photograph shows a worker repairing a road near Beltsville.

Another program built new communities. In 1937, the national government built Greenbelt, Maryland, near Washington, D.C. This was a planned community in which streets and homes were all built based on a design. This project provided employment for many Marylanders.

Over time, the economy of Maryland and the nation improved. The Great Depression finally ended in the early 1940s.

REVIEW Why did Marylanders begin growing their own fruits and vegetables during World War I?

World War II

Main Idea Marylanders helped the United States win World War II.

During the 1930s, a dictator named **Adolf Hitler** took control of Germany. A dictator is a ruler who has total power over a country. Hitler wanted to build Germany into a strong country. Italy and Japan became Germany's allies. Together, the three countries planned to become world powers by taking over other countries. They started World War II by invading other countries.

Most Americans, however, did not want to go to war again. Then, on December 7, 1941, Japanese warplanes bombed United States planes and ships at Pearl Harbor, Hawaii. The next day, the United States entered the war.

Maryland Supports the War

During World War II, more than 200,000 Marylanders served in the military forces such as the Army, Navy, and Air Force. Military camps in the state trained troops from all over the country. Many soldiers trained at the army base in Aberdeen. In 1940, the National Naval Medical Center in Bethesda was built to help wounded sailors.

Most Maryland factories began to make war supplies, such as ships and airplanes. While men fought overseas, women went to work in factory jobs. Marylanders also used less food and other products so that the troops would have more supplies. For example, families were allowed only small amounts of shoes, tires, and gasoline.

On May 7, 1945, Germany surrendered to the United States and its allies. The war ended in September 1945 after Japan surrendered as well.

A Wartime Factory Thousands of Maryland workers helped build airplanes during World War II, including these women.

Post-War Maryland

After the war, Marylanders tried to return to normal life. Soldiers returned to factory jobs.

As Marylanders started new families, they looked for new places to live. New communities called suburbs attracted young families. A **suburb** is a community outside a large city. Most suburbs were built in areas that had been woods or trees. Roads, sidewalks, and buildings replaced the trees that had grown there naturally. The automobile made traveling to the city for work easier, so the suburbs kept growing.

REVIEW What event brought the United States into World War II?

New Housing Many people who worked in Washington, D.C., moved to nearby suburbs, such as Greenbelt.

Lesson Summary

- Marylanders fought for the United States in World War I.
- The New Deal helped Marylanders during the Great Depression.
- Maryland's suburbs grew after World War II.

Why It Matters . . .

Maryland continued to grow after World War II.

Lesson Review

1. **VOCABULARY** Complete each sentence with one of the following words.

   depression **suburb**

   Many people moved to a ______ after 1945.

   During a ______, jobs are hard to find.

2. **READING SKILL** How did Marylanders help during World War I? Use your list of **details** to help you find the answer.

3. **MAIN IDEA: Economics** Why did Marylanders use less of items such as tires and gasoline during World War II?

4. **MAIN IDEA: History** In what ways did growth of the suburbs affect Maryland's natural resources?

5. **TIMELINE SKILL** How many years passed between the United States entering World War I and the attack on Pearl Harbor?

6. **CRITICAL THINKING: Evaluate** Explain how the growth of suburbs would have been different without automobiles.

HANDS ON **ART ACTIVITY** Draw a poster that would encourage people to help in the war effort by working in a factory or planting a garden.

Skillbuilder

Make a Line Graph

VOCABULARY
data
line graph
axis

Sometimes information, especially data, is easier to understand when it is presented as a graph or a chart. Data are facts or numbers. A line graph shows changes in data over time. Read the steps below to learn how to make a line graph.

Learn the Skill

Step 1: Collect the data you will use. Arrange the data in a table, such as the one here.

Year	Population in Baltimore-Washington, D.C., suburbs
1940	400,000
1950	700,000
1960	1,450,000
1970	2,250,000
1980	2,600,000

Step 2: Draw and label each axis of your line graph. An **axis** is a vertical or horizontal line on a graph that shows the units of measurement.

Step 3: Create a grid for your graph.

Step 4: Divide each axis into equal segments, and label each grid line with a number. For each axis, the lowest and highest numbers should be the lowest and highest value that will be shown on that axis. For each year, draw a dot where the grid line for that year and the correct value meet.

Step 5: Draw a line to connect the dots.

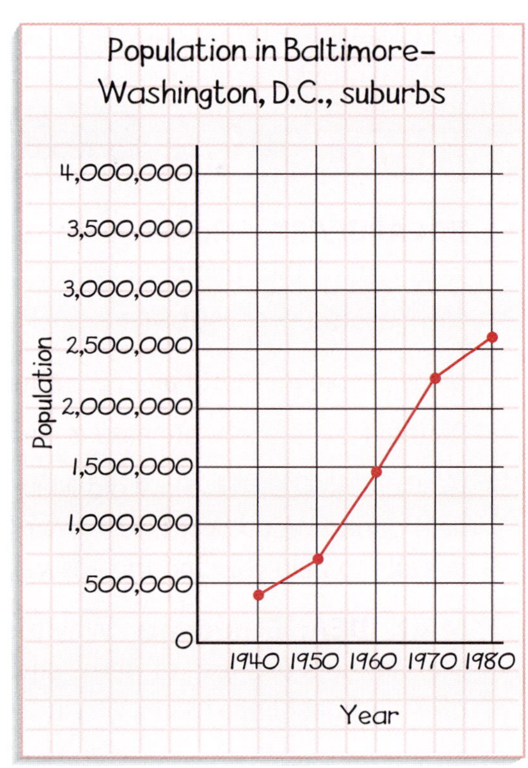

Practice the Skill

Use the data below to make a line graph. Show how the population of the city of Baltimore changed between 1940 and 1980. Label the vertical axis "population" and label the horizontal axis "year."

Year	Population
1940	860,000
1950	950,000
1960	940,000
1970	900,000
1980	790,000

Apply the Skill

Collect data that shows change over a period of time. For example, you might collect data showing your class's attendance every day for a week, or the number of people in your classroom during each period. Arrange the data in a table, and then show the information on a line graph.

Core Lesson 3

Modern Maryland

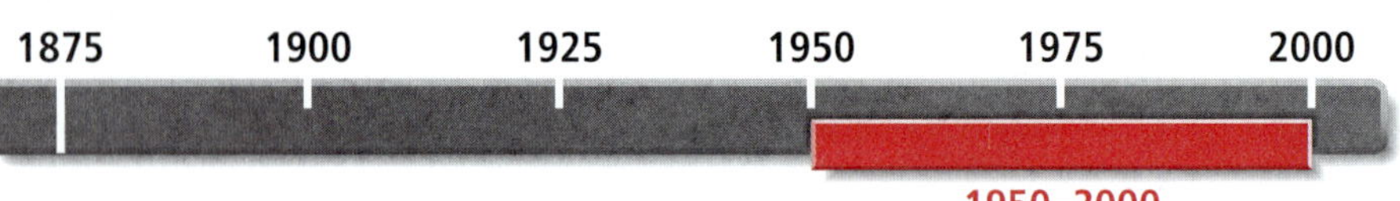

VOCABULARY

civil rights
integration
beltway

Vocabulary Strategy

civil rights

The word **civil** comes from a Latin word meaning "relating to citizens." The rights that each citizen should have are called **civil rights.**

READING SKILL

Sequence Write the events of the civil rights movement in Maryland in the order in which they happened.

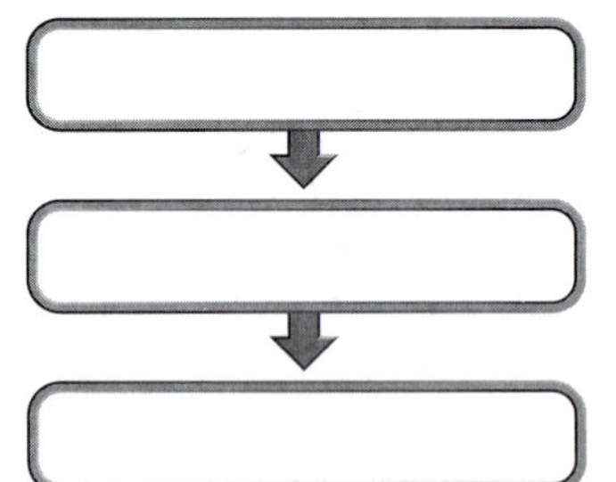

Build on What You Know Can you think of a time when you were not treated fairly? Before the Civil Rights movement, many people in Maryland were not treated fairly.

Civil Rights in Maryland

Main Idea In the mid-1900s, African Americans worked to gain equal rights.

In the early 1950s, segregation was legal in many places in the United States. Segregation is the separation of people on the basis of their race. African Americans could not use the same restaurants and schools as whites. Many jobs were closed to African Americans.

Segregation took away important civil rights from African Americans. **Civil rights** are the rights that the government guarantees its citizens, such as the right to vote freely. After World War II, African Americans began to work together in the civil rights movement.

Protesting in Maryland This family is protesting the way African Americans who served their country during the war were treated when they returned home.

School Integration

One issue that was important to the civil rights movement was the integration of schools. **Integration** means bringing together people of different races. In 1954, the United States Supreme Court considered whether all schools in the United States should be integrated.

One of the lawyers working on the case was **Thurgood Marshall,** an African American lawyer from Maryland. He argued that because the public schools for African Americans were not as good as schools for white children, African American children should be allowed to go to the schools for white children. The Supreme Court agreed, deciding that all school segregation was wrong. Starting with schools in Baltimore, schools throughout Maryland and the nation began to integrate.

Learning Together In the 1950s, Maryland classrooms became integrated.

Protests Lead to Change

Schools were integrated, but many other places were not. Dr. **Martin Luther King Jr.** called for an end to segregation and other unfair treatment of African Americans. In 1963, King organized a peaceful protest march in Washington, D.C. More than 200,000 people took part.

In July 1964, the U.S. Congress passed the Civil Rights Act of 1964. This law helped to protect the civil rights of all Americans.

REVIEW What did Thurgood Marshall do to help the civil rights movement?

The March on Washington, D.C. Martin Luther King Jr. led a protest for civil rights on August 28, 1963. He delivered his famous "I Have a Dream" speech at this protest.

Maryland's Highway System

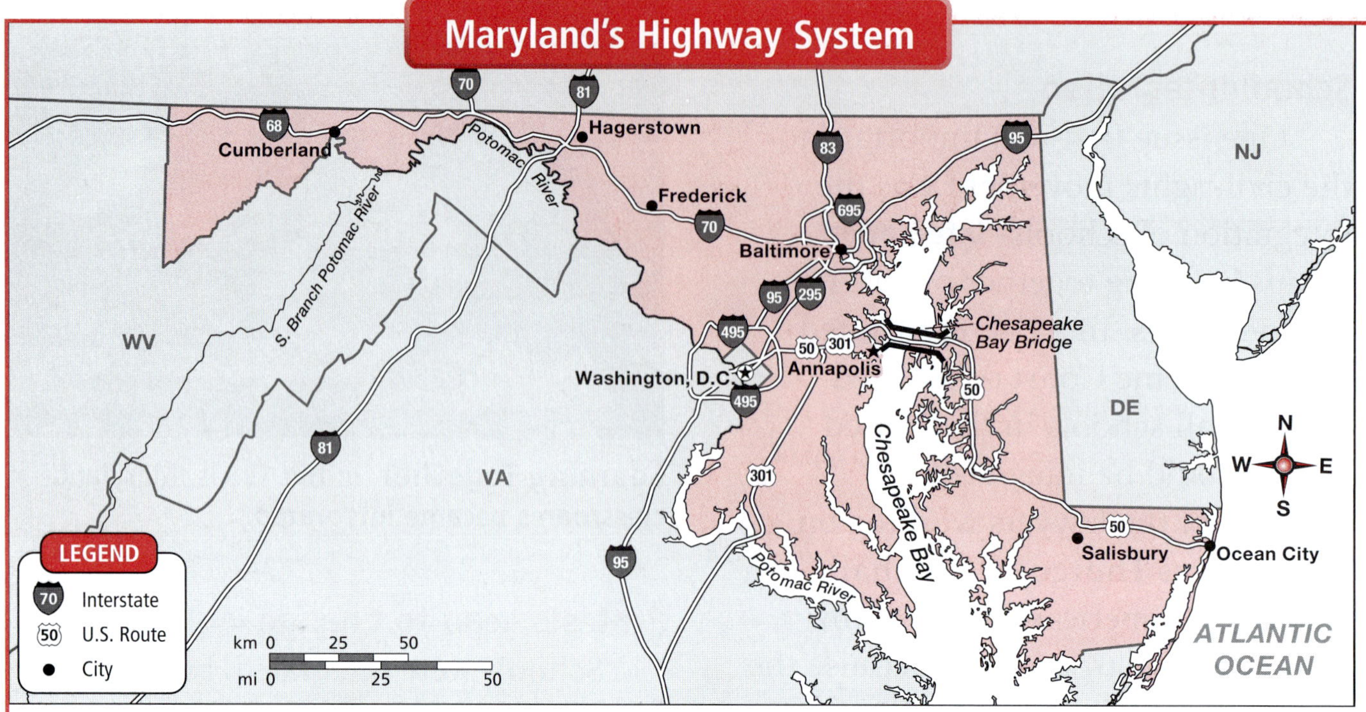

Transportation System Highways made travel in Maryland easier.

SKILL Reading Maps Which route goes from Washington, D.C., to Ocean City?

A Growing State

Main Idea Maryland's population and economy grew in the 20th century.

In the years after World War II, the number of government and military jobs in the area increased. As people moved to work in these new jobs, the population of Washington, D.C., Baltimore, and Annapolis continued to grow. This affected Maryland's environment in many ways.

Between 1950 and 1980, thousands of new homes, shopping centers, and other buildings were built in Maryland. Many buildings, parking lots, and roads were built in places that previously had been woods or fields. This affected the way that rainwater and other liquids drained into streams, rivers, and the Chesapeake Bay.

The New Bridge

Beginning in 1945, the number of cars on the roads in Maryland increased greatly. Traffic between Washington, D.C., and Baltimore increased. Traffic between Baltimore and Annapolis grew, too. The government of Maryland built new roads and bridges to handle the traffic.

On July 30, 1952, the Chesapeake Bay Bridge opened between Sandy Point and Kent Island. Marylanders paid a toll to use the bridge.

The opening of the bridge allowed Eastern shore farmers and seafood producers to get their products to Baltimore and Washington markets quickly. Marylanders also began vacationing on the Eastern shore in the summer, as it was now so much easier to get there. Eastern Shore workers could now sell more and earn more.

The Beltways

Other major road projects included the Baltimore and Washington beltways. A **beltway** is a major road that travels around a city rather than through it. The beltways helped people reach Baltimore and Washington, D.C., more quickly. Unfortunately, exhaust fumes from the traffic caused air pollution in and near the large cities. The new roads also affected the ways that water drained into Maryland's streams and rivers.

REVIEW What effect did the building of the Chesapeake Bay Bridge have on how some Marylanders spent their summers?

Lesson Summary

People throughout the United States worked to protect civil rights for all United States citizens.

Between 1945 and 2000, Maryland's economy and population grew. More people owned cars, so more roads and bridges were built.

Why It Matters . . .

Actions of the civil rights movement and growth of the suburbs have shaped life in Maryland today.

The Chesapeake Bay Bridge The bridge is also known as the William Preston Lane Jr. Memorial Bridge. Lane was governor of Maryland from 1947 to 1951.

Lesson Review

1. **VOCABULARY** Write a sentence describing **integration.** Give an example.
2. **READING SKILL** Choose one event from your **sequence** chart and explain its importance.
3. **MAIN IDEA: History** In what way did the civil rights movement affect schools in Maryland?
4. **MAIN IDEA: Economics** What effect did the Chesapeake Bay Bridge have on the Eastern Shore's economy?
5. **TIMELINE SKILL** In what year did the Supreme Court integrate schools?
6. **CRITICAL THINKING: Infer** What impact might the growth of suburbs and new roads have had on life in the Chesapeake Bay?

RESEARCH ACTIVITY Find out about a community that was started in Maryland after World War II. Write a short report that describes when the community was founded, the closest large city, and where most of the people in the community work.

Skillbuilder

Resolve Conflicts

VOCABULARY
conflict
compromise

Conflicts occur when people want different things. A **conflict** is a disagreement. To resolve, or settle, a conflict, people should listen to one another. Then they can find a compromise that works for everyone. A **compromise** is a plan to which everyone agrees.

Learn the Skill

Use the steps below to help you resolve conflicts.

Step 1: Identify the conflict. For example, students in your class may have different ideas about where to go on a field trip.

Step 2: Allow time for each group to explain what it wants. For example, one group may want to go to a museum. Another group may want to visit a park or the zoo.

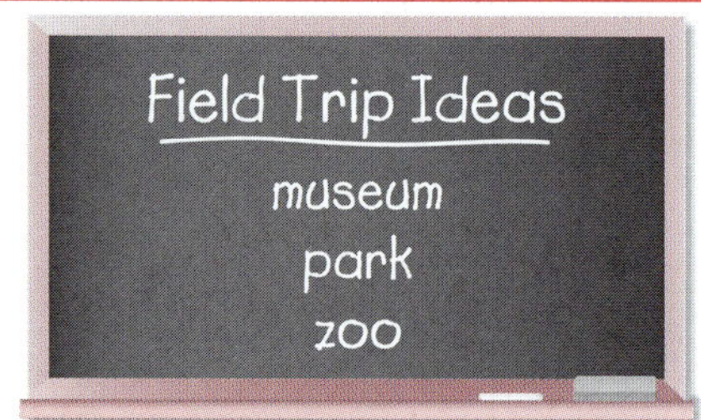

Step 3: Brainstorm different solutions. Make sure that you consider what each group wants. For example, you might decide to visit one place now and another place at a later time.

Step 4: Agree to one of the solutions. To do so, some people may have to compromise and accept something other than what they wanted. Keep working until most people can accept the plan.

Practice the Skill

Read about a conflict between some Maryland landowners and people who wanted to protect parts of Maryland that were still natural.

For many years, farms, homes, and roads have changed the land in Maryland. Some people wanted to protect Maryland's remaining woods and natural areas. Other people wanted to keep building and changing the land. Maryland did not have one overall plan that protected natural lands and protected the rights of landowners at the same time.

In 2001, the Maryland legislature created a program called GreenPrint. This program considered the needs of Marylanders as well as the needs of the natural environment. It even set money aside to purchase and protect important natural lands.

1. What was the conflict between landowners and those who wanted to protect remaining natural lands?
2. What did each side want?
3. What was the solution?

Apply the Skill

Suppose that a piece of land in your community is being sold. One group would like to build a shopping center on the land. Another group would like to use the land for a park. Write several possible solutions that would satisfy both sides.

Chapter 6 Review and Test Prep

Visual Summary

1 – 3. Write a description for each item or event named below.

Chesapeake Oyster Wars

Great Depression

Civil Rights

Facts and Main Ideas

TEST PREP Answer each question below.

4. **Government** What effect did the reforms of the late 1800s and early 1900s have on the lives of Marylanders?
5. **Geography** List three countries that immigrants to Maryland came from.
6. **Economics** What effect did the New Deal have on Maryland?
7. **Citizenship** What argument did Thurgood Marshall use to persuade the Supreme Court to integrate schools?

Vocabulary

TEST PREP Choose the correct word from the list below to complete each sentence.

immigrant, p. 114
suburb, p. 119
integration, p. 123

8. A person who moved to Maryland from another country was an ______.
9. After World War II, many families chose to live in a ______.
10. Many African Americans who became involved in the civil rights movement wanted ______ of public places.

CHAPTER SUMMARY TIMELINE

1917
U.S. enters World War I

1929
Great Depression begins

1964
Civil Rights Act of 1964

1875 | 1900 | 1925 | 1950 | 1975 | 2000

Apply Skills

TEST PREP Make a Line Graph Read the data below. Then use what you have learned about making a line graph to answer each question.

Year	Population
1940	860,000
1950	950,000
1960	940,000
1970	900,000
1980	790,000

11. If you were making a line graph by using the data above, what label would you give the horizontal axis?

A. 1950
B. Year
C. Baltimore
D. 1980

12. If you were making a line graph by using the data above, what number would you place at the top of the vertical axis?

A. 1,000,000
B. 2,000,000
C. 5,000,000
D. 6,000,000

Critical Thinking

TEST PREP Write a short paragraph to answer each question below. Use details from the chapter to support your response.

13. Summarize How did Marylanders help during World War I and World War II?

14. Evaluate How have the reforms of the late 1800s and early 1900s had an impact on your life?

Timeline

Use the Chapter Summary Timeline above to answer the question.

15. When did the Great Depression begin?

Activities

Research Activity Make a timeline of important events for the civil rights movement.

Writing Activity Suppose it is 1950. Write a persuasive essay to the U.S. government explaining how a bridge across the Chesapeake Bay will help Maryland.

Technology
Writing Process Tips
Get help with your essay at
www.eduplace.com/kids/hmss/

UNIT 3

Review and Test Prep

Vocabulary and Main Ideas

TEST PREP Write a sentence to answer each question.

1. What was the main goal of an **abolitionist?**
2. What is one reason that the country fought the **Civil War?**
3. Why did Maryland become a **border state** during the Civil War?
4. What was one **reform** that took place in Maryland during the late 1800s and early 1900s?
5. Why might someone move to a **suburb?**
6. How did African Americans gain their **civil rights?**

Critical Thinking

TEST PREP Write a short paragraph to answer each question.

7. **Analyze** In the mid-1800s, was Maryland's economy similar to the economy in the South or in the North? Explain.
8. **Compare and Contrast** What are some ways in which the experiences of World War I and World War II were alike for Marylanders?

Apply Skills

TEST PREP Use what you have learned about fact and opinion to answer each question.

After World War II, the suburbs of Baltimore were a great place to live. Automobiles and railroads made it easy to get into the city. People thought that they could have all the space they wanted in the suburbs. New families thought that children should have yards in which to play. Everyone believed that suburban peace and quiet was a great reason to move.

9. Which of the following is a fact?

   A. Children should have yards in which to play.
   B. Suburban peace and quiet was a great reason to move.
   C. Automobiles and railroads improved transportation from the suburbs to the city.
   D. People could have all the space they wanted in the suburbs.

10. Which of the following words from the passage signals an opinion?

   A. was
   B. improved
   C. suburbs
   D. believed

Unit Activity

Create and Present a Courage Award

- Choose a person mentioned in this unit who you think showed great courage.
- Write a short paragraph telling why this person deserves an award for courage.
- Use construction paper to create a certificate for this person.
- Present the award by reading your certificate aloud.

At the Library

You may find these books at your school or public library.

Harriet Tubman: Freedombound (History of the World) by Janet Benge and Geoff Benge
Learn more about Harriet Tubman.

Oh, Freedom! Kids Talk About the Civil Rights Movement with the People Who Made It Happen by Linda Barrett Osborne
Discover more about people involved in the civil rights movement.

CURRENT EVENTS
WEEKLY WR READER

Connect to Today

Make a display of people in the news who have shown leadership.

- Find information describing the actions of at least two leaders.
- Find photographs or draw pictures of the people you chose.
- Beneath each picture, write a sentence or two in which you describe how the person led other people well.
- Discuss with a partner why you chose each person.

Technology
Weekly Reader online offers social studies articles. Go to **www.eduplace.com/kids/hmss/**

UNIT 4

Maryland Today

What part will you play in Maryland's future?

"*Together we have the chance to change Maryland.*"

Robert Ehrlich Jr., governor of Maryland, 2003

H.L. Mencken

1880–1956

Writer H.L. Mencken was known for his sense of humor and strong views. He spent his life writing and worked at two Baltimore newspapers. **page 179**

History Makers

Thurgood Marshall
1908–1993

Marylander Thurgood Marshall was the first African American to serve on the United States Supreme Court. He helped all Americans earn equal rights. **page 178**

Martha Clarke
1944–

Dance is Baltimore-born Martha Clarke's life. She has thrilled people around the world with ballets that she directed. She also creates dances for others to perform. **page 179**

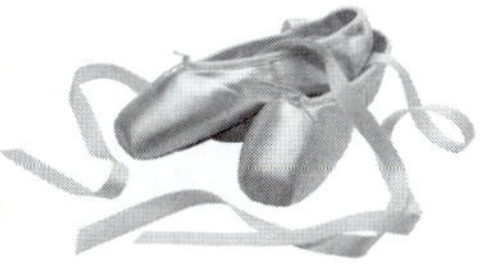

Chapter 7

The Government in Maryland

Vocabulary Preview

citizen

A **citizen** of a country has rights as well as responsibilities. Immigrants often want to become citizens, or official residents, of their new country. **page 136**

democracy

Democracy is government by the people. The United States government is a form of democracy. **page 137**

Chapter Timeline

1776 Maryland's first constitution

1787 United States Constitution

1770 | 1790 | 1810

Reading Strategy

Summarize Use this strategy to help you understand important information in this chapter.

A summary includes only the most important information. Look for main ideas as you read.

jury

Serving on a **jury** is one way to take part in government. Citizens on a jury decide court cases.

page 141

responsibility

Voting is an important **responsibility** of citizens in a democracy. Citizens elect people to represent them in government.

page 154

1867
Maryland's fourth constitution

1830 | 1850 | 1870

Core Lesson 1

United States Government

VOCABULARY

citizen
common good
democracy
election
rule of law

Vocabulary Strategy

election

The verb **elect** means "to choose or decide." In an **election,** voters choose people to serve in government.

READING SKILL

Problem and Solution Identify and describe the problems that government is supposed to solve.

Problem	Solution

Build on What You Know A United States flag probably hangs in your classroom. Schools in all 50 states have the same national flag. We are all part of the same nation, even when we live many miles apart.

Government by the People

Main Idea The government is made by the people, of the people, and for the people of the United States.

The United States government is "by the people." This means that the people hold the power to govern. People create the government. The government is also "of the people" because each American citizen has a say in what the government does. A **citizen** is someone who is born in a country or who promises to be loyal to the country. The United States government is supposed to protect people's rights and serve the common good. The **common good** means the good of the whole population. That is why we say the United States government is "for the people."

American Citizenship People make a promise of loyalty to become American citizens.

United States Congress American voters elect people to represent them in the government. The U.S. Congress is made up of the Senate and the House of Representatives. In this photograph, the President of the United States is speaking to both parts of Congress.

How the People Rule

The United States is a **democracy.** A democracy is a system in which the people hold the power of government. The people decide who will lead them and what the government will do.

Democracy can take several forms. In many small towns, every person votes on every rule and decision. This does not work well, however, for a huge nation. Think about what might happen if millions of citizens had to vote on every law. It would take far too long to make a decision.

Instead, the government of the United States is a representative democracy. Citizens choose representatives to vote for them. These representatives make day-to-day decisions for the government. They represent the voters. That is what makes this country a democracy.

Citizens decide who will represent them in elections. An **election** is the way voters choose people to serve in government. On election day, citizens cast their votes for the people they want to represent them. Whoever gets the most votes usually wins the election. Voting is both a right and a duty of citizens in a democratic system.

REVIEW What is the job of representatives in our democratic system?

Liberty, Equality, and Justice for All

United States citizens generally agree on some basic ideas. They agree on the value of liberty. This is the freedom from control by others. They agree on the idea of justice and the **rule of law.** This means that laws should apply to everyone in the same way.

Before 1776, the states were colonies controlled by Great Britain. Many colonists wanted more liberty. They wrote the Declaration of Independence. It states that all people are equal and that the people have a right to "life, liberty, and the pursuit of happiness." Colonists fought the British to win these rights and establish the United States.

The Constitution

Main Idea The United States Constitution limits the power of the government and divides the government into three branches.

The leaders of the United States wrote a constitution in 1787. Our constitution tries to ensure liberty, equality, and justice for all. It includes the Bill of Rights, which protects our rights and liberties. It sets firm limits on the power of government.

Bill of Rights Americans have certain rights and freedoms.

SKILL **Reading Charts** What does the freedom of speech allow Americans to do?

The Three Branches of Government

The Constitution sets up three branches, or sections, for our government. This helps prevent any one part of the government from getting too powerful.

The legislative branch is the U.S. Congress. It makes the nation's laws. Congress has two parts, the House of Representatives and the Senate. Voters elect senators and members of the House. **Elijah E. Cummings** is one of the people who has represented Maryland in the U.S. Congress. He became a Congressman in 1996.

The executive branch carries out the nation's laws. It is headed by the President, who is elected.

The judicial branch includes the federal courts. It decides questions about the nation's laws. The Supreme Court is the country's highest court. It has the power to decide which laws are allowed by the Constitution. Judges and Justices in the judicial branch are not elected. They are chosen by the President and approved by the Senate.

REVIEW Why are there three branches of government?

Lesson Summary

- The many people of the United States are united under one government.
- The United States government is based on the values of liberty, equality, and justice.
- The Constitution limits the power of the branches of government.

Why It Matters . . .

The United States government unites Americans through shared values of liberty and justice.

Lesson Review

1. **VOCABULARY** Write a paragraph about the United States government that uses the terms **election** and **citizen.**
2. **READING SKILL** In what ways does the Constitution solve the **problem** of the government's becoming too powerful?
3. **MAIN IDEA: Citizenship** What is a representative democracy?
4. **MAIN IDEA: Government** What are the three branches of government?
5. **FACTS TO KNOW** What was the purpose of the Declaration of Independence?
6. **CRITICAL THINKING: Infer** Why do you think judges in the national government are not elected?

WRITING ACTIVITY Write a "Declaration of Unity" for the United States. Describe how the government brings people together. Explain why it is important for the country to stay united.

Core Lesson 2

Maryland's State Government

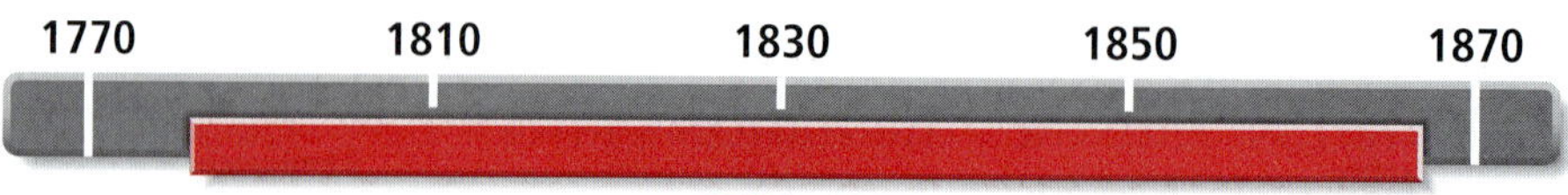

VOCABULARY

due process
jury
delegate

Vocabulary Strategy

due process

Process means the steps that lead to a result. **Due process** is the right to all the steps that will lead to a fair legal decision.

READING SKILL

Main Idea and Details

List details that support this main idea: Government has many important roles, or jobs.

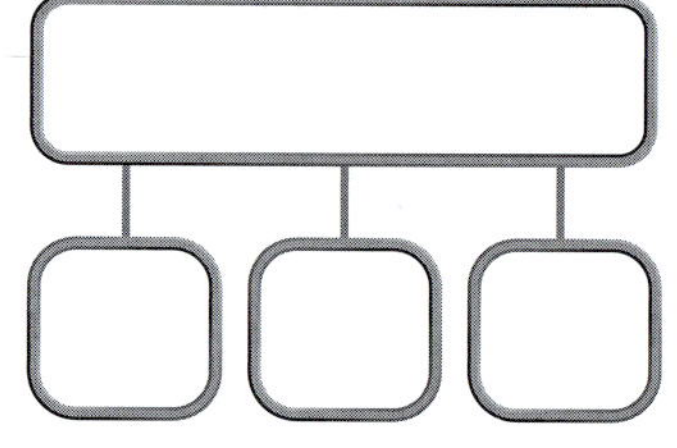

Build on What You Know As a member of your class in school, you follow certain rules. The citizens of Maryland also follow rules, the laws of the state.

Maryland's Constitution

Main Idea Maryland's constitution is a plan for state government that provides fairness and order.

Like other states, Maryland has its own constitution. Maryland's constitution provides a written plan for state government. It also explains the role, or job, of state government.

Maryland's first constitution was written in 1776, soon after the United States declared its independence from Britain. As Maryland grew and changed over time, the constitution needed to change as well. In 1867, Marylanders approved the state's fourth constitution. This constitution is still used today.

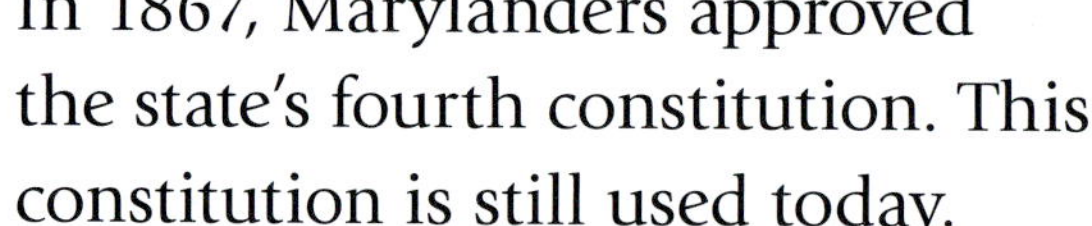

State Capitol Maryland state leaders work in the state capitol building in Annapolis.

Your Rights

Right	U.S. Constitution	Maryland Constitution
Freedom of religion	First Amendment	Article 36
Freedom of speech	First Amendment	Article 40
Right to refuse to testify against oneself	Fifth Amendment	Article 22
Right to trial by jury	Sixth Amendment	Article 21

Rights and Freedoms
The United States Constitution and the Maryland Constitution protect many of the same rights.

SKILL Reading Charts
Which constitution describes rights in articles? Which describes rights in amendments?

Roles of Government

The governments of Maryland and the United States have many of the same roles. One important role of government is to work for the common good. Maryland's state government works for the common good by making laws that make Maryland a better place for all citizens to live.

Some laws keep order by making certain that people behave responsibly. For example, laws require people to get drivers' licenses. Other laws require businesses to operate in ways that are safe and fair. Laws even help people handle disagreements or conflicts.

Governments not only govern citizens, but they also protect them. The United States Constitution includes a Bill of Rights to protect people's rights. Maryland's constitution also protects the rights of individuals in a section called the Declaration of Rights. A declaration is an official announcement.

Like the Bill of Rights, Maryland's Declaration of Rights guarantees people's freedom to voice their opinions and to choose and practice any religion. It also states that people have a right to ask the government to make changes.

Both the Bill of Rights and the Declaration of Rights give people the right to due process. **Due process** means that the government must protect the legal rights of anyone who goes to court. One of these rights is the right to a trial decided by a jury. A **jury** is a group of citizens who decide a case in court. Another right is the right to refuse to testify, or answer questions, about yourself when you are on trial.

The Bill of Rights and the Declaration of Rights guard many other rights that are important in a democracy, such as the right to vote.

REVIEW What are some rights the Maryland Constitution guarantees?

Public Policy

Main Idea The Maryland state government serves citizens in many ways, including helping to protect the Chesapeake Bay.

The Maryland government protects the rights of citizens as well as the land and environment in which they live. One way the government does this is through public policy. Public policy is the rules and laws a government makes about certain issues.

For example, one of the most valuable natural areas in Maryland is the Chesapeake Bay. There, salt water from the ocean mixes with fresh water draining from surrounding land. This helps make the bay home to many unusual animals and plants.

Unfortunately, pollution and human activity have harmed the bay's environment. This pollution hurt Maryland's economy, because many people depend on the bay to earn their living.

In 1980, the state governments of Maryland and Virginia formed the Chesapeake Bay Commission. Pennsylvania joined the commission in 1985, because its waters drain into the Chesapeake Bay. The commission helps the states work together to clean the Chesapeake Bay and to help its wildlife.

Helping the Chesapeake Bay **The Maryland government made cleaning up the Chesapeake Bay part of its public policy. Governor Ehrlich has led clean-up efforts.**

Land Use

The way that Marylanders use the land affects how much pollution reaches the Chesapeake Bay. Harmful chemicals from human activity, such as driving and using fertilizer, can drain into the bay. The Maryland government has made laws about land use to help protect the Chesapeake Bay environment.

People can also harm the environment by overusing natural resources. For many years, too many oysters were harvested from the bay. Pollution also damaged the remaining oyster beds. Now, the governments of Maryland and Virginia are cooperating to help the oyster population grow. They decide how many oysters may be harvested from the bay each year.

Working Together

Scientists, government officials, and citizens from all over the region are working together to restore the bay. In 1983, the Chesapeake Bay Program was started. Maryland, Virginia, Pennsylvania, the District of Columbia, the Chesapeake Bay Commission, and the U.S. Environmental Protection Agency established the program.

The Chesapeake Bay Program tries to protect the animals, plants, and their habitats. It also works to clean up the water, and to make smart decisions about how to use land around the Chesapeake Bay. The program works to get citizens involved by educating them on what they can do to help.

REVIEW Why is it important for the government to make decisions about how land near the Chesapeake Bay can be used?

Protecting Animals **Volunteers protected these baby turtles (left) until they were large enough to survive in the wild. Others (below) bring oysters back to parts of the bay where they have become scarce.**

Maryland's Laws Members of the General Assembly discuss and vote on new laws for Maryland.

Branches of State Government

Main Idea Maryland's government is divided into three branches.

Like the national government, Maryland's government is divided into three branches. Also like the national government, each branch checks, or limits, the power of the other two branches.

Maryland's legislative branch is the General Assembly. It makes laws for the state. The General Assembly is divided into the Senate and the House of Delegates. A **delegate** is a representative. The Senate has 47 members. The House of Delegates has 141 members. All members serve four-year terms.

The governor is the leader of Maryland's executive branch. This branch carries out state laws. The governor signs, or approves, laws made by the General Assembly. Every four years, Maryland voters choose the governor in a state election. Other members of the executive branch are also elected.

State courts and judges make up Maryland's judicial branch. The judicial branch explains what state laws mean. The highest state court is the Maryland Court of Appeals. Seven judges serve on this court. They are chosen by Maryland's governor, but they must win an election to stay in office. These judges settle disagreements about the meaning of state laws.

Comparing State and National Governments

Maryland's state government and the United States government have different duties. Maryland's government makes laws that only apply to people in the state. The United States government makes laws that apply to people in all states. Maryland's constitution lists rights for Marylanders. The United States Constitution lists rights guaranteed to all citizens of the United States.

Most laws that affect the safety and property of individuals are made by state or local governments. This includes laws about driving. For example, a Maryland law requires all children riding in a car to be fastened in a child's safety seat or wearing a seat belt.

REVIEW Describe the job of each branch of state government.

Lesson Summary

The Maryland Constitution provides a plan for state government. It gets involved in public policy issues such as protecting the Chesapeake Bay. Maryland's government includes the legislative, executive, and judicial branches.

Why It Matters . . .

The state constitution protects the rights of Marylanders. The state government makes laws that protect Marylanders.

Police Protection The Maryland State Police protect the property and safety of citizens.

Lesson Review

1776	1867
Maryland's first constitution written	Maryland's fourth constitution approved

Timeline: 1770, 1790, 1810, 1830, 1850, 1870

1. **VOCABULARY** Describe the part that a **delegate** plays in Maryland government.
2. **READING SKILL Main Idea and Details** Use **details** from your chart to explain what you think is the most important role of government.
3. **MAIN IDEA: Government** What are some of the rights protected by Maryland's constitution?
4. **MAIN IDEA: Citizenship** How do workers and volunteers work together to protect the Chesapeake Bay?
5. **MAIN IDEA: Government** What are the three branches of Maryland's government?
6. **CRITICAL THINKING: Analyze** On what democratic idea is the Maryland Declaration of Rights based? Explain.

ART ACTIVITY Make an illustrated chart that shows the three branches of state government and what each branch does.

Skillbuilder

Write a Report

VOCABULARY
report

Why was the constitution of Maryland written before the U.S. Constitution? Why was the state constitution changed three times? One way to answer questions such as these is to research and write a report. A report is a piece of writing that provides facts and information about a topic.

Learn the Skill

Step 1: Choose a topic, such as Maryland's first constitution. Write questions that you would like answered about the topic.

Step 2: Look through reference materials to find answers to your questions. Reference materials may include encyclopedias, atlases, books, or official websites.

Step 3: Take notes on index cards to help you remember your findings. Be sure to include the name of each source you used. Group your notes according to the questions they answer.

Step 4: Start your report by turning your questions into statements. These are the main ideas. Fill in details about each main idea from your notes. Remember that each main idea should be a paragraph.

Practice the Skill

Name a topic related to Maryland's government that interests you. Then use what you know about writing reports to answer the following questions.

1. What are some questions that you want to answer about the topic?
2. What reference materials will you use to find answers to your questions?
3. How will you organize the information you find?

Apply the Skill

Write a report about the topic you chose. Go to a library or go online to do some research. Find at least two sources of information that will help you answer your questions. Take notes and write a short report that answers your questions about the topic.

Core Lesson 3

Local Government in Maryland

VOCABULARY

county
municipality

Vocabulary Strategy

county

County comes from the word **count.** A long time ago, a county was the land controlled by a count.

READING SKILL

Draw Conclusions
Record details that lead to this conclusion.

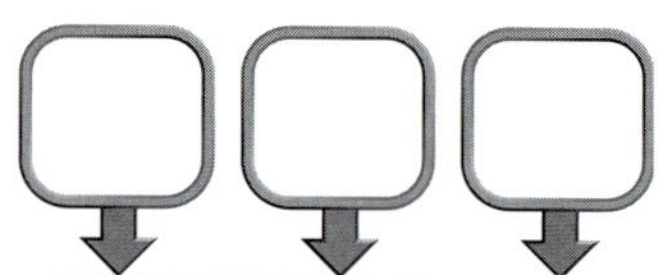

Build on What You Know Do you ride the bus to school? Who do you think pays for the bus and the driver? Your local government provides such services.

Counties and Municipalities

Main Idea Counties and municipalities in Maryland have their own governments.

Maryland is divided into 23 counties. A **county,** like a city or town, is a unit of local government. The government meets in a city or town known as the county seat. The large municipality of Baltimore is treated as a county in many ways.

A **municipality** is a city or town that has its own government. There are 157 municipalities in the state. There are many cities and towns that do not have their own governments, but are governed only by county governments.

Serving Maryland Wayne K. Curry spoke to citizens in Hyattsville when he was county executive for Prince George's County.

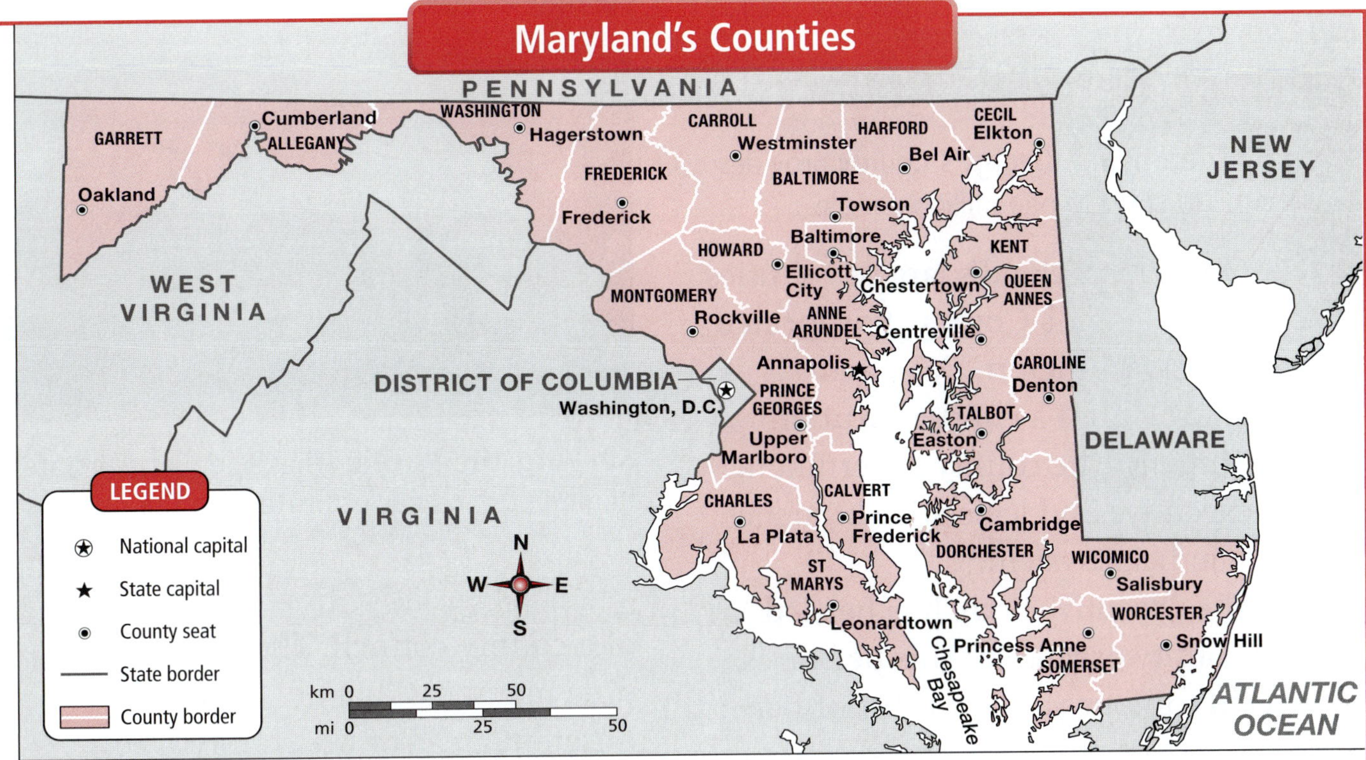

Counties and County Seats Each of Maryland's counties has a county seat, where decisions for that county are made.

Types of Counties

Maryland's counties all provide services to their citizens. However, they do not all operate in the same way.

Eight counties are commissioner counties. They are run by commissioners, or representatives who are elected by the citizens of each county. These counties may not make laws without the permission of the Maryland General Assembly.

Nine counties are charter counties. The voters in these counties have approved a plan for the county government. Six counties are code counties. The commissioners in a code county are elected by county citizens. They have the power to make laws without approval from the General Assembly.

Local Services

Counties and municipalities provide services to their residents. These services are paid for by taxes.

Counties in Maryland must provide certain services. These services include providing public schools, community colleges, and libraries. County governments also provide county health departments and supervise elections.

Municipalities may choose what services to provide their citizens. Each municipality has a charter, or written document describing how it operates and what services it provides.

Many people work for county or municipal governments. These include schoolteachers and police officers.

REVIEW What is an example of a job that someone who works for local government in Maryland may have?

Prince George's County

Main Idea Prince George's County provides services to close to one million people.

One of Maryland's largest counties is Prince George's County. It is located between Washington, D.C., and Baltimore. It has a charter form of government. The county government has executive and legislative branches and a judicial system.

The executive branch is headed by a county executive. This person is elected for four years. It is his or her job to enforce the laws of the county. Over 30 executive branch departments help provide services, such as police protection and transportation services, to county citizens.

County Seat **This courthouse is the center of government for Prince George's County. It is located in the county seat, Upper Marlboro.**

Serving the Public **These new officers are beginning a career of protecting the public safety.**

The legislative branch is made up of a county council. The council has nine members that are elected from different areas of the county. The council makes laws for the county. For example, the council makes decisions about how land and resources in the county may be used.

The judicial system in the county has two main courts—district courts and circuit courts. District courts hear cases involving traffic tickets and other small criminal cases. There is no jury. The circuit court handles larger cases that are tried by a jury.

Education

One of the most important tasks of a county government is to provide education to students in the county. Prince George's County public school system is the second largest system in the state. It is the 17th largest system in the United States.

The schools are run by a 10-member Board of Education. The board members are appointed by the governor and county executive. The board makes decisions about teachers, students, school buildings, and programs.

The public school system is an important part of Maryland's economy. Thousands of people work in Prince George's County schools in many different jobs, such as teachers, mechanics, secretaries, and nurses.

REVIEW In what way does the Prince George's County school system affect the economy of the county and state?

Public School Classroom The public schools in Maryland educate about one million students.

Lesson Summary

- Counties and municipalities in Maryland have their own local governments.
- Local governments provide services such as police protection, education, and transportation services.
- Local governments contribute to Maryland's economy through the number of jobs they provide.

Why It Matters . . .

Local governments in Maryland provide important services to citizens.

Lesson Review

1. **VOCABULARY** Write a sentence about local government in Maryland using the words **municipality** and **county.**
2. **READING SKILL** Give two details that lead to the **conclusion** that local governments provide needed services.
3. **MAIN IDEA: Economics** In what way does Prince George's County government contribute to Maryland's economy?
4. **MAIN IDEA: Government** In what way do local governments help protect natural resources in Maryland?
5. **CRITICAL THINKING: Compare and Contrast** In what way is Prince George's County government similar to the Maryland state government?
6. **CRITICAL THINKING: Evaluate** Do you think it is useful to divide Maryland government into counties? Why or why not?

HANDS ON **RESEARCH ACTIVITY** Research the type of government in your county. Write a short report about it.

Core Lesson 4

Government and Citizens

VOCABULARY

responsibility
candidate
volunteer

Vocabulary Strategy

responsibility

Think of **respond** when you see **responsibility.** One responsibility of citizens in a democracy is to respond to the needs of their community.

READING SKILL

Categorize As you read, list information about services provided by national, state, and local governments.

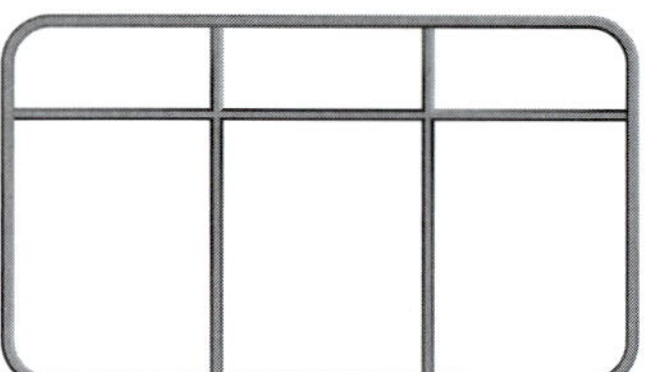

Build on What You Know Think of some workers who help people in your community. Workers such as firefighters and police officers provide valuable services to you and others in your community.

Governments Serve the People

Main Idea National, state, and local governments provide a variety of services for citizens.

It is the job of government to serve the common good. One way in which governments work for the common good is by providing services for people.

The national government provides many kinds of services. For example, it maintains armed forces to protect the United States and its citizens. It sets up health care, housing, and other programs for people in need. The national government provides money to build and maintain the interstate highway system. It also runs national parks for people to enjoy.

National Parks Maryland has several national parks. Assateague Island National Seashore is a favorite of both Marylanders and visitors from other states.

State and Local Services State and local governments provide services such as public libraries and fire protection.

State and Local Services

The state government provides services only for the people of Maryland. It provides money to public schools, as well as to state colleges and universities. The government of Maryland also repairs state roads, operates state parks, and provides state police to enforce state laws.

Local governments run maintain correctional facilities and libraries. They also provide police officers and firefighters. Some cities and counties provide public transportation. Local governments may also collect trash and provide water.

Paying for Services

Governments collect taxes from citizens to pay for services and government workers. Taxes also help public schools by paying for teachers, school buildings, and supplies.

Sales tax, income tax, and tolls are several ways that Maryland raises the money to pay for services. A sales tax is an amount of money added to the price of items that people buy. Income tax is money that people pay from their earnings to the federal, state, and local governments. Maryland also raises money by charging tolls for travel on highways, tunnels, and bridges.

REVIEW Why must citizens pay taxes?

Elections Voting in elections gives citizens a voice in how their government is run.

Your Role in Government

Main Idea Democracy depends on people taking an active part in their government.

United States citizens have many rights. Along with these rights come responsibilities. A **responsibility** is a duty that someone is expected to carry out.

Citizens have a responsibility to take part in their government. Citizens can participate in many ways. They pay taxes so that the government has money for services. They serve on juries when called to do so. Citizens also obey laws and can work to change unfair laws.

One way that citizens can work for change is by writing or signing a document called a petition. Citizens write an idea, such as a plan for a new law, in a petition and ask others to read and sign it. The signed petition is given to government officials. They may use the ideas in it to make new laws.

Voting in elections is another way that citizens take part in government. Some people get involved in elections in other ways. They may become candidates for public office. A **candidate** is a person who is running in an election for a government office.

If you are too young to vote, you can still take part in government and volunteer in your community. To **volunteer** is to provide a service without pay.

Volunteers who want to take part in government may talk to people about issues, put up signs, help in a candidate's office, or write letters to newspapers. The Bill of Rights guarantees free speech and freedom of the press to any citizen, even those too young to vote.

Staying Informed

Responsible citizens stay informed about issues and current events. To get information, they read newspapers and magazines. They watch the news on television, read it on the Internet, or listen to it on the radio. They share information and ideas with one another.

Citizens use the information they gather to decide how to vote and which candidates to support. They use it to form opinions about issues. They may share their views with government officials. Well-informed citizens help officials decide what action to take on the issues. They may contact officials directly or write letters to the editors of local newspapers.

REVIEW In what ways can you take part in government if you are too young to vote?

Lesson Summary

Ways To Take Part in Government

• Pay Taxes	• Support Candidates
• Serve on Jury	• Volunteer in Community
• Obey Laws	• Stay Informed
• Vote in Elections	• Share Ideas
• Speak Out on Issues	• Write Letters to Newspapers or Officials

Why It Matters . . .

Involved citizens make their community, state, and country stronger.

Lesson Review

1. **VOCABULARY** Use **responsibility** and **volunteer** in the same sentence.
2. **READING SKILL** Would you put firefighters in the **category** of national services or local services?
3. **MAIN IDEA: Government** Name three services that the national government provides.
4. **MAIN IDEA: Government** How does the government of Maryland pay for the services that it provides?
5. **MAIN IDEA: Citizenship** Where can citizens get information about important issues?
6. **CRITICAL THINKING: Synthesize** Why is voting both a right and a responsibility of citizens in a democracy?

HANDS ON **ART ACTIVITY** Think of an activity in which citizens can help make their community a better place. Then make a poster persuading volunteers to participate.

Skillbuilder

Make Decisions

VOCABULARY
consequence

Maryland's leaders have to make many decisions, or choices, about issues in the state. The decisions they make have consequences. A consequence is something that happens because of a decision or an action. Consequences can be good or bad. Use the steps and a chart like the one below to think about consequences and make good decisions.

Learn the Skill

Step 1: Identify the decision that you must make.

Step 2: List the possible actions that you could take.

Step 3: Predict the good and bad consequences of each action.

Step 4: Consider the consequences of each action. Then make a decision about the best action to take.

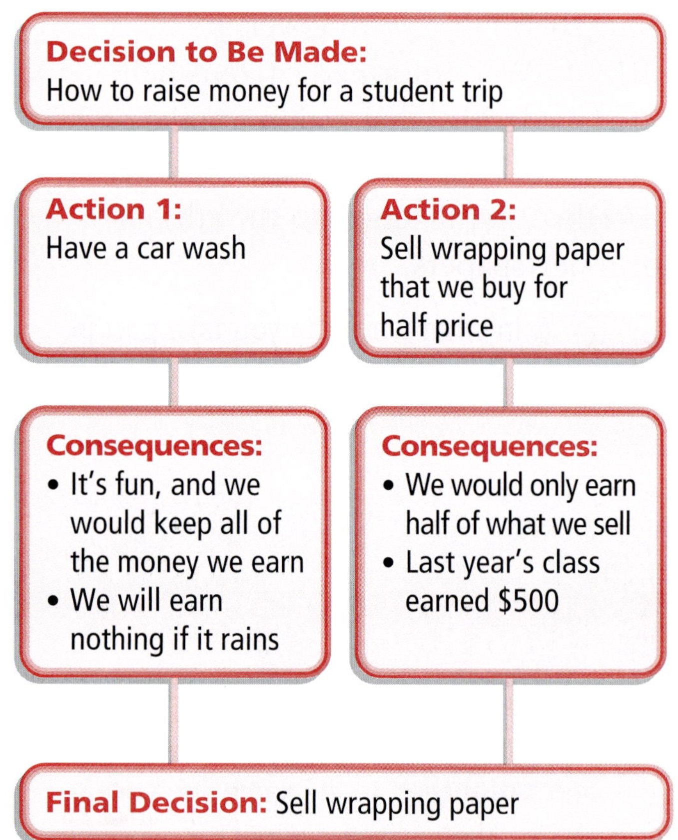

Practice the Skill

Suppose that a river in your town has a great deal of garbage around it. Make a decision about what you could do about it. You could organize a river cleanup or write a letter about the problem to a local politician. Think about the possible outcome of each of these actions. Use a chart like the one on page 156 to decide on the best action.

Apply the Skill

In a group or on your own, choose an issue that your school or community must make a decision about. Use the steps you have learned to think about the choices. Fill in a chart like the one on page 156 to help you make a decision. Then write a paragraph about the decision. Explain why you think it is the best decision.

Chapter 7 Review and Test Prep

Visual Summary

1 – 3. Write a description of each item named below.

United States Government

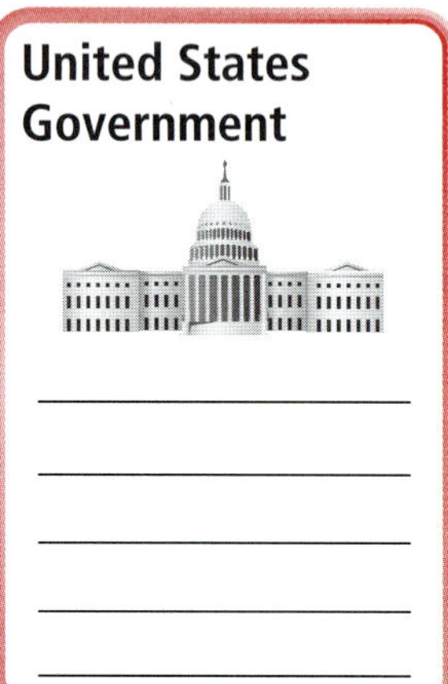

Maryland Government

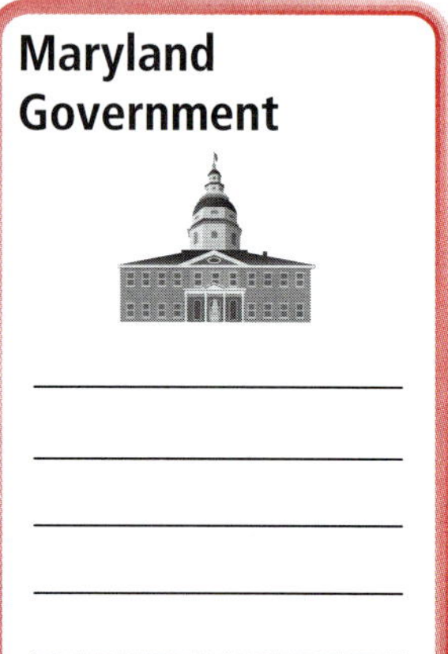

Local Government

Facts and Main Ideas

TEST PREP Answer each question below.

4. **Citizenship** Why does the United States use representatives to help make decisions?
5. **Government** Why does the Maryland constitution include a Declaration of Rights?
6. **Government** What are the three branches of Maryland's government? Why do they share power?
7. **Government** How does the state government pay for services?
8. **Citizenship** How can citizens work to change unfair laws?

Vocabulary

TEST PREP Choose the correct word from the list below to complete each sentence.

election, p. 137
rule of law, p. 138
responsibility, p. 154
volunteer, p. 154

9. A duty that someone is expected to carry out is a _____.
10. In an _____, voters choose people to serve in government.
11. When you _____, you provide a service without being paid.
12. The _____ means that laws apply to everyone the same way.

CHAPTER SUMMARY TIMELINE

1776
Maryland's first constitution

1787
United States Constitution

1867
Maryland's fourth constitution

1750 1770 1790 1810 1830 1850 1870

Apply Skills

TEST PREP Make Decisions Use the organizer below and what you have learned about making decisions to answer each question.

Decision to be made:
Should I vote in an election?

Option 1:
Read about the people who are running and vote.
Consequences:
- Reading will take time.
- I will have a say in my government.

Option 2:
Don't vote.
Consequences:
- I won't have a say in my government.

Final Decision:

13. Which of the following is the first step in making a decision?

A. Think about all of the possible actions that can be taken.
B. Identify the decision to be made.
C. Predict an action's consequences.
D. Decide on the best action to take.

14. What should the citizen do after considering possible consequences?

A. Create a chart.
B. Predict more consequences.
C. Identify a decision that has to be made.
D. Make a final decision.

Critical Thinking

TEST PREP Write a short paragraph to answer each question below.

15. Synthesize Why is the United States government said to be "of the people," "by the people," and "for the people"?

16. Draw Conclusions What responsibility does each citizen have as a result of our right to free speech?

Timeline

Use the Chapter Summary Timeline above to answer the question.

17. How many years after the first Maryland Constitution was the United States Constitution written?

Activities

Math Activity Maryland's state government sales tax is 5¢ for every $1.00. Find how much total tax would be collected if everyone in your class bought a notebook that cost $3.00.

Writing Activity Use your First Amendment rights by writing a letter to the editor of a school or local newspaper about an important issue.

Technology
Writing Process Tips
Get help with your letter at **www.eduplace.com/kids/hmss/**

Chapter 8

Maryland's Economy

Technology

e • glossary
e • word games
www.eduplace.com/kids/hmss/

Vocabulary Preview

producer

A person who makes or sells goods or services is a **producer.** Maryland farmers raise and sell crops and livestock.
page 163

human resources

Maryland businesses require **human resources** to produce goods and services. Marylanders bring special knowledge and skills to their work. **page 169**

Reading Strategy

Question As you read the lessons in this chapter, ask yourself questions about important ideas.

List any questions you have. When you finish reading, go back to find the answers.

metropolitan area

Most Marylanders today live in a **metropolitan area.** The Washington-Baltimore metropolitan area includes suburbs as well as urban centers. **page 175**

tradition

A **tradition** is a way of doing something that has been passed down for many years. Many Marylanders come together to celebrate their traditions. **page 176**

Core Lesson 1

Using Maryland's Resources

VOCABULARY

producer
consumer
scarcity
opportunity cost
supply
demand

Vocabulary Strategy

producer consumer

Producer and **consumer** end in **-er**. This suffix means "a person who does something."

READING SKILL

Categorize As you read, list producers and goods.

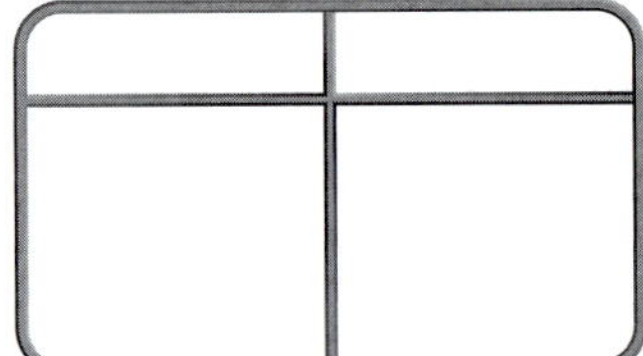

Build on What You Know What are some of your favorite foods? Do you like corn, chicken, or crab? These foods and many more are produced in Maryland.

Water, Soil, and Minerals

Main Idea Maryland's waters, soils, and minerals provide products and jobs.

Maryland has many natural resources, including water, rich soil, and minerals. Maryland's resources have helped the state's economy grow over time.

People use Maryland's water resources in many ways. The state's waterways provide transportation. The rushing waters of rivers at the fall line are used to produce electricity. Maryland's rivers and the Chesapeake Bay also provide special areas where people can enjoy boating, fishing, and swimming.

Water Power Water moving through the Conowingo Dam on the Susquehanna River is used to produce electricity.

Shellfish Maryland watermen gather crabs, oysters, and other shellfish in the Chesapeake Bay.

Fishing

Many people make a living by fishing in the waters of the Chesapeake Bay. These Marylanders are known as watermen.

Watermen are important producers in Maryland's economy. A **producer** is someone who makes or sells goods or services. Goods are material items. Services are useful things people do for others, such as repairing a car.

In manufacturing, producers turn raw materials into goods. Maryland's watermen catch crabs, oysters, clams, and many kinds of fish in the Chesapeake Bay. They sell what they catch to consumers. A **consumer** is someone who buys or uses goods or services. Consumers in Maryland and other states buy fish and crabs from Maryland waters.

Maryland's fishing industry is not as strong as it once was because there are fewer fish to catch. The Chesapeake Bay Commission is working to reduce pollution in the bay and increase the number of fish.

Farming

Farmers in Maryland are also important producers. They raise crops and livestock to sell. Maryland's crops include flowers, corn, soybeans, and fruit such as apples, peaches, and strawberries. Maryland's livestock includes chickens, turkeys, dairy cows, beef cattle, and pigs. Most farmland is in the Piedmont and the upper part of the Eastern Shore.

Mining

Miners are another group of producers in Maryland. They produce sand, gravel, and stone. Sand and gravel come mainly from the Western Shore. Stone is found in northern and western Maryland. All three materials are used for building.

Maryland miners also provide coal and minerals for making cement. Coal is mined in western Maryland. It is used as a fuel, or energy source.

REVIEW In what way has pollution affected fishing in the Chesapeake Bay?

Resources and Economics

The way in which people use their resources is called economics. Economics is based on the idea of **scarcity.** Scarcity means that there are not enough resources, goods, or services for everyone to have all that they would like to have. Because of scarcity, people have to make choices. What will they produce? Who will receive the goods or services? And, perhaps most important, who will make these decisions?

Opportunity Cost

Making economic choices involves an idea known as opportunity cost. An **opportunity cost** is the thing you give up when you decide to do or have something else. In other words, the real cost of an item is not just its dollar value. It's also the value of what you must give up to obtain the item. For example, your teacher might want to buy new books and new art supplies. There may not be enough money for both. If your teacher chooses the books, he or she gives up the opportunity to buy the art supplies. The art supplies are called an opportunity cost.

To deal with the problems caused by scarcity and opportunity costs, a society develops an economic system, or economy. Three common types of economic systems are traditional, market, and command.

Opportunity Cost

1. You see a pair of shoes you want on sale for $20.

2. You have just enough money to buy the shoes.

3. You also see a poster you want for $2.

4. If you buy the poster, you will still have $18. But you will lose the opportunity to own the shoes. This is called "opportunity cost." Many decisions you must make include an opportunity cost.

SKILL Reading Charts What is the opportunity cost in the example above? List examples of opportunity costs you have had recently.

Traditional Economy

A traditional economy is based on farming and barter. Barter is a way of trading goods and services without using money. For example, one family may trade part of its grain harvest for a cow from another family's cattle herd. Services can also be traded for goods or other services. For example, a laborer may receive part of the harvest in exchange for working on someone's farm.

Market Economy

A market economy is based on supply and demand. **Demand** is the amount of a product that consumers are willing to buy at different prices. At higher prices, consumers buy less. At lower prices, consumers buy more. **Supply** is the amount of a product that businesses are willing to sell at different prices. At higher prices, companies produce more. At lower prices, they produce less.

In a market economy decisions are made by the producers and consumers. If consumers demand a product, producers tend to supply that product. For example, if red sweaters become popular and many people are buying them, producers will see an opportunity to make money by making and selling red sweaters. As long as there is a scarcity of red sweaters, their price will be high because demand is larger than supply. As producers make more red sweaters, soon there are more red sweaters than there are people to buy them. Now, the supply is larger than demand and the prices drop. Prices and the availability of goods and services, then, are determined by supply and demand.

Command Economy

A command economy is controlled by a strong central government, which controls all of the resources as well as the way goods are produced and sold. The government, not the consumer or the producer, decides what type of goods are produced and how much to produce, as well as how much the consumer pays for the product. This may seem to be more efficient. However, without knowing what the consumer actually wants or needs, it is difficult for a central government to know what to produce. For example, in the former Soviet Union, which had a command economy, shortages of basic products were common. People waited for hours in lines to buy shoes or bread. At the same time, Soviet factories were busy producing goods for which there was little consumer need.

Market Economy
This Maryland business decides what to sell and what price to charge. The supply of fish affects the price.

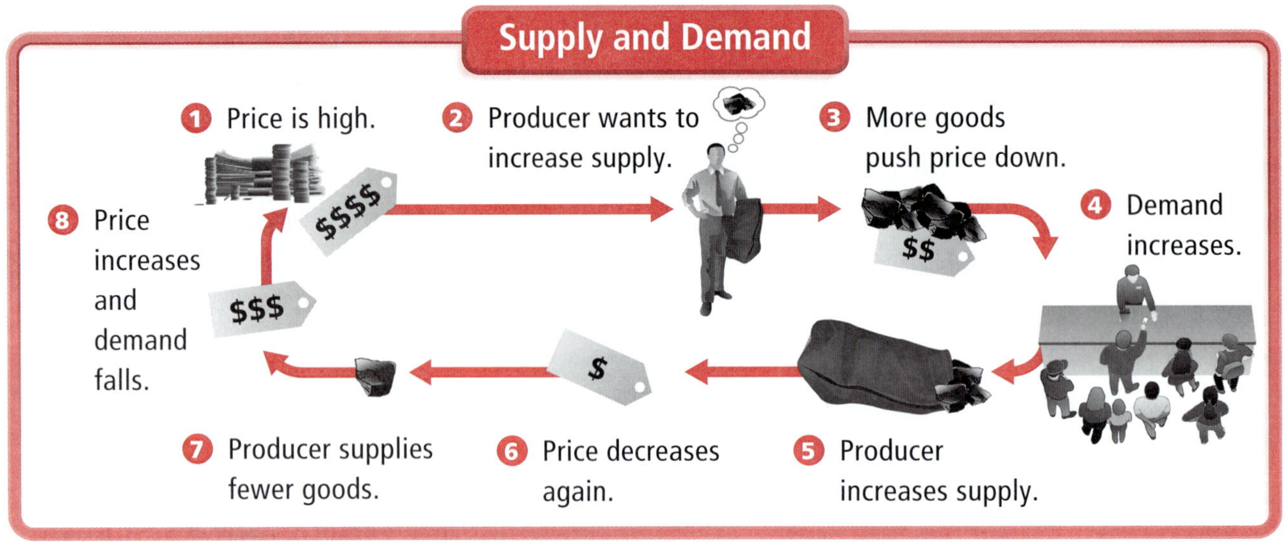

Supply and Demand When supply is greater than demand, prices fall. When demand is greater than supply, prices rise.

Supply and Demand

Main Idea Supply and demand affect how people use Maryland's resources.

The economy of Maryland has always depended on markets. A market is anywhere that producers and consumers exchange products. A grocery store and the Internet are examples of markets.

Supply and Demand of Coal

The history of coal production in Maryland shows how supply and demand affect each other. In the late 1800s and early 1900s, many people used coal to heat their homes. Factories also used coal as a fuel. Demand for coal was high, so coal mining companies in Maryland increased production to create a greater supply of coal.

After 1945, however, demand for coal fell. New homes were using natural gas or electricity instead of coal for heat. Railroads were replacing engines that used coal with engines that used oil. Now there was more coal on the market than there were customers for it. As a result, coal prices fell. Coal mining companies cut back production.

In the late 1970s and early 1980s, supplies of oil and natural gas fell. People needed another fuel, so the demand for coal rose again. Now there were more customers than there was coal on the market. Coal prices rose. In response, Maryland's mining companies produced more coal.

The example of coal production shows that supply and demand can change from year to year and even from month to month. This creates a challenge for producers.

Finding a Balance

Maryland farmers also face challenges related to supply and demand. They create a supply of many products, including chickens, eggs, and milk. When demand is greater than supply, prices rise. This helps farmers earn more. When supply is greater than demand, prices fall.

How do farmers find a balance? It's not easy for one farmer to limit supply by cutting production. Another farmer could tip the balance again by increasing his or her production. Supplies would stay high and prices stay low.

It is rare that the United States government would get involved in the balance between supply and demand. However, sometimes the government steps in to help. By paying some farmers to produce less, the government can keep prices from falling too low.

REVIEW When do consumers pay high prices for farm products?

Lesson Summary

Some producers in Maryland use the state's natural resources to make goods to sell. Consumers in Maryland, other states, and other countries buy and use Maryland products. The prices of these products are affected by supply and demand.

Why It Matters . . .

Everyone in Maryland is a producer, a consumer, or both. This means that everyone in Maryland is part of the economy. The way you buy food, clothing, and other goods depends on the economy and supply and demand.

Farm Products
The price of eggs and other farm products changes as supply and demand change.

Lesson Review

1. **VOCABULARY** What is the difference between a **producer** and a **consumer?**
2. **READING SKILL** Name two types of producers in Maryland and the goods they produce.
3. **MAIN IDEA: Economics** Give an example of how supply affects demand.
4. **MAIN IDEA: Economics** Why did Maryland mining companies increase coal production in the late 1970s and early 1980s?
5. **CRITICAL THINKING: Draw Conclusions** Why might a command economy produce goods that consumers do not want to buy?

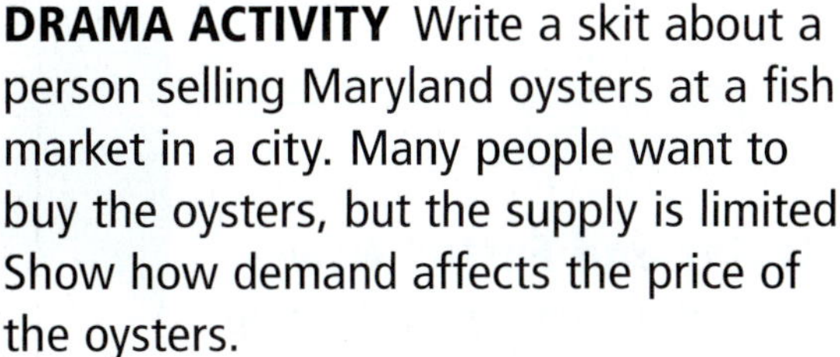

HANDS ON **DRAMA ACTIVITY** Write a skit about a person selling Maryland oysters at a fish market in a city. Many people want to buy the oysters, but the supply is limited. Show how demand affects the price of the oysters.

Core Lesson 2

Industry in Maryland

VOCABULARY

technology
manufacturing
human resources
capital resources
retail

Vocabulary Strategy

techno*logy*

The word part **techno-** in **technology** means "skill." Using technology sometimes involves learning new skills.

READING SKILL

Main Idea and Details

Chart the main idea under Manufacturing Today. What details support it?

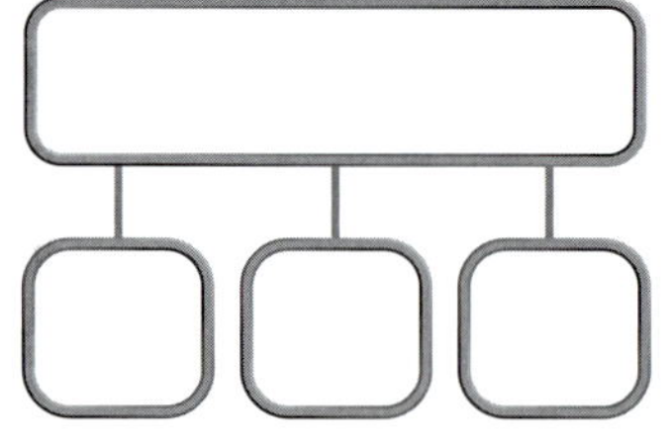

Build on What You Know What kind of work would you like to do someday? Marylanders find jobs in the state's many different industries.

Changes in the Economy

Main Idea New ways of working have changed Maryland's economy.

For most of the 1800s, farming was the occupation of most Marylanders. An occupation is a type of paying job.

Over time, new technology changed the state's economy. **Technology** is the use of scientific knowledge and tools to do things better and faster. In the 1800s, the steam engine helped railroads and factories to grow. Later, electricity helped many businesses to grow. Today, computers and the Internet are creating new kinds of jobs in Maryland. Some of those jobs involve buying and fixing computers. All of these examples show how changes in technology affect the economy.

Better and Faster New technology continues to help Maryland's economy grow.

Resources at Work **In this factory, skilled workers are human resources. The factory building and equipment are capital resources.**

Manufacturing Today

In the 1800s, new technology helped manufacturing grow in Maryland. **Manufacturing** is the process of making goods from other materials. Soon manufacturing was bringing more money to Maryland than farming was. By 1900, more people in Maryland were working in factories than on farms.

Today, manufacturers in Maryland use various resources to produce the goods that people want or need. One of these resources is called human resources. **Human resources** are the knowledge, skills, and intelligence that workers provide. Workers in Maryland's factories use natural resources and other materials to make goods. They also use capital resources such as tools, machines, and other equipment. **Capital resources** include new technology, such as robotics, that help Maryland workers produce better goods quickly.

Maryland Manufacturing

Most manufacturing in Maryland takes place in or near cities. Cities with many factories include Baltimore, Cumberland, Hagerstown, Frederick, and Salisbury. Workers at factories in the Piedmont and the Atlantic Coastal Plain make food products using crops, livestock, and seafood from Maryland.

Other workers make steel at metal factories in the Baltimore area. They use iron and other materials from Canada, South America, and Asia as well as the United States.

Other major industries in Maryland include printing and publishing as well as manufacturing of electrical products, chemicals, industrial machinery, and transportation equipment.

REVIEW Describe the resources used in manufacturing in Maryland.

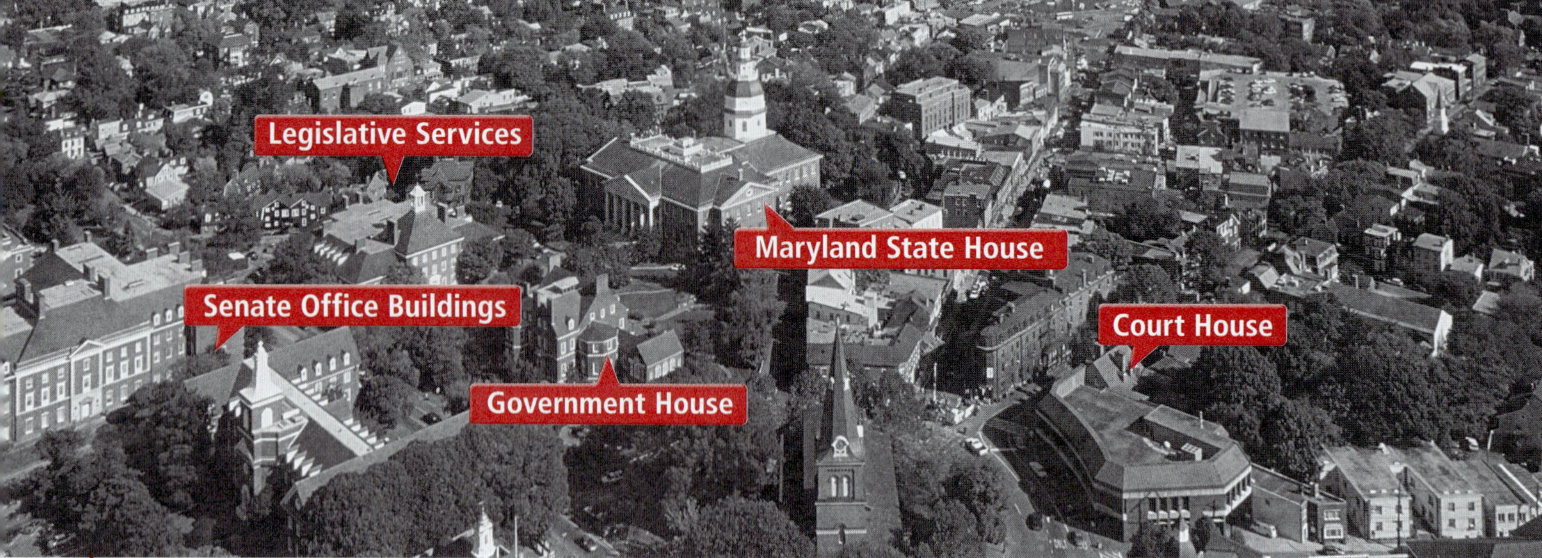

Maryland's Capital State government leaders work in the many state government buildings in Annapolis. **SKILL Reading Visuals** In which building would judges hear court cases?

Service Industries

Main Idea Maryland's economy includes a wide variety of service industries.

Many Marylanders work in service industries. Service workers have jobs in the tourism, trade, and transportation industries. Others are doctors, nurses, teachers, and restaurant workers. Some work in the retail industry. **Retail** businesses sell products directly to the consumer.

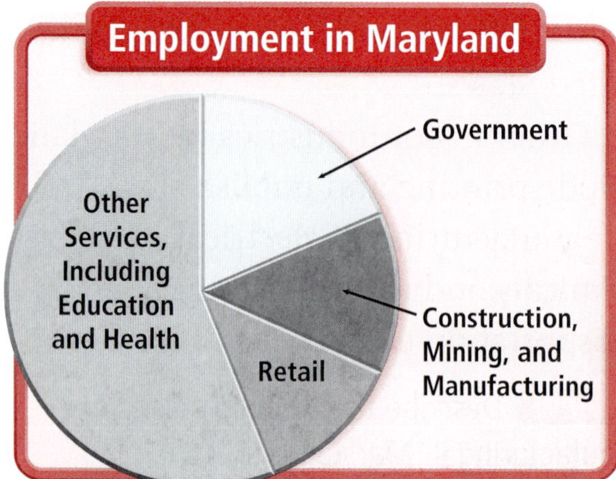

SKILL Reading Graphs Which industry shown here employs the fewest people?

Government Workers

Service workers also include the large number of Marylanders who work for the government. Many people who live in Maryland work for the national government in Washington, D.C.

Maryland is home to important parts of the national government. Some Marylanders gather information at the National Institutes of Health in Betheseda and the U.S. Census Bureau in Suitland. Others work at Maryland offices of the Department of Defense, which is in charge of the country's military. Some work at the United States Naval Academy in Annapolis and at the National Naval Medical Center in Bethesda.

Many workers in Maryland have jobs in state or local government. These workers do jobs that help the people of Maryland, or help people in a particular community.

High-Tech Occupations

Main Idea Many people in Maryland are employed in high-tech occupations.

When people speak of "high tech" they are talking about the most advanced technology that is available today. Most of Maryland's high-tech service jobs are based on computer sciences, or information technology. Information technology occupations in Maryland include designing, building, installing, and using computer systems. Those systems are used in universities, factories, and offices, including government offices.

Not all high-tech workers have computer-related jobs, however. Some high-tech jobs are in biomedical research, looking for new treatments for diseases. Other high-tech jobs can be found in Maryland's aerospace industry. People with those jobs develop new technology for airplanes, satellites, or vehicles that are used for exploring the planets. Some of Maryland's high-tech jobs are with government agencies or laboratories such as the NASA Goddard Space Flight Center in Greenbelt.

REVIEW In what ways do Maryland's high-tech industries affect how people live and work?

Lesson Summary

New technologies changed Maryland's economy over time. At first people depended on farming. By the 1900s they were depending more on manufacturing. Today, Maryland's economy depends mostly on the service industries, including government and high-tech industries.

Why It Matters . . .

Maryland's many different industries form the basis of the state's economy. They provide jobs and present many opportunities to young people who are making choices about their future careers.

Lesson Review

1. **VOCABULARY** Write a sentence using the words **technology** and **manufacturing.**
2. **READING SKILL** Give three **details** about manufacturing today.
3. **MAIN IDEA: History** What effect did new technology have on Maryland's economy in the 1800s?
4. **MAIN IDEA: Economics** What do high-tech workers in Maryland do?
5. **CRITICAL THINKING: Infer** In what ways do you think changes in technology have affected jobs in Maryland?

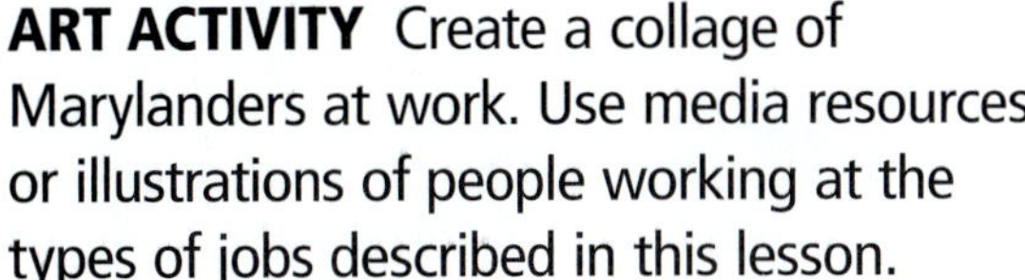

ART ACTIVITY Create a collage of Marylanders at work. Use media resources or illustrations of people working at the types of jobs described in this lesson.

Skillbuilder

Draw Conclusions

VOCABULARY
conclusion

Good readers often use what they already know about a topic to draw conclusions. A conclusion is a judgment or decision that is based on facts and ideas. To draw a conclusion, use your own experience and decide how the facts and ideas you read are connected.

Learn the Skill

Step 1: Carefully read and study the facts and ideas that the writer presents.

Step 2: Think about what you already know about the topic. Look for connections between the facts and ideas presented and what you already know.

Step 3: Draw a conclusion. Your conclusion should state your opinion about what the facts and ideas mean.

Fact: John likes computers.	+	**Fact:** High-tech workers invent and build computers.	=	**Conclusion:** John would probably like to work in the high-tech industry.

Practice the Skill

Read the following paragraph about Maryland's economy. Then answer the questions.

At one time, farming, fishing, and mining made up a large part of Maryland's economy. Today, fewer Marylanders have occupations in these industries than had them in the past. On the other hand, nearly 450,000 people work in the retail industry. It is one of the biggest industries in Maryland. Service industries are the most important part of the state's economy today. In addition to retail, government jobs and the high-tech industry employ many Marylanders.

1. What conclusion can you draw about farming, fishing, and mining in Maryland today?
2. What conclusion can you draw about whether the retail industry has grown in the last century?
3. What conclusion can you draw about the future of service industries?

Apply the Skill

Reread Lesson 1 and study the information that it presents about Maryland's economy. Use the information to draw a conclusion about Maryland's economy today.

Core Lesson 3

The People of Maryland

VOCABULARY

metropolitan area
multicultural
tradition

Vocabulary Strategy

multicultural

The prefix **multi-** means "many." **Multicultural** means "having many cultures."

READING SKILL

Draw Conclusions Note facts about where people live in Maryland. Think about why they live where they do. Record your conclusions.

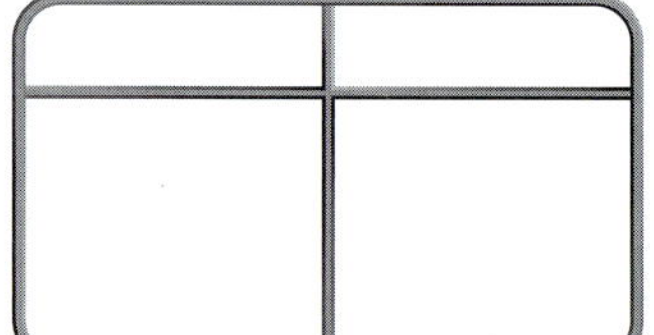

Build on What You Know Maryland's population is growing. Its cities are getting larger. New areas are being developed. What are some of the changes you have noticed in your community?

Where People Live

Main Idea Most Marylanders live in or around major cities.

More than 5 million people live in the state of Maryland. Some areas of Maryland are more densely populated, or crowded, than others. The average number of people who live within a square mile is called population density.

Garrett County, in far western Maryland, is the least densely populated area in the state. Its population density is about 46 people per square mile. Baltimore City is the most densely populated place in Maryland, with about 8,000 people per square mile.

Urban Areas Millions of people live in Baltimore (below), Washington, D.C., and the surrounding communities.

Maryland's Urban Areas

Baltimore is Maryland's largest city. In 2000, more than 650,000 people lived there. The population of the Washington, D.C.-Baltimore metropolitan area is more than 7.5 million. A **metropolitan area** is a region that includes one or more urban centers and the surrounding suburbs. The Washington, D.C.-Baltimore metropolitan area stretches from Baltimore through the center of Maryland. The area includes the communities of Silver Spring, Bethesda, Columbia, and Dundalk.

Why do metropolitan areas have so many people? Many people who live in suburbs work in a nearby city.

Maryland's Largest Cities

City	Population
Baltimore	651,154
Frederick	52,767
Gaithersburg	52,613
Bowie	50,269
Rockville	47,388

Maryland's Rural Areas

In addition to Maryland's metropolitan areas, Maryland has many areas in which there are few large cities. Although Frederick is a large city, it is surrounded by a large rural area.

Maryland has several other cities in rural areas, including Cumberland and Hagerstown, which are located in the western part of the state. Many of the industries that support these cities depend on farming or natural resources. All of the cities are connected to Maryland's urban centers by railroads and highways.

Urban and Rural Areas Although most of Maryland's land is rural, most people live in metropolitan areas.

Many Cultures These photographs show Marylanders celebrating their own cultures at public events.

A Multicultural State

Maryland's population is made up of people from many different cultures. These groups include American Indians, Europeans, Africans, Hispanics and Asians. The different languages and backgrounds of these groups have made Maryland a multicultural state. **Multicultural** means "having many cultures."

The Earliest Marylanders

Long before Europeans came to Maryland, American Indians lived here, including groups that belonged to Algonquian and Haudenosaunee cultures. Today, Accohannock, Assateague, Nanticoke, Piscataway, Pocomoke, and other American Indians live in Maryland. Modern American Indian organizations honor their traditions in many ways.

A **tradition** is a way of doing things that has been passed down through the years. To keep Acconnock traditions alive, for example, one Accohannock organization runs a museum and sponsors annual gatherings of American Indians.

Settlers and Immigrants

Beginning in the 17th century, European settlers brought new cultures and traditions to Maryland. Most of Maryland's early European settlers were from England. People from other Western European countries soon followed. German Lutherans and Catholics settled in Maryland because they were allowed to practice their religions here. Each group that settled in Maryland kept their heritage alive. Heritage includes the language, songs, beliefs, and customs of a family, a group of people, or a nation.

Marylanders Celebrate Their Heritage

Today Marylanders celebrate our differences. We also celebrate our common heritage as citizens of Maryland and of the United States.

Our ancestors have affected the way we speak, the things we believe, and many other parts of Maryland's culture. For example, the heritage of Maryland's American Indians is shown in many names of places and rivers, such as the Potomac and Piscataway rivers. The heritage of the English settlers is seen today in the language most Marylanders speak. It is also shown in our state flag, which displays the family crest of our founders. Modern Maryland also shows the heritage of people from other European nations, as well as people from Africa, Latin America, and Asia.

Common Heritage Marylanders celebrate our country's history in a July 4th parade (below). The state flag (right) reminds people of our state's history and the role of the Calvert family.

Our American Heritage

Although our ancestors came from many places and cultures, events that happened in Maryland have also given us a common heritage. For example, all Marylanders share our rights as citizens of Maryland and of the United States. Those rights include the right to free speech.

Marylanders also celebrate our state and national history. Maryland Day, on March 25, reminds us of our history as a colony. Fourth of July parades remind us of the United States' struggle for independence.

REVIEW What makes Maryland a multicultural state?

Famous Marylanders

Main Idea Marylanders have made contributions in many areas.

Marylanders are proud of their state and its citizens. Many famous musicians, artists, dancers, writers, politicians, business people, and sports figures have called Maryland home.

People from Maryland have been in office in our nation's government. Marylander **Spiro Agnew** was elected vice president of the United States. **Thurgood Marshall** was the first African American to serve on the U.S. Supreme Court. Marshall was born in Baltimore.

Marylanders have also become well-known figures in other jobs. **Tom Jones,** from Baltimore, is an astronaut. He once set a record for circling Earth on the space shuttle. He and the rest of the shuttle crew circled Earth for almost 18 days.

Edgar Allan Poe Poe's poems and short stories were written over 150 years ago, but they are still popular today.

Baltimore Oriole player **Cal Ripken Jr.** was born in Havre de Grace. Ripken helped his team win the World Series in 1983. He also set many records, including playing baseball for nearly 17 seasons without missing a game.

Jim Henson, who studied at the University of Maryland, made television shows and movies. He entertained children and adults with puppets. Henson came up with a new word for the combination of marionettes and puppets that he used. The Muppets have been teaching and entertaining children since 1969.

Jim Henson The characters that Jim Henson created are favorites of both children and adults.

Writers and Artists

Marylanders have always been active in the arts. Writers **Edgar Allan Poe** and **H.L. Mencken** have ties to Maryland. Many readers have enjoyed Poe's short stories and recognize one of his most famous poems, "The Raven." Mencken was a Baltimore newspaper writer and author who often wrote about politics.

Baltimorean **Eubie Blake** played the piano and became a popular jazz performer. The great jazz singer **Billie Holiday** was also from Baltimore. Maryland ballet dancer **Martha Clarke** has directed ballet performances all over the world.

REVIEW In what areas have Marylanders made contributions to the country and to the world?

Lesson Summary

- Most Marylanders live in urban areas.
- Maryland's population is multicultural.
- Marylanders have made many contributions to this country and to the world.

Why It Matters . . .

Learning about Maryland's multicultural population helps Marylanders understand and respect one another.

Billie Holiday Singer Billie Holiday had a natural gift for singing. Her recordings influenced many other jazz singers.

Lesson Review

1. **VOCABULARY** Explain how the **traditions** of many groups help make Maryland a **multicultural** state.
2. **READING SKILL** What **conclusion** can you draw about available jobs in less densely populated parts of Maryland?
3. **MAIN IDEA: Geography** What large metropolitan area is located partly in Maryland, and why do so many people live there?
4. **MAIN IDEA: History** Name two Marylanders who served in the national government.
5. **CRITICAL THINKING: Analyze** Name some features of your community that help you know that Maryland is a multicultural state.

RESEARCH ACTIVITY Find out more about a famous Marylander. Write a one-page report about his or her achievements.

Skillbuilder

Read a Circle Graph

A circle graph is a circle that is divided into sections to show how information is related. Circle graphs are sometimes called pie charts. Circle graphs can help you see how the whole of something is broken up into different parts. For example, a circle graph can show you how a state's population works in a variety of industries. It also allows you to see how these groups compare with one another.

VOCABULARY
circle graph

Learn the Skill

Step 1: Read the title to find out what information the graph presents. This graph gives information about jobs in Maryland.

Maryland Employment by Industry

Step 2: Read the labels for each section of the circle. Each section of this graph represents a specific industry.

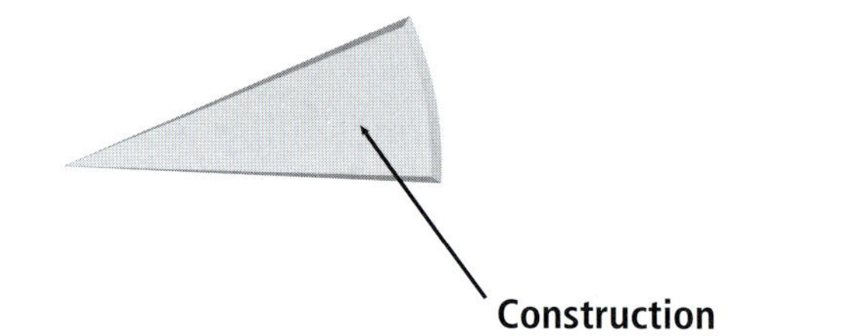

Step 3: Compare the sizes of the different sections. In this type of graph, a larger section means that more people in the state work in that industry. A smaller section means that fewer people in the state work in that industry.

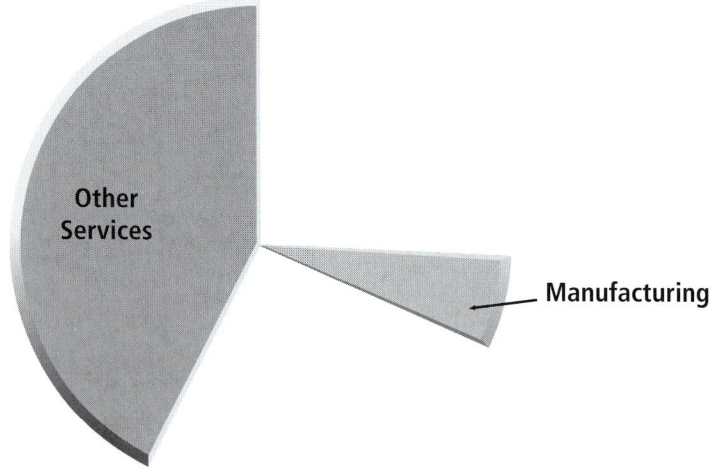

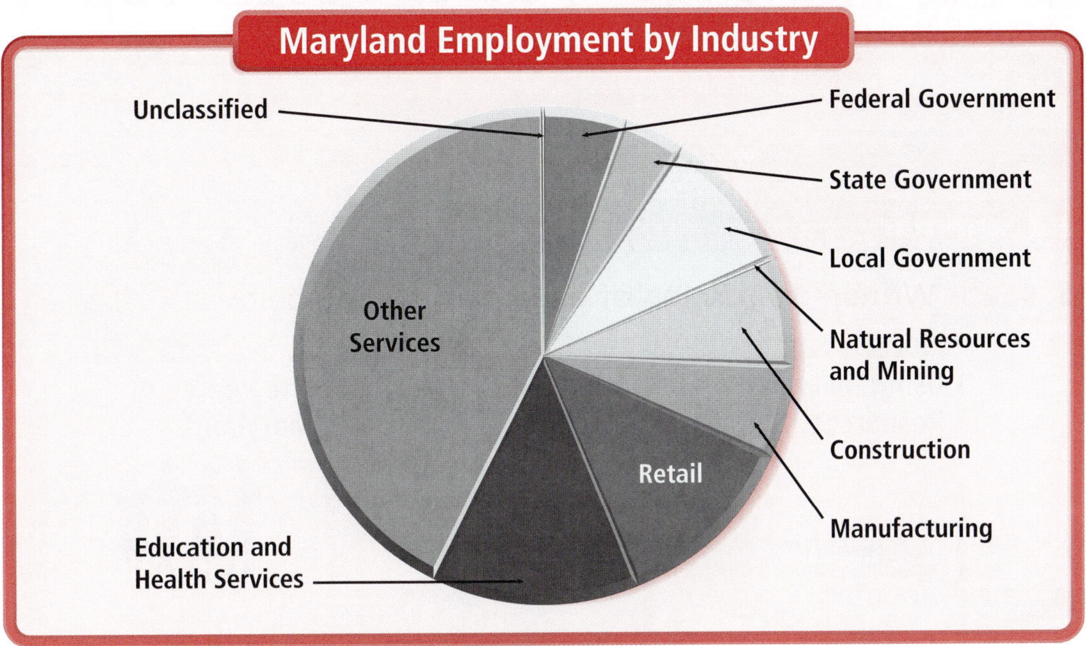

Practice the Skill

Use the circle graph to answer the questions.

1. Which industry employs the most Marylanders?
2. How many groups are represented in the circle graph?
3. Are there more total jobs in the three government categories or in education and health services?

Apply the Skill

Create a circle graph to show how you spend your time during a typical school day. First, draw a circle that stands for the 24 hours in a whole day. Then divide the circle into sections to show all of your activities and the amount of time that you spend on each one.

Chapter 8 Review and Test Prep

Visual Summary

1 – 3. Write a description of each item named below.

Using Maryland's Resources

Industry in Maryland

The People of Maryland

Facts and Main Ideas

TEST PREP Answer each question below.

4. **Economics** Describe a group of producers in Maryland, the goods they produce, and how consumers use the goods.
5. **Economics** What happens to prices when the supply of Maryland farm products is greater than the demand for them?
6. **Technology** What occupation did many Marylanders have for most of the 1800s?
7. **Geography** What is the most densely populated place in Maryland?
8. **Culture** In what ways do Marylanders celebrate their different heritages?

Vocabulary

TEST PREP Choose the correct word from the list below to complete each sentence.

consumer, p. 163
manufacturing, p. 169
metropolitan area, p. 175
tradition, p. 176

9. Most _____ in Maryland takes place in or near cities.
10. A _____ in Maryland can purchase goods or services.
11. Urban centers and suburbs make up a _____.
12. A _____ is a way of doing things that has been passed down through the years.

Apply Skills

TEST PREP Draw Conclusions Read the paragraph below. Then use what you have learned about drawing conclusions to answer each question.

When people come to live in Maryland from other parts of the world, they bring their cultures with them. Some people continue to speak the language of their first country at home. They also keep practices such as holidays, religious customs, and other traditions. Often these practices become family traditions, passed down from parents to children.

13. What conclusion can you draw from the facts in the passage?

- **A.** Marylanders usually give up their original cultures.
- **B.** Some Marylanders are proud of their original cultures.
- **C.** Marylanders dislike holidays.
- **D.** All Marylanders have the same culture.

14. All of the following facts support this conclusion except

- **A.** Marylanders keep certain practices from their original cultures.
- **B.** Traditions pass from parents to children.
- **C.** People have come to Maryland from other countries.
- **D.** Most Marylanders speak English.

Critical Thinking

TEST PREP Write a short paragraph to answer each question below.

15. Summarize How have jobs in Maryland's economy changed since the 1800s?

16. Compare and Contrast In what ways are traditional economies and command economies similar? In what ways are they different?

Activities

RESEARCH ACTIVITY Identify a local cultural festival. Create a fact sheet that tells when and why the festival takes place and what it celebrates.

WRITING ACTIVITY Write an essay about the ways that technology affects your daily life.

Technology

Writing Process Tips
Get help with your essay at **www.eduplace.com/kids/hmss/**

UNIT 4

Review and Test Prep

Vocabulary and Main Ideas

TEST PREP Write a sentence to answer each question.

1. Why is it important for **citizens** to vote in an **election?**
2. Name three ways that government works for the **common good.**
3. How can citizens learn about a **candidate?**
4. Give an example of a Maryland **producer** and **consumer.**
5. In what ways has **technology** changed the occupations of Marylanders?
6. Why is Maryland considered a **multicultural** state?

Critical Thinking

TEST PREP Write a short paragraph to answer each question.

7. **Draw Conclusions** Why do you think the writers of the U.S. Constitution thought it was important to limit the power of government?
8. **Cause and Effect** In what ways does Maryland's location near the national capital affect how Marylanders live and work?

Apply Skills

TEST PREP Fact and Opinion Use what you have learned about fact and opinion to answer each question.

9. Which of the following is an opinion?
   - **A.** Voting is a right of citizens in a democracy.
   - **B.** Citizens in our democracy vote for people to represent them.
   - **C.** If you are too young to vote, you can work to help elect a candidate.
   - **D.** Working to elect a candidate is better than voting.

10. Which of the following is a fact?
    - **A.** The Washington-Baltimore area is the best place to live.
    - **B.** A big city is more fun to live in.
    - **C.** Many people who live near Baltimore work there.
    - **D.** It costs more to live in the city, but it is worth the extra money.

11. "The best place to live in Maryland is on the Chesapeake Bay." What clue tells you that this statement is an opinion?
    - **A.** It includes the word *best.*
    - **B.** It is supported by facts.
    - **C.** It gives an exact location.
    - **D.** It can be proved true.

Unit Activity

Create a "Dream Job" Comic Strip

- Think about a job that you would like to have in the future.
- Write answers to these questions: Where will you work? What will you do in your job? What skills will you need? What will you like most about your job?
- Write a comic strip called "My Dream Job" in which you tell a friend all about your job without naming it. Have the class guess your dream job.

At the Library

Learn more by finding these books at your school or public library.

Landslide! A Kid's Guide to the U.S. Elections by Dan Gutman

Find answers to your questions about elections in our country.

Maryland 24/7 by Rick Smolan and David Elliott Cohen

Explore Maryland through photographs.

CURRENT EVENTS

WEEKLY WR READER

Create a jobs bulletin board.

- Find information about a job that you don't know much about.
- Read about what it is like to do the job. Learn what skills and education are needed for it.
- Write a description of the job.
- Post your description on the bulletin board.

Technology

Weekly Reader online offers social studies articles. Go to: **www.eduplace.com/kids/hmss/**

UNIT 5

Maryland and the East

The Big Idea

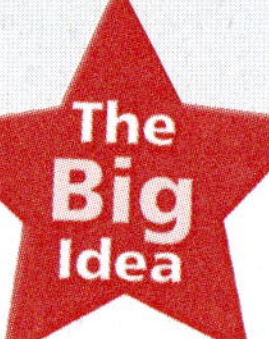

What do you like most about the place where you live?

"*The thing that struck me most all over the United States was the physical beauty of the country, and the great beauty of the cities.*"

Gertrude Stein, writer, 1937
From *Everybody's Autobiography* from *America the Quotable* by Mike Edelhart
Published by Facts on File Publications

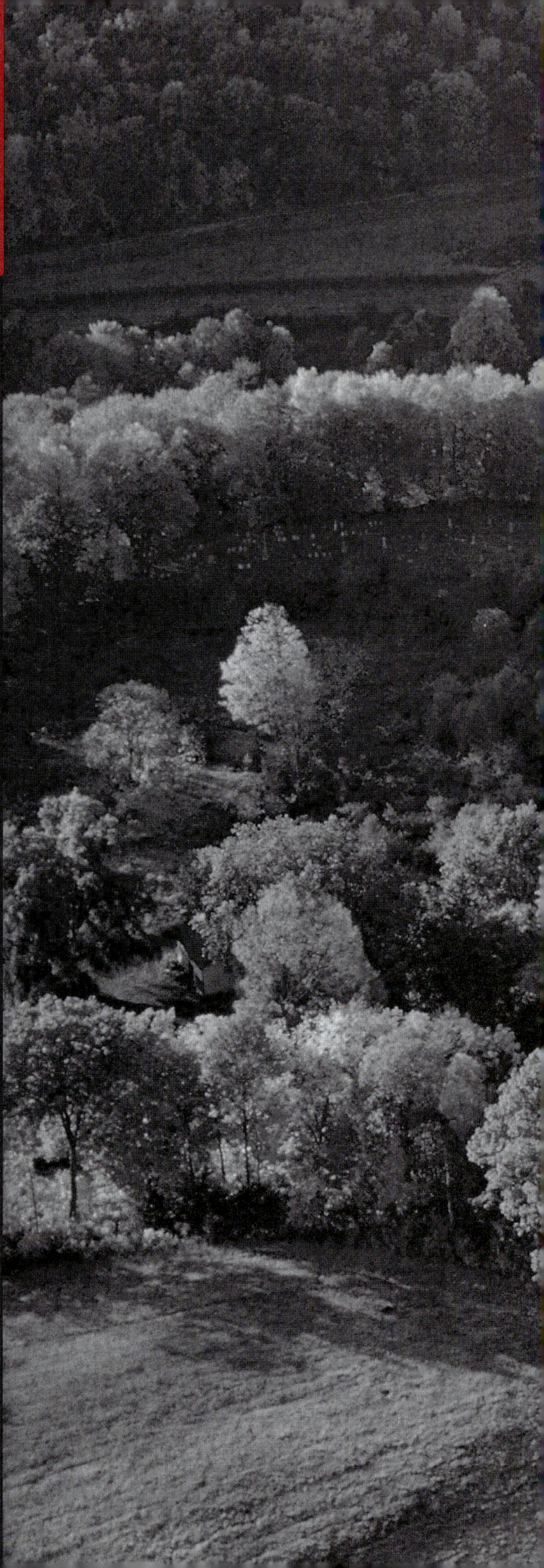

Chapter 9

Exploring the East

Technology

e • glossary
e • word games
www.eduplace.com/kids/hmss/

Vocabulary Preview

glacier

Much of the eastern United States was shaped by a **glacier.** Glaciers formed valleys and flat lands found throughout this region. **page 191**

entrepreneur

An **entrepreneur** is a person who starts a business, such as a store, a factory, or a restaurant.
page 198

Reading Strategy

Summarize As you read, use the summarize strategy to focus on important ideas.

Review the main ideas to get started. Then look for important details that support the main idea.

capitol

Lawmakers meet in a building called a **capitol.** The Maryland state capitol is the oldest that is still in use in the United States. **page 204**

heritage

People share many traditions that make up their **heritage.** Heritage includes language, food, music, and holidays. **page 210**

Core Lesson 1

Land and Climate

VOCABULARY

glacier
cape
temperate

Vocabulary Strategy

temperate

Temperate is related to the word **temper,** to make something less severe. A temperate climate has temperature without extremes.

READING SKILL

Main Idea and Details

List details that describe the mountains of the East.

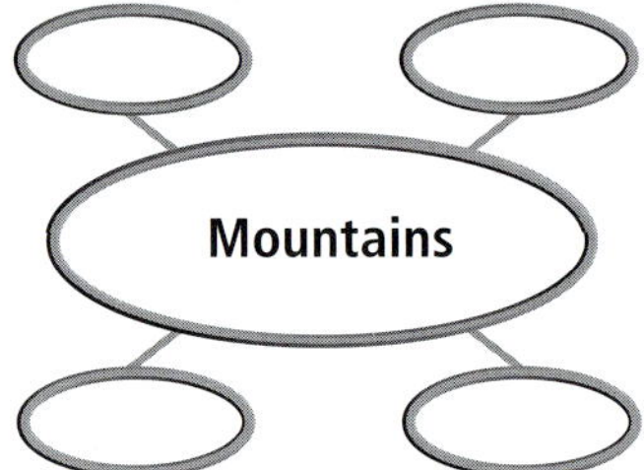

Build on What You Know Think of a road that cuts through a mountain. You would see many layers of rock. Scientists can tell the age of mountains by looking at these layers. The Appalachian Mountains are hundreds of millions of years old.

Land and Water of the East

Main Idea The East has many landforms and bodies of water.

The region between the Atlantic Ocean and the Great Lakes is known as the East. Canada borders the region to the north. Our nation's capital, Washington, D.C., is at the southern tip.

The East includes six states in New England and five Mid-Atlantic states. Some of our nation's oldest cities are in the New England region. The nation's largest city, New York, is in the Mid-Atlantic region.

Nine states in the East are on the coast. A coast is land that borders an ocean. Coastal areas form a landform region called the coastal plain. A coastal plain is flat, level land along a coast.

Western New York **The Genesee River flows between steep cliffs and thick forests. The cliffs show layers of rock.**

The East Two main landform regions are the Appalachian Mountains and the coastal plain.

Mountains and Plains

The Appalachian Mountains were formed by the movement of the earth. Over millions of years, two moving continents came together. The land between them slowly buckled and rose up. These huge piles of rocks became the Appalachians.

Wind, weather, and the water flowing in rivers slowly wore the Appalachians down. Glaciers also changed the mountains' shape. A **glacier** is a sheet of ice that carves out valleys or levels the land with the rocks and dirt it leaves behind.

East of the Appalachians is the coastal plain. In northern New England, this plain lies mostly underwater. It is wider from Massachusetts to Florida. Here, the plain has major cities, farms, and factories. Rock and sand left from glaciers formed islands with sandy beaches, such as Long Island. They also formed capes, such as Cape Cod. A **cape** is a point of land that sticks out into the water.

More people live on the coastal plain than in the mountains. The land is less rugged and closer to water routes. In the mountains, some people mine coal or cut down trees for timber. People also farm on the mountainsides and in the mountain valleys.

REVIEW Why are more cities built on the coastal plain than in the mountains?

Winter Nor'easter **Waves pounded the Massachusetts coast in this March 2001 storm. Heavy snow forced many schools to close.**

Bodies of Water

The East is a land of lakes, rivers, and ocean. As rivers flow from mountains down to the plain, great changes in elevation create waterfalls. Waterfalls made early travel on rivers difficult. However, people learned to use the water's force to power machines in mills and factories. The usefulness of water power led to the growth of major cities on these waterways.

People built settlements near the best harbors along the Atlantic coast. These settlements grew into cities. Ships carrying people and goods from other continents arrived in the harbors and bays. A bay is a body of water partly surrounded by land but open to the sea. The Chesapeake Bay, which reaches into Maryland, is important for shipping. It also supports thousands of plants and animals.

Climate and Its Effects

Main Idea The East has a temperate climate.

The East lies in the middle latitudes, about halfway between the North Pole and the equator. This location gives it four seasons and a temperate climate. **Temperate** means without extremes, such as the very cold weather in the Arctic or the very hot weather near the equator. Cool breezes blow from the Atlantic Ocean on hot days, and warm breezes blow on cold days. Winters in the East are cold and snowy, though, and summers are warm and humid.

The East sometimes has storms called "nor'easters." These storms bring strong winds from the northeast. Nor'easters also bring high ocean waves and heavy snow or rain. People need warm clothing and snow shovels to help them cope with winter conditions.

Plants and Animals

Climate affects the plants and animals that can live in a region. In the East, trees such as maple, birch, hickory, and oak drop their leaves before winter. This helps them survive the lack of water in the frozen soil.

Eastern animals must cope with both cold winters and changing food supplies. Squirrels bury nuts during the warmer months. In the winter, when food is hard to find, they can dig up the nuts and eat them. Other animals, such as black bears, hibernate during the winter. They use leaves and twigs to make a den in a cave or other shelter. Then they sleep for up to 100 days. Raccoons, skunks, and chipmunks also hibernate during the winter.

REVIEW In what ways does the climate of the East affect people, animals, and plants?

Lesson Summary

- The landforms of the East include mountains and plains.
- Rivers, harbors, and bays are important for development.
- The climate of the East is temperate, but winters are cold and snowy.

Why It Matters . . .

Water power, travel routes, and a temperate climate helped the East develop.

Black Bear Bears sleep through the coldest part of eastern winters.

Lesson Review

1. **VOCABULARY** Write a paragraph about how a **glacier** helped form the land in the East.
2. **READING SKILL** List two **details** that support this **main idea**: People learned to use bodies of water in the East.
3. **MAIN IDEA: Geography** Describe two landforms and two waterways that a visitor to the East might see.
4. **MAIN IDEA: Culture** Explain one effect of the climate on people's lives in the East.
5. **CRITICAL THINKING: Fact and Opinion** Write one fact about New England. Then write an opinion based on that fact.

HANDS ON **SCIENCE ACTIVITY** Use a reference book, such as an encyclopedia, to find out why the leaves of certain trees change color in the fall. Draw a diagram to show the process.

Core Lesson 2

Resources and Economy

VOCABULARY

profit
factors of production
entrepreneur

Vocabulary Strategy

profit

The word **profit** comes from the Latin **pro,** which means *to make.* Someone who makes a profit makes money.

READING SKILL

Classify Use a chart to list some natural resources of the East.

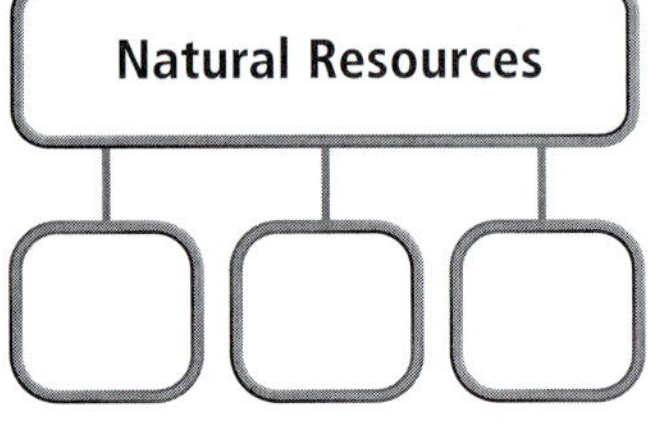

Build on What You Know Suppose you want to sell lemonade in your neighborhood. What price will you charge? Every business owner must choose what to sell, where to sell it, and for how much.

Natural Resources of the East

Main Idea The natural resources of the East include forests, soil, and minerals.

The East has fewer of some natural resources than other regions. For example, western states have more minerals than eastern states. However, the East has rivers, forests, farmland, fish, and an ocean. People use these resources to make goods for themselves and to sell to other people.

The Appalachian Mountains contain coal. Workers mine coal in Pennsylvania. Power plants burn it to make electricity. In Maine and Vermont, workers dig out granite and marble. These kinds of stone are used in buildings and monuments.

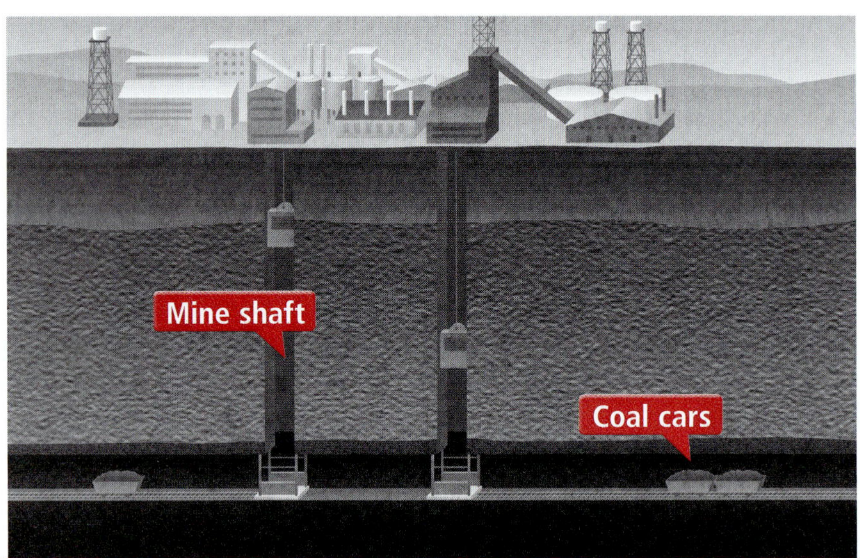

Coal Mine Workers take coal from mine shafts dug deep into the ground.

Natural Resources of the East

Resource	Uses
Granite	Stones for building
Marble	Monuments, tombs, parts of buildings
Coal	Fuel to make electricity, steel, iron, glass, stone, paper
Forests/Wood	Building materials, furniture, paper, fuel, maple syrup
Soil	Fruits, vegetables, grain, dairy cows
Fish	Food, fertilizer
Rivers/Ocean	Moving goods or people, source of water and power, fish

SKILL Reading Charts **Which resources are used for fuel or power?**

Apple Picking in New York **In the fall, easterners can pick their own apples.**

Using the East's Resources

In the East, many houses are made of wood. Forests provide wood for buildings, paper, furniture, and fuel. Wood can also be used to make chemicals for many other products, including plastics and textiles.

Do you like pancakes with syrup for breakfast? Maple syrup comes from sugar maple trees. Vermont produces more maple syrup than any other state. Maine, Massachusetts, New York, and New Hampshire also produce syrup.

The soil and climate of the East allow farmers to use their land in different ways. Blueberries grow well in the soil of Maine and New Hampshire. The soil of the Aroostook Valley in Maine is perfect for potatoes. Massachusetts and New Jersey have sandy marshes where farmers can grow cranberries. The warm, rainy summers in New York and Vermont make grasses grow well. These conditions are good for dairy cows, which eat the grasses. Eastern farmers also grow vegetables such as tomatoes, corn, and beans. Some farmers raise fruit trees, including apple and peach trees.

The Atlantic Ocean is an important resource for the East. From Maine to Maryland, people catch lobsters, sardines, flounder, and bass. Maryland and Delaware produce many blue crabs.

REVIEW Why is the farmland of the East an important natural resource?

Working in the East

Main Idea In a market economy, people decide what to make, buy, and sell.

A nation's economy is the system in which it uses resources to meet its needs and wants. The United States has a market economy. In a market economy people are free to decide what to make, how to make it, and for whom to make it. If the law allows it, they can run any business they want.

A market economy is different from a command economy. In a command economy, the government decides what to make, who will make it, and who will get it. The government also sets the prices for goods.

Business owners keep their profits in a market economy. **Profit** is the money left over after a business pays its expenses. Some businesses make profits by selling natural resources. Others make goods from resources. Then they sell the goods. Paper, maple syrup, and furniture are goods.

Some businesses sell services that people want. A service is any kind of work that one person does for another person as a job. Lawyers, plumbers, and engineers all provide services. In recent years, more and more people have worked in service businesses. Many of these service jobs involve computers, or information technology.

Market Economy In a market economy, people have many choices.

Trading Resources

Businesses use trade to get the resources they want. Trade begins when one person has what another wants. These people exchange resources or money for goods or services. In that way, both people get what they want. When people trade a lot, the economy grows.

Moving goods is important for trade. Imagine that a chemical factory in Maryland needs to buy raw materials from an owner in another region. The factory must pay a trucking company to bring the materials to the factory. Many businesses settle near big cities because the roads, waterways, and airports in these cities make trade easier.

Factories in the East make many kinds of goods. For example, New Jersey businesses make chemicals, medicines, machinery, and clothing. In Connecticut, factory workers make weapons, sewing machines, jet engines, and clocks.

Many eastern businesses provide services. For example, banks offer a safe place for people to keep their money. Banks also lend money to people. Many banks started in eastern cities. Today, Philadelphia and New York City are important banking centers. In banks, people can work as bank tellers, loan officers, and even computer programmers.

REVIEW How is making goods different from performing services?

Service Businesses in the East

Banking	Insurance
Communication	Legal services
Education	Recreation
Engineering	Repairs
Health care	Restaurants
Hotels	Tourism

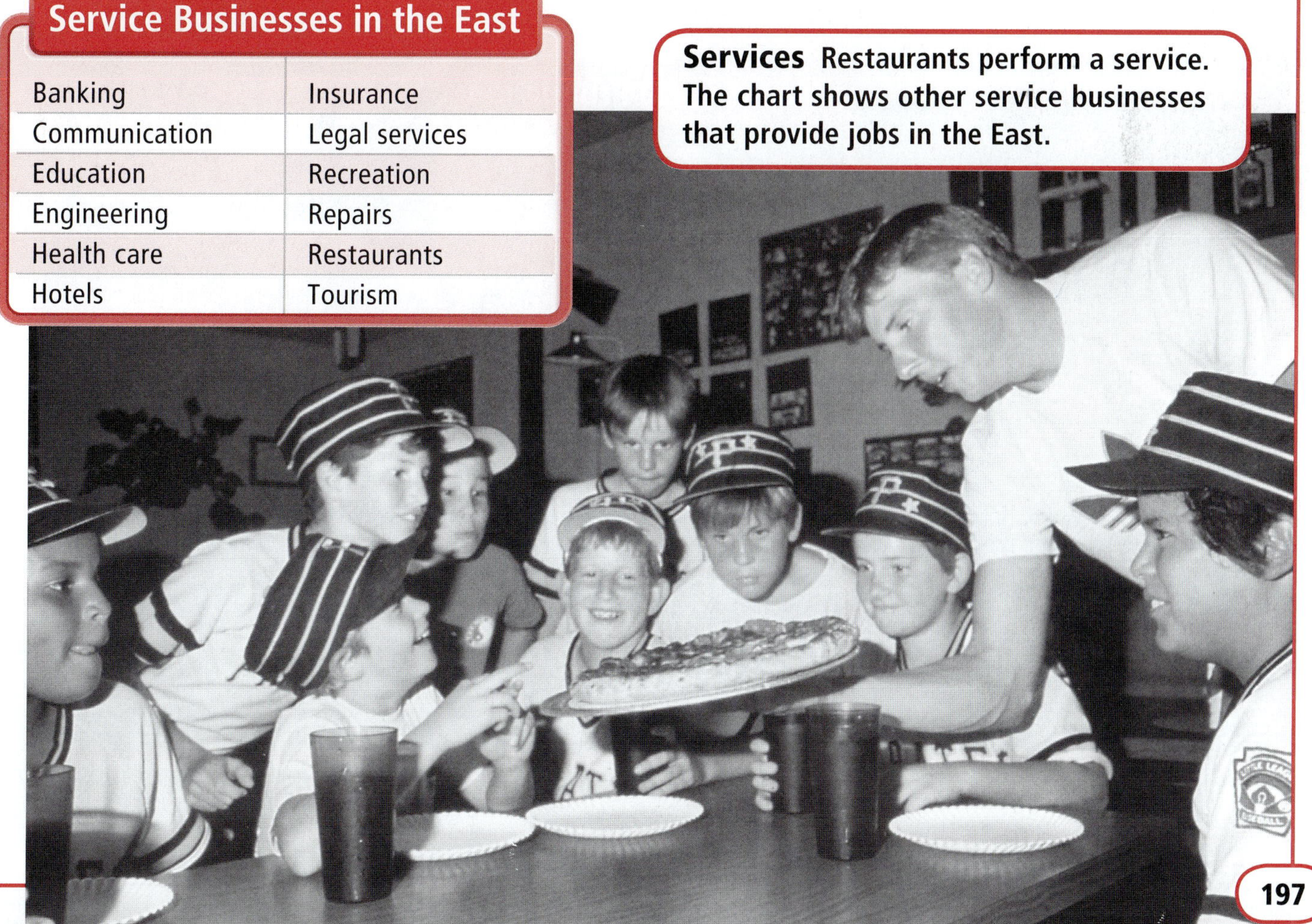

Services Restaurants perform a service. The chart shows other service businesses that provide jobs in the East.

Elements of Business

Main Idea In a system of private ownership, individuals own the factors of production.

A business needs equipment, workers, and often some raw materials. These things are the factors of production. **Factors of production** are the people and materials needed to make goods or provide services. The four factors are labor, capital, land, and entrepreneurship (ahn truh pruh NUHR ship). An **entrepreneur** is a person who is willing to take the risk of starting a new business.

Some businesses use natural resources. All businesses use human resources and capital resources. Human resources are the services, knowledge, skills, and intelligence that workers provide. Capital resources are the tools, machines, buildings, and other equipment that a business uses to make goods or provide services.

The East has a long tradition of successful businesses. Settlers near York, Maine, built the nation's first sawmill in 1623. Philadelphia had the nation's first bank and its first daily newspaper in the 1780s. Some of the nation's oldest companies still operate in the East today.

Factors of Production Skilled workers are needed to make sap into maple syrup.

SKILL **Reading Visuals** What capital resources do you see in the pictures below?

Maple Syrup Production

Natural and capital resources + Human resource = Product

Entrepreneurs and Ownership

Entrepreneurs are people who use the factors of production to start new businesses. Entrepreneurs take risks when they start new businesses. They invest their time and money in their businesses. However, people might not want to buy their goods or services. Then, instead of making a profit, the entrepreneurs could lose money. Entrepreneurs must plan carefully and work hard to have the best chance of earning a profit.

Entrepreneurs own their own businesses. Private ownership is an important part of a market economy. Private ownership means that individual people, not the government, own the factors of production. Individuals also make their own business decisions, hoping to earn a profit.

REVIEW Why is private ownership important in a market economy?

Entrepreneurship A person who opens a new store is an entrepreneur.

Lesson Summary

- People use the natural resources of the East to make products and trade with businesses in other areas.
- Businesses make profits by selling resources, goods, and services.
- Entrepreneurship and resources—natural, human, and capital—are necessary in any business.

Why It Matters ...

A market economy can give people more freedom to choose how they work and live.

Lesson Review

1. **VOCABULARY** Explain why **factors of production** are needed to make goods or provide services.
2. **READING SKILL** List two things that can be **classified** as human resources and two that can be classified as capital resources.
3. **MAIN IDEA: Geography** What are two natural resources of the East, and how are they used?
4. **MAIN IDEA: Economics** In what way is a market economy different from a command economy?
5. **CRITICAL THINKING: Analyze** Why might someone start a business near a city?

HANDS ON **INTERVIEW ACTIVITY** Interview several adults who work in different jobs. Ask each person if his or her job involves making a product or providing a service. Make a chart of these products and services.

Skillbuilder

Read a Table

VOCABULARY
table

Sometimes information is easier to understand if it is sorted into a chart. A table is a kind of chart in which information is listed in columns and rows. Tables make it easier to find and remember information.

Learn the Skill

Step 1: Read the title to learn what the whole table shows.

Step 2: Look at how the table is set up. In this table, the information is arranged in rows and columns. You can see that each column has a heading. The headings name two types of information.

Step 3: Read across a row to find information about one of the natural resources.

Jobs from Natural Resources

Natural Resource	Service Jobs
Granite and Marble	Stone cutter, stone carver, builder
Coal	Coal miner, coal hauler
Forests/Wood	Home builder, furniture maker
Rich Soil	Farmer, grocery worker
Fish	Fisher, restaurant worker
River/Bay	Boat pilot, water transportation worker

Practice the Skill

Use the table on page 200 to answer these questions.

1. What jobs are made possible by natural resources that are found underground?
2. What natural resources create jobs that have to do with food?
3. What natural resources provide products used by people who build things?

Apply the Skill

Read this paragraph about products made from various natural resources. Write the information as it would appear in a table like the one on page 200.

People of the Eastern states depend on our natural resources to create many products. From the wood grown in our forests we make furniture and houses. From the marble and granite we make monuments and important buildings. From the crops grown in our fields we make cotton clothing and many kinds of food products.

Core Lesson 3

The Mid-Atlantic

VOCABULARY

skyscraper
mass transit
capitol

Vocabulary Strategy

skyscraper

Skyscraper is a compound word of **sky** and **scraper.** Skyscrapers are tall buildings that look like they scrape the sky.

READING SKILL

Compare and Contrast List details that compare and contrast each area of the Mid-Atlantic region.

New York City	Suburbs	Rural Areas

Build on What You Know How tall is your school? If it were 100 stories tall, it would hold a lot of students! In large cities, many people work in buildings even taller than that.

Where People Live

Main Idea People in the Mid-Atlantic region live and work in big cities, suburbs, and rural areas.

The Mid-Atlantic region contains Delaware, Maryland, New Jersey, New York, Pennsylvania, and the nation's capital, Washington, D.C. It is the most thickly settled region in the nation. Many major cities are found in the Mid-Atlantic. One is New York City, the largest city in the United States.

New York's location at the mouth of the Hudson River led to its growth. European settlers used the river and New York's harbor to move goods from inland North America to Europe. Shipping led to the growth of trade. Today, New York is a world center for banking, publishing, advertising, and technology.

Grand Central Terminal
More than 150,000 commuters use this train station in New York each day.

Living in New York City

New York City started on an island called Manhattan. As the city grew, people settled in four new neighborhoods—Queens, Staten Island, the Bronx, and Brooklyn. Today, skyscrapers fill Manhattan. A **skyscraper** is a very tall building.

More than eight million people live in New York. Millions of others visit each year. They come to shop, to go to museums, and to attend plays. Most people rely on mass transit to move around this crowded city. **Mass transit** is transportation for many people at once, on buses, subways, or trains.

Suburbs of the Mid-Atlantic

Suburbs surround the major cities of the Mid-Atlantic region. People began to move from cities to the suburbs in the 1800s. They wanted to find less crowded places to live.

Some people commute from their homes in the suburbs to jobs in the city. Others work in businesses near their homes. People in suburbs often drive their cars to work, to schools, and to shopping malls.

REVIEW Why was New York's location important to its growth?

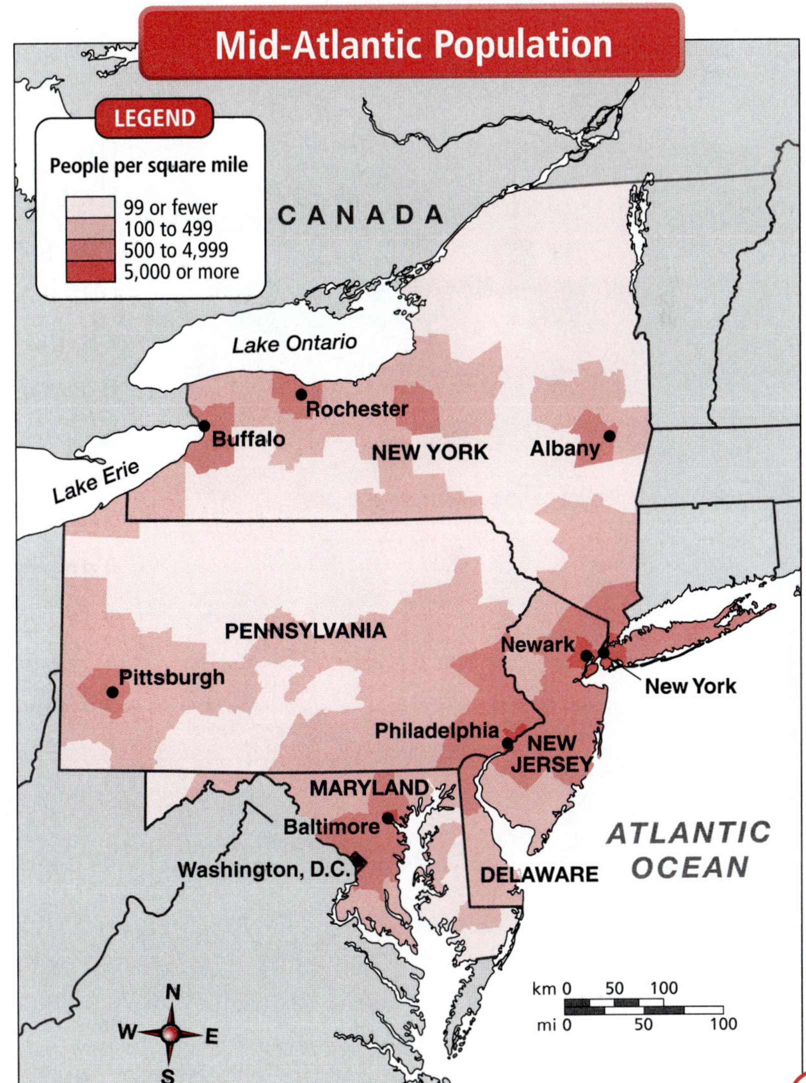

Mid-Atlantic Population The coastal plain of the Mid-Atlantic region is the most populated.

SKILL Interpreting Maps Are the highest populations closer to the Atlantic Ocean or to the Great Lakes?

Rural Areas

Although urban and suburban areas cover much of the Mid-Atlantic, forest and farmland fill large areas, too. The soil here is much easier to farm than it is in New England. Mid-Atlantic farms produce flowers, chickens, and many dairy products. Mines in Pennsylvania rank fourth in producing the most coal in the United States.

The natural environment and historic landmarks draw millions of visitors to the Mid-Atlantic states. They enjoy winter sports in the mountains of New York and Pennsylvania. They sunbathe on Delaware and New Jersey beaches. They boat and fish in the Chesapeake Bay. Many visitors also tour our nation's capital.

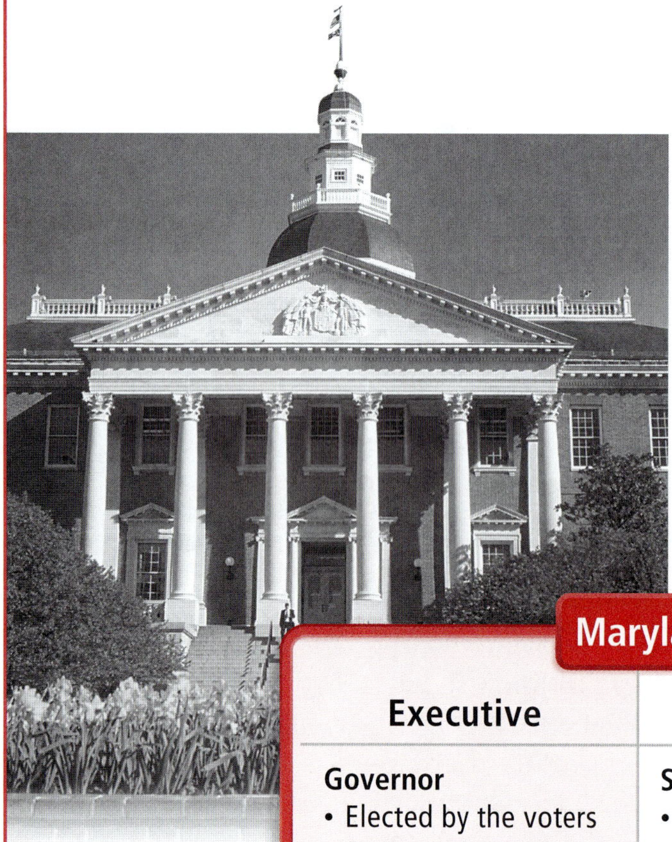

State Governments

Main Idea State government is divided into three branches.

Each state has a capital city where the state government is located. Within the state capital is a state house or a building called the capitol. The **capitol** is where lawmakers, or legislators, meet.

Each state has a constitution. The constitution divides state government into three parts, or branches. These are the legislative, executive, and judicial branches. The legislative branch makes laws. The executive branch puts the laws into action. The judicial branch interprets, or explains, the laws in the courts.

Suppose the legislative branch of the New Jersey government made a law that provided money for new parks. The governor would sign the law to put it into action. The governor is the official who leads the executive branch. If people disagreed about the law, the judicial branch would have to decide exactly what the law meant.

Annapolis, Maryland Maryland's capitol is the oldest still in use. It was built in 1772.

SKILL **Reading Chart** Which people in Maryland's government are not elected?

Maryland State Government

Executive	Legislative	Judicial
Governor • Elected by the voters • Serves a 4-year term	**Senators, Delegates** • Elected by the voters • Serve 4-year terms	**Judges** • Some elected by voters • Some appointed to 10-year terms

Public and Private Services

State governments are public institutions. That means they serve the state's people and communities. State services for the public include education, fire and police protection, and highways. States pay for public services by collecting taxes. A tax is a fee paid to the government. States may tax the money people earn, the property they own, and the things they buy.

State services are public. Services provided by a group or individual are private. For example, New Jersey builds public roads for everyone to use. However, private companies sell the cars and trucks that travel on the roads.

REVIEW What are the three branches of state government, and what do they do?

Lesson Summary

- The Mid-Atlantic has many large cities surrounded by suburbs.
- New York City, a financial and industrial center, is the biggest city in this region.
- Rural regions of the Mid-Atlantic support farming, mining, and tourism.
- State governments divide power among three branches.

Why It Matters . . .

Millions of people live and work in the Mid-Atlantic region. Workers in this region provide goods and services to the entire nation and the world.

Lesson Review

1. **VOCABULARY** Match each vocabulary term with its description.

   skyscraper **capitol** **mass transit**

   (a) transportation for many people; **(b)** very tall building; **(c)** building in which legislators meet

2. **READING SKILL Compare and contrast** public and private services.

3. **MAIN IDEA: Culture** In what ways is living in a city different from living in a rural area?

4. **MAIN IDEA: Geography** What is one difference between a capital city and other cities?

5. **CRITICAL THINKING: Infer** Why do you think more people rely on mass transit in a city than in a suburb?

HANDS ON **CURRENT EVENTS ACTIVITY** Read about what is happening in one Mid-Atlantic state. What is one major issue the state's government is dealing with?

Skillbuilder

Use a Special Purpose Map

Some maps have a special purpose. They use different symbols to tell about the special features of a place. The map below tells you about agricultural areas in the East.

Agricultural Areas in the East

CANADA
MAINE
VERMONT
NEW HAMPSHIRE
NEW YORK
MASSACHUSETTS
CONNECTICUT
RHODE ISLAND
PENNSYLVANIA
NEW JERSEY
MARYLAND
DELAWARE
Lake Ontario
Lake Erie
ATLANTIC OCEAN
Augusta
Montpelier
Concord
Albany
Boston
Hartford
Providence
Buffalo
New York
Pittsburgh
Harrisburg
Trenton
Philadelphia
Baltimore
Annapolis
Dover
Washington, D.C.
N
E
S
W
km 0 50 100
mi 0 50 100

LEGEND

- State capital
- National capital
- Large city
- Apple-growing areas
- Peach-growing areas
- Cherry-growing areas
- Grape-growing areas

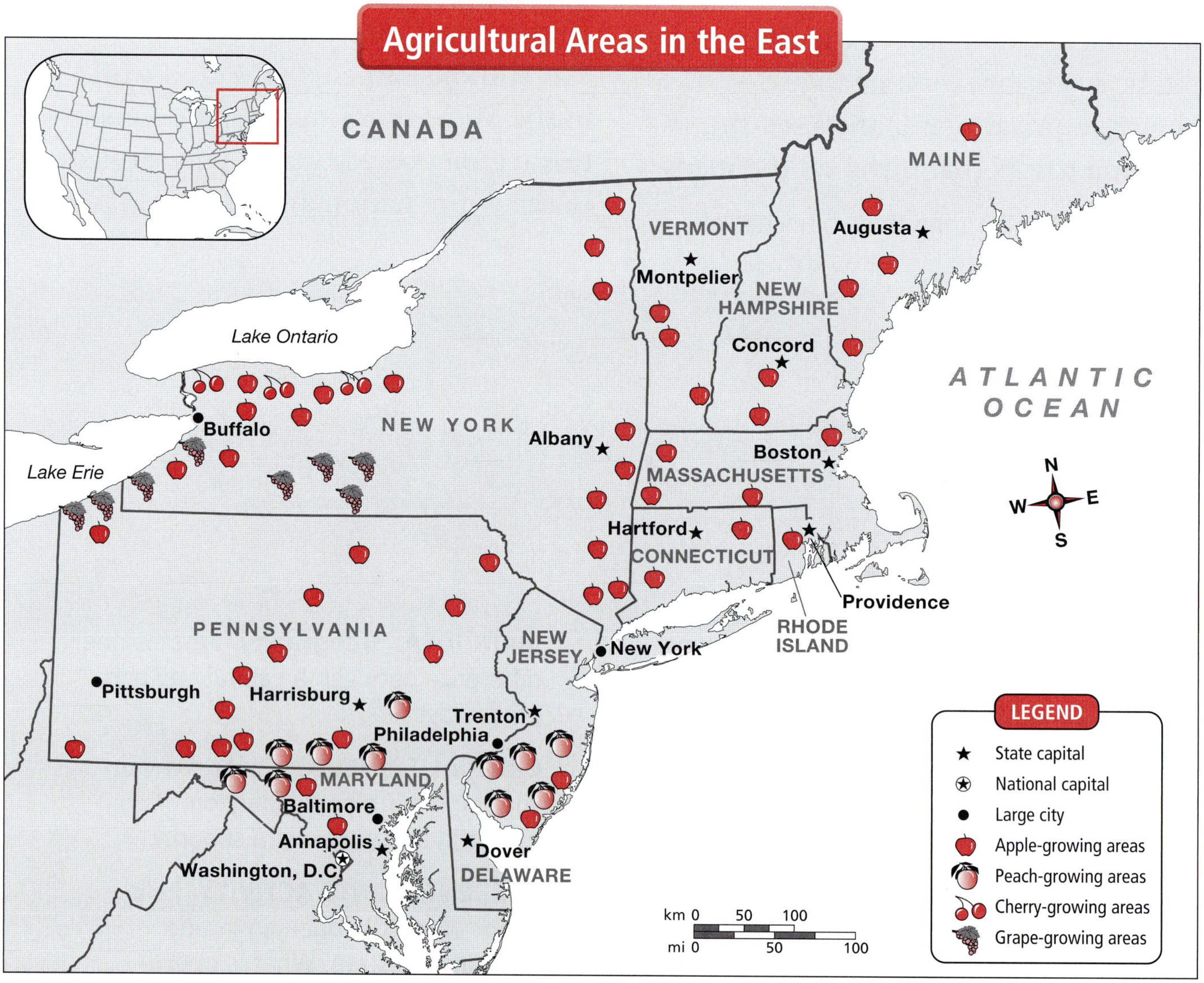

Learn the Skill

Step 1: Read the map title to find out what kind of information is shown on the map.

Step 2: Study the map's legend. Notice that each symbol represents one of the different fruits grown in the East. There are also symbols for cities and capitals.

Step 3: Note where the symbols for the legend appear on the map. For example, the peach symbol appears in Maryland.

Practice the Skill

Use the map on page 206 to answer these questions.

1. What helps you to know that apples are grown throughout the East?
2. According to the map, which fruits are grown in the state of New York?
3. Which two of the fruits are grown farthest south?

Apply the Skill

Study the special purpose map on page 203. Then write a paragraph that summarizes the information shown on the map.

Core Lesson 4

Many Regions, One Nation

VOCABULARY

interdependence
prosperity
heritage

Vocabulary Strategy

interdependence

The prefix **inter–** means "between." **Interdependence** can mean dependence between people, or people needing each other.

READING SKILL

Draw Conclusions As you read, list facts that support this conclusion.

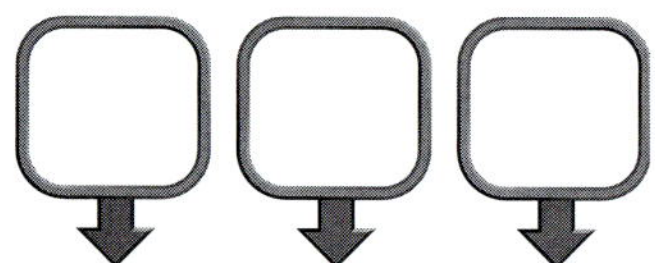

The government helps create links between Americans.

Build on What You Know Do you have friends or relatives who live in other parts of the country? Although you live far apart, do you feel connected? People all across our nation are connected, too.

Linking Regions

Main Idea Networks of communication, transportation, and trade link people of the United States.

Americans are linked in many ways. We live in the United States. We have a national government. We share the values of liberty, equality, and justice.

Our government has always searched for new ways to link states and regions. For example, early leaders created a postal system even before there was a United States. Our nation has built roads, canals, and railroads. We have phone systems, airports, and the Internet. These links change over time, but they have always had the same goal of connecting the states and regions of the country.

Making Connections The Internet and the United States Postal Service are two systems that link Americans.

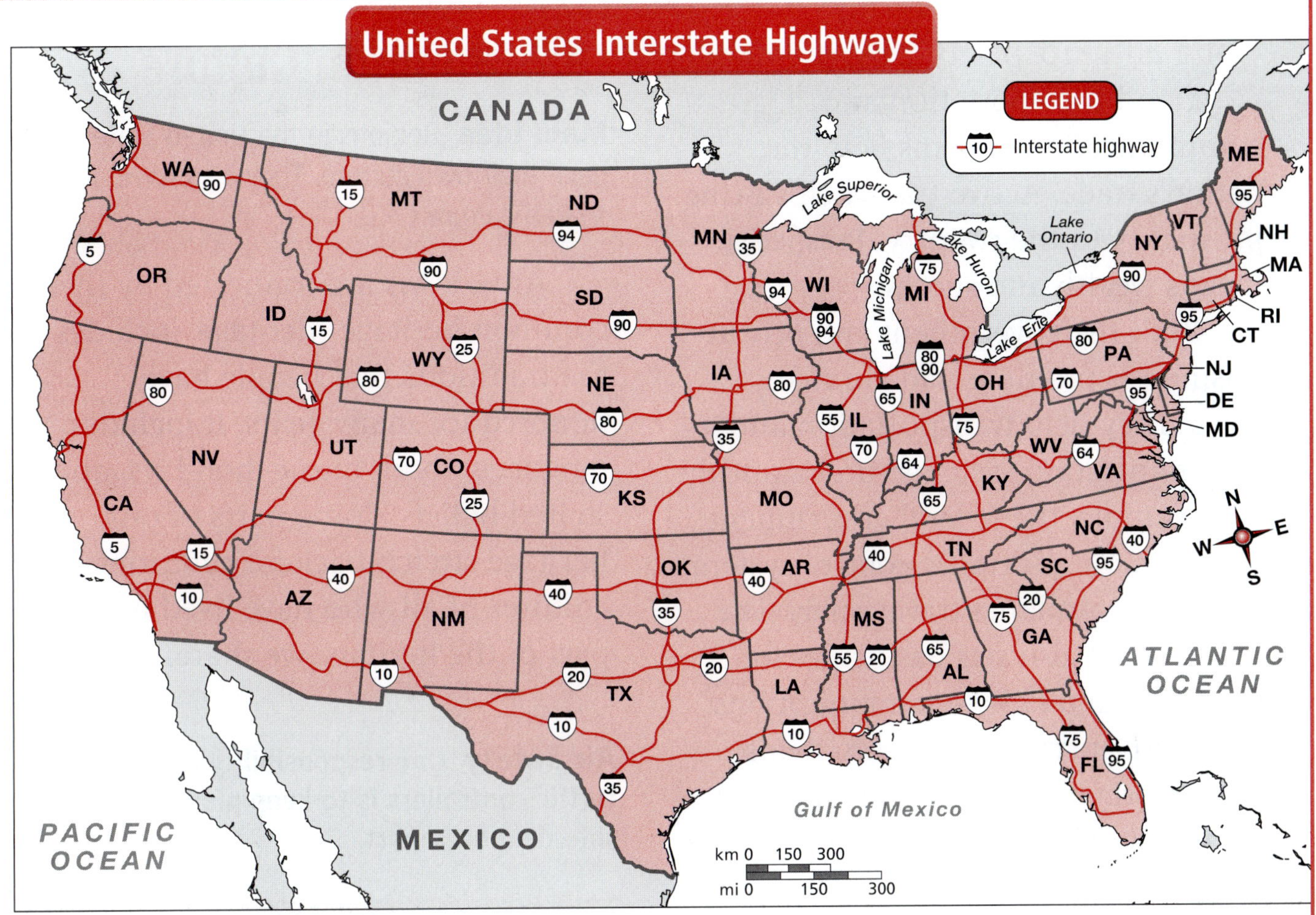

Interstate Highways The interstate highway system has made transportation much easier.

Interdependence of Regions

Each link that connects states and regions leads to more interdependence. **Interdependence** is a relationship in which people depend on each other. For example, think about farmers in Maryland and families living in New Jersey. Because roads connect the states, Maryland farmers can sell crops to New Jersey families who eat the farmers' crops. Both depend on each other. These kinds of links are found across the country. They help unite us and help us live better lives.

The United States government has worked hard to create these links. Today, the United States Postal Service connects people and businesses across the country. It helps people communicate and transport goods. The mail handles billions of dollars in business every day.

The United States government has also helped build a network of roads called the Interstate Highway System. Many of these roads were built in the 1950s and 1960s. Interstate highways help people and goods move easily across the country.

REVIEW In what way does the United States Postal Service link different parts of the country?

Trade and Prosperity

Good transportation and communication systems help the nation's trade. Active trade helps bring prosperity to the country. **Prosperity** means wealth and success.

Both the government and private businesses promote trade in many ways. They help transportation and communication systems run smoothly. For example, the federal government manages our air-traffic control system. This helps airplanes travel safely. The government also sets basic rules for television and radio communications. Some private companies ship items. Others provide phone service and air transportation. The Internet also allows people to communicate.

Another way our government helps trade is by providing a system of money and banking. This makes trade easier. Everyone agrees on how to pay for goods and services. People know what the money is worth.

Our Common Culture

Main Idea Regions in the United States have their own culture. They also have a shared culture.

Americans are connected by their common heritage. **Heritage** includes the traditions that people have honored for many years. It includes language, food, music, holidays, and shared beliefs. Some parts of our heritage stretch back for centuries. The cultures of all who have lived here are part of the heritage we share.

Air Safety One responsibility of air traffic controllers is to keep planes a safe distance apart.

Sharing Traditions

Holidays show our shared heritage. People in every state celebrate Independence Day. Memorial Day parades happen all across the country.

People also share a tradition of helping others. After the attacks of September 11, 2001, volunteers from around the country came to New York City. A volunteer is someone who agrees to provide a service without pay.

Helping Out **These volunteers prepared food for rescue workers in New York City.**

One volunteer was Timothy Mottl of Illinois. He said,

> **“The experience made me really look at . . . what being an American means to me.”**

REVIEW In what ways do we show our shared culture?

Lesson Summary

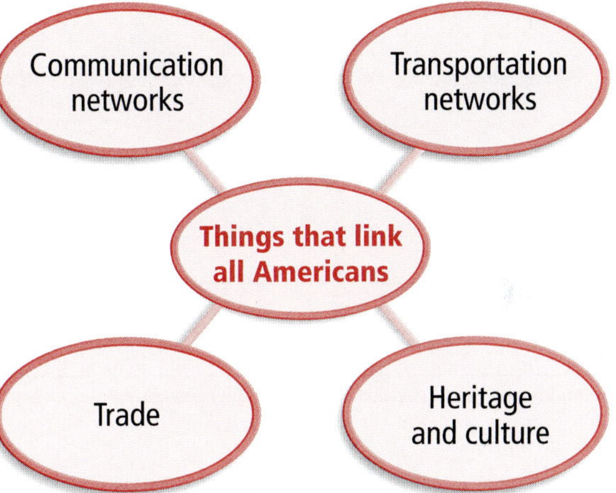

Why It Matters . . .

Though each region of the United States is different, we are linked together in many ways.

Lesson Review

1. **VOCABULARY** Write a short paragraph that shows you know what **interdependence** and **prosperity** mean.
2. **READING SKILL** What can you conclude about the ways government helps the economy?
3. **MAIN IDEA: Geography** List three ways the government helps link the different parts of the country.
4. **MAIN IDEA: Culture** In what ways does heritage connect people?
5. **CRITICAL THINKING: Draw Conclusions** In an emergency, why do you think people volunteer to help each other?

ART ACTIVITY What do you think it means to be an American? Create a poster with words and images that show our shared culture and heritage.

Chapter 9 Review and Test Prep

Visual Summary

1 – 4. Write a description of each item named below.

Climate

Resources

Skyscraper

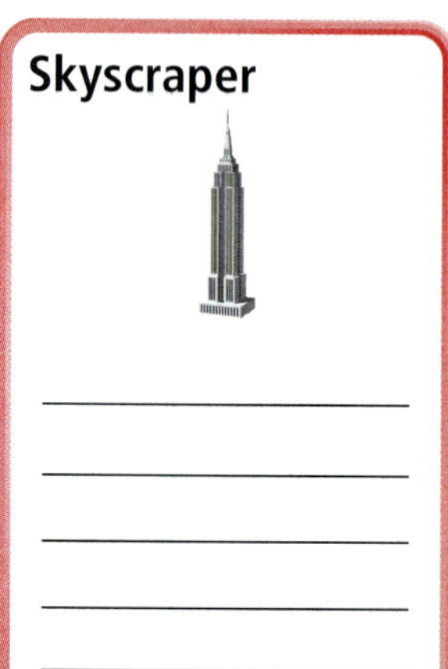

Prosperity

Facts and Main Ideas

TEST PREP Answer each question below.

5. **Geography** In what ways have glaciers affected landforms in the East?
6. **Economics** In a market economy, what decisions must a business owner make?
7. **Culture** How do Americans celebrate their shared heritage?
8. **Technology** Who sets rules for television and radio communications?
9. **Government** What happens if someone challenges or disagrees with a state law?

Vocabulary

TEST PREP Choose the correct word from the list below to complete each sentence.

cape, p. 191
entrepreneur, p. 198
capitol, p. 204
prosperity, p. 210

10. An _____ is a person who is willing to take the risk of starting a new business.
11. A point of land that sticks out into the water is a _____.
12. _____ means wealth and success.
13. A _____ is a building where legislators meet.

Apply Skills

TEST PREP **Read a Special Purpose Map** Study the Crystal Lake Beach map below. Then use your map skills to answer each question.

14. What is the purpose of the map?

A. to sell boats
B. to provide a guide for visitors
C. to keep people out of the lake
D. to identify wildlife

15. How many places for people to put their boats into the water does the map show?

A. two
B. three
C. four
D. none

Critical Thinking

TEST PREP Write a short paragraph to answer each question below.

16. **Cause and Effect** Why must resources often be moved from one area to another before they are used?

17. **Infer** Why might some people prefer commuting to work rather than living near their jobs?

18. **Compare and Contrast** How are lives of people who live in the suburbs different from the lives of people who live in large cities?

19. **Summarize** How do interdependence and a common culture bring the people of the United States together?

Activities

Art Activity Draw pictures of some of the natural resources of the East that show how people have used them.

Writing Activity Write a description of what an eastern city in the early 1900s might have been like. Include why people came to cities and from where they came. Tell what kind of work they might find.

Technology
Writing Process Tips
Get help with your description at **www.eduplace.com/kids/hmss/**

UNIT 5

Review and Test Prep

Vocabulary and Main Ideas

TEST PREP **Write a sentence to answer each question.**

1. What are some features of a **cape?**
2. In what ways might a **glacier** change the geography of a region?
3. What is an example of **mass transit?**
4. In what ways does trade help bring **prosperity** to our region?
5. What are some of the **factors of production?**
6. What happens in a **capitol?**

Critical Thinking

TEST PREP **Write a short paragraph to answer each question.**

7. **Cause and Effect** What are some natural resources of the East? How do they help determine the jobs that people do?
8. **Evaluate** Why is our shared American heritage important?

Apply Skills

TEST PREP **Use the table below and what you have learned about tables to answer each question.**

Places to Live

Region	Characteristics
Urban	Many people, large buildings, many museums and other reasons to visit
Suburban	Many single-family homes, people commuting to work
Rural	Few people, many farms, natural attractions

9. What kind of region would you visit to see many museums?

   A. urban
   B. suburban
   C. rural

10. What kind of region would you visit to see many natural attractions?

   A. urban
   B. suburban
   C. rural

11. In what kind of region would you see many single-family homes?

   A. urban
   B. suburban
   C. rural

Unit Activity

Make a State Government Poster

- Make a chart of the three branches of your state government. List the name of the governor and other top officials.
- Find out when and where the state legislature meets and what law they are planning to vote on. Add the information to your poster.
- Write a sentence stating how you think they should vote on the issue.
- Present your poster to the class.

At the Library

You may find this book at your school or public library.

Capital by Lynn Curlee

This history of Washington, D.C., provides information on the National Mall.

Current Events Project

Create a bulletin board about the freedoms that Americans have.

- Find information about the Constitution and the Bill of Rights.
- Pick one of the 10 amendments. Think about how it keeps Americans free today.
- Write a paragraph about your amendment. Include drawings of people using their freedom.
- Post your paragraph on a bulletin board.

Technology

Weekly Reader online offers social studies articles. Go to: **www.eduplace.com/kids/hmss/**

References

Citizenship Handbook

Resources

Pledge of Allegiance

I pledge allegiance to the flag
of the United States of America
and to the republic for which it stands,
one Nation, under God, indivisible,
with liberty and justice for all.

Spanish

Prometo lealtad a la bandera
de los Estados Unidos de América,
y a la república que representa,
una nación bajo Dios, indivisible,
con libertad y justicia para todos.

Maryland Constitution Excerpts

The Constitution of the State of Maryland

ADOPTED 1867

Preamble

We, the People of the State of Maryland, grateful to Almighty God for our civil and religious liberty, and taking into our serious consideration the best means of establishing a good Constitution in this State for the sure foundation and more permanent security thereof, declare:

Article 1

DECLARATION OF RIGHTS

That all Government of right originates from the People, is founded in compact only, and instituted solely for the good of the whole; and they have, at all times, the inalienable right to alter, reform or abolish their Form of Government in such manner as they may deem expedient.

Article 8

SEPARATION OF POWERS

That the Legislative, Executive and Judicial powers of Government ought to be forever separate and distinct from each other; and no person exercising the functions of one of said Departments shall assume or discharge the duties of any other.

Article 5

TRIAL BY JURY

That the Inhabitants of Maryland are entitled to . . . trial by Jury. . . .

Article 40

FREEDOM OF THE PRESS

That the liberty of the press ought to be inviolably preserved; that every citizen of the State ought to be allowed to speak, write and publish his sentiments on all subjects, being responsible for the abuse of that privilege.

Character Traits

Character includes feelings, thoughts, and behaviors. A character trait is something people show by the way they act. To act bravely shows courage, and courage is one of several character traits.

Positive character traits, such as honesty, caring, and courage, lead to positive actions. Character traits are also called "life skills." Life skills can help you do your best, and doing your best leads to reaching your goals.

Duke Ellington

Respect Jazz musician Duke Ellington helped many other musicians achieve success. He was known for treating himself and others with respect.

Clara Barton

Caring Barton spent most of her life working to get medical help to people suffering as a result of war or natural disaster. She founded the American Red Cross organization.

Courage means acting bravely. Doing what you believe to be good and right, and telling the truth, requires courage.

Patriotism means working for the goals of your country. When you show national pride, you are being patriotic.

Responsibility is taking care of work that needs to be done. Responsible people are reliable and trustworthy, which means they can be counted on.

Respect means paying attention to what other people want and believe. The "golden rule," or treating others as you would like to be treated, shows thoughtfulness and respect.

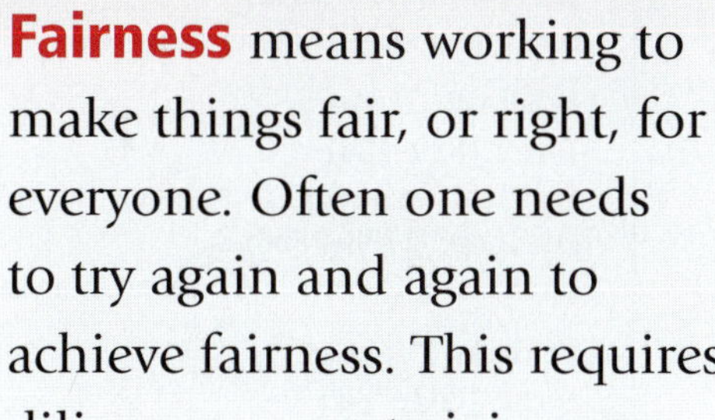

Fairness means working to make things fair, or right, for everyone. Often one needs to try again and again to achieve fairness. This requires diligence, or not giving up.

Civic virtue is good citizenship. It means doing things, such as cooperating and solving problems, to help communities live and work well together.

Caring means noticing what others need and helping them get what they need. Feeling concern or compassion is another way to define caring.

Maryland Governors

State Governors

Thomas Johnson
Term: 1777–1779
Political Party: Federalist
Lifespan: (1732–1819)
Birthplace: Calvert County, Maryland

Thomas Sim Lee
Term: 1779–1782
Political Party: Federalist
Lifespan: (1745–1819)
Birthplace: Upper Marlboro, Maryland

William Paca
Term: 1782–1785
Political Party: Anti-Federalist
Lifespan: (1740–1799)
Birthplace: near Abingdon, Maryland

William Smallwood
Term: 1785–1788
Political Party: None
Lifespan: (1732–1792)
Birthplace: Charles County, Maryland

John Eager Howard
Term: 1788–1791
Political Party: Federalist
Lifespan: (1752–1827)
Birthplace: Baltimore, Maryland

George Plater
Term: 1791–1792
Political Party: Federalist
Lifespan: (1735–1792)
Birthplace: St. Mary's County, Maryland

James Brice
Term: 1792
Political Party:
Lifespan: (1746–1801)
Birthplace: Annapolis, Maryland

Thomas Sim Lee
Term: 1792–1794
Political Party: Federalist
Lifespan: (1745–1819)
Birthplace: Upper Marlboro, Maryland

John H. Stone
Term: 1794–1797
Political Party: Federalist
Lifespan: (1750–1804)
Birthplace: Charles County, Maryland

John Henry
Term: 1797–1798
Political Party: Democrat
Lifespan: (1750–1798)
Birthplace: Dorchester County, Maryland

Benjamin Ogle
Term: 1798–1801
Political Party: Federalist
Lifespan: (1749–1809)
Birthplace: Annapolis, Maryland

John Francis Mercer
Term: 1801–1803
Political Party: Democratic-Republican
Lifespan: (1759–1821)
Birthplace: Marlborough, Maryland

Robert Bowie
Term: 1803–1806
Political Party: Democratic-Republican
Lifespan: (1750–1818)
Birthplace: Mattaponi, Maryland

Robert Wright
Term: 1806–1809
Political Party: Democrat
Lifespan: (1752–1826)
Birthplace: Queen Anne's County, Maryland

Edward Lloyd
Term: 1809–1811
Political Party: Democratic-Republican
Lifespan: (1779–1834)
Birthplace: Talbot County, Maryland

Robert Bowie
Term: 1811–1812
Political Party: Democratic-Republican
Lifespan: (1750–1818)
Birthplace: Mattaponi, Maryland

Levin Winder
Term: 1812–1816
Political Party: Federalist
Lifespan: (1757–1819)
Birthplace: Somerset County, Maryland

Charles Ridgely
Term: 1816–1819
Political Party: Federalist
Lifespan: (1760–1829)
Birthplace: Baltimore County, Maryland

Charles Goldsborough
Term: 1819
Political Party: Federalist
Lifespan: (1765–1834)
Birthplace: Dorchester County, Maryland

Samuel Sprigg
Term: 1819–1822
Political Party: Democrat/Whig
Lifespan: (1783–1855)
Birthplace: Prince George's County, Maryland

Samuel Stevens, Jr.
Term: 1822–1826
Political Party: Democrat
Lifespan: (1778–1860)
Birthplace: Talbot County, Maryland

Joseph Kent
Term: 1826–1829
Political Party: Democratic-Republican
Lifespan: (1779–1837)
Birthplace: Calvert County, Maryland

Daniel Martin
Term: 1829–1830
Political Party: Whig
Lifespan: (1780–1831)
Birthplace: Talbot County, Maryland

Thomas King Carroll
Term: 1830–1831
Political Party: Democrat
Lifespan: (1793–1873)
Birthplace: Somerset County, Maryland

Daniel Martin
Term: 1831
Political Party: Whig
Lifespan: (1780–1831)
Birthplace: Talbot County, Maryland

George Howard
Term: 1831–1833
Political Party: Whig
Lifespan: (1789–1846)
Birthplace: Annapolis, Maryland

James Thomas
Term: 1833–1836
Political Party: Whig
Lifespan: (1785–1845)
Birthplace: St. Mary's County, Maryland

Thomas W. Veazey
Term: 1836–1839
Political Party: Whig
Lifespan: (1774–1842)
Birthplace: Cecil County, Maryland

William Grason
Term: 1839–1842
Political Party: Anti-Jacksonian
Lifespan: (1788–1868)
Birthplace: Queen Anne's County, Maryland

Francis Thomas
Term: 1842–1845
Political Party: Democrat
Lifespan: (1799–1876)
Birthplace: Frederick County, Maryland

Thomas G. Pratt
Term: 1845–1848
Political Party: Whig
Lifespan: (1804–1869)
Birthplace: Georgetown, Maryland

Philip Francis Thomas
Term: 1848–1851
Political Party: Democrat
Lifespan: (1810–1890)
Birthplace: Easton, Maryland

Enoch L. Lowe
Term: 1851–1854
Political Party: Democrat
Lifespan: (1820–1892)
Birthplace: Frederick County, Maryland

State Governors (continued)

Thomas W. Ligon
Term: 1854–1858
Political Party: Democrat
Lifespan: (1810–1881)
Birthplace: Prince Edward County, Virginia

Thomas H. Hicks
Term: 1858–1862
Political Party: Unionist/Republican
Lifespan: (1798–1865)
Birthplace: East New Market, Maryland

Augustus W. Bradford
Term: 1862–1866
Political Party: Unionist
Lifespan: (1806–1881)
Birthplace: Bel Air, Maryland

Thomas Swann
Term: 1866–1869
Political Party: Democrat
Lifespan: (1809–1883)
Birthplace: Alexandria, Virginia

Oden Bowie
Term: 1869–1872
Political Party: Democrat
Lifespan: (1826–1894)
Birthplace: Prince George's County, Maryland

William P. Whyte
Term: 1872–1874
Political Party: Democrat
Lifespan: (1824–1908)
Birthplace: Baltimore, Maryland

James B. Groome
Term: 1874–1876
Political Party: Democrat
Lifespan: (1838–1893)
Birthplace: Elkton, Maryland

John Lee Carroll
Term: 1876–1880
Political Party: Democrat
Lifespan: (1830–1911)
Birthplace: Baltimore, Maryland

William T. Hamilton
Term: 1880–1884
Political Party: Democrat
Lifespan: (1820–1888)
Birthplace: Boonsboro, Maryland

Robert M. McLane
Term: 1884–1885
Political Party: Democrat
Lifespan: (1815–1898)
Birthplace: Wilmington, Delaware

Henry Lloyd
Term: 1885–1888
Political Party: Democrat
Lifespan: (1852–1920)
Birthplace: Dorchester County, Maryland

Elihu E. Jackson
Term: 1888–1892
Political Party: Democrat
Lifespan: (1837–1907)
Birthplace: Delmar, Maryland

Frank Brown
Term: 1892–1896
Political Party: Democrat
Lifespan: (1846–1920)
Birthplace: Carroll County, Maryland

Lloyd Lowndes
Term: 1896–1900
Political Party: Republican
Lifespan: (1845–1905)
Birthplace: Clarksburg, West Virginia

John W. Smith
Term: 1900–1904
Political Party: Democrat
Lifespan: (1845–1925)
Birthplace: Worcester County, Maryland

Edwin Warfield
Term: 1904–1908
Political Party:
Lifespan: (1848–1920)
Birthplace: Howard County, Maryland

Austin L. Crothers
Term: 1908–1912
Political Party: Democrat
Lifespan: (1860–1912)
Birthplace: Conowingo, Maryland

Phillips L. Goldsborough
Term: 1912–1916
Political Party: Republican
Lifespan: (1865–1946)
Birthplace: Cambridge, Maryland

Emerson C. Harrington
Term: 1916–1920
Political Party: Democrat
Lifespan: (1864–1945)
Birthplace: Madison, Maryland

Albert C. Ritchie
Term: 1920–1935
Political Party: Democrat
Lifespan: (1876–1936)
Birthplace: Richmond, Virginia

Harry W. Nice
Term: 1935–1939
Political Party: Republican
Lifespan: (1877–1941)
Birthplace: Washington, D.C.

Herbert R. O'Conor
Term: 1939–1947
Political Party: Democrat
Lifespan: (1896–1960)
Birthplace: Baltimore, Maryland

William P. Lane, Jr.
Term: 1947–1951
Political Party: Democrat
Lifespan: (1892–1967)
Birthplace: Hagerstown, Maryland

Theodore R. McKeldin
Term: 1951–1959
Political Party: Republican
Lifespan: (1900–1974)
Birthplace: Baltimore, Maryland

J. Millard Tawes
Term: 1959–1967
Political Party: Democrat
Lifespan: (1894–1979)
Birthplace: Crisfield, Maryland

Spiro T. Agnew
Term: 1967–1969
Political Party: Republican
Lifespan: (1918–1996)
Birthplace: Baltimore, Maryland

Marvin Mandel
Term: 1969–1979
Political Party: Democrat
Lifespan: 1920–
Birthplace: Baltimore, Maryland

Blair Lee III (acting governor)
Term: 1977–1979
Political Party: Democrat
Lifespan: (1916–1985)
Birthplace: Silver Spring, Maryland

Harry R. Hughes
Term: 1979–1987
Political Party: Democrat
Lifespan: 1926–
Birthplace: Easton, Maryland

William D. Schaeffer
Term: 1987–1995
Political Party: Democrat
Lifespan: 1921–
Birthplace: Baltimore, Maryland

Parris N. Glendening
Term: 1995–2003
Political Party: Democrat
Lifespan: 1942–
Birthplace: Bronx, NY

Robert L. Ehrlich, Jr.
Term: 2003–present
Political Party: Republican
Lifespan: 1957–
Birthplace: Arbutus, Maryland

Maryland Counties

County	County Seat	Year Organized	Population	Origin of Name
Allegany	Cumberland	1789	74,930	from an American Indian word meaning "beautiful stream"
Anne Arundel	Annapolis	1650	489,656	named for Anne Arundel, wife of the Second Lord Baltimore, Cecil Calvert
Baltimore	Towson	1659/60	754,292	from the name of the Proprietor's Estate in Ireland
Baltimore City	Baltimore	1851	651,154	from the Proprietor Irish Barony
Calvert	Prince Frederick	1654	74,563	from the family name of Lord Baltimore, the Proprietor of the Maryland colony
Caroline	Denton	1773	29,772	for Lady Caroline Eden, the wife of Maryland's last colonial governor, Robert Eden
Carroll	Westminster	1837	150,897	for Charles Carroll of Carrollton
Cecil	Elkton	1674	85,951	for Cecil Calvert, Second Lord Baltimore, and founder of the Maryland colony
Charles	La Plata	1658	120,546	for Charles Calvert, 3rd Lord Baltimore
Dorchester	Cambridge	1668/69	30,674	for the Earl of Dorset, a family friend of the Calverts
Frederick	Frederick	1748	195,277	Frederick Calvert, 6th Lord Baltimore
Garrett	Oakland	1872	29,846	for John Work Garrett, railroad executive, industrialist, and financier
Harford	Bel Air	1773	218,590	for Henry Harford, last Proprietor of Maryland
Howard	Ellicott City	1851	247,842	for John Eager Howard, Revolutionary War officer, Maryland governor, and statesman
Kent	Chestertown	1642	19,197	for the county of the same name in the southeast of England
Montgomery	Rockville	1776	873,341	for Revolutionary War General Richard Montgomery

County	County Seat	Year Organized	Population	Origin of Name
Prince George's	Upper Marlboro	1695	801,515	for Prince George of Denmark, the husband of Queen Anne, who ruled Great Britain and Ireland from 1702 to 1714
Queen Anne's	Centreville	1706	40,563	for Queen Anne, who ruled Great Britain and Ireland from 1702 to 1714
St. Mary's	Leonardtown	1637	86,211	for Mary, the mother of Jesus
Somerset	Princess Anne	1666	24,747	for Lady Mary Somerset, the sister of Lady Anne Arundell, who was the wife of Cecil Calvert, Second Lord Baltimore
Talbot	Easton	1661/62	33,812	for Lady Grace Talbot, sister of Cecilius Calvert, Second Lord Baltimore
Washington	Hagerstown	1776	131,923	for George Washington, first United States president
Wicomico	Salisbury	1867	84,644	from the American Indian words "wicko" and "mekee" meaning "a place where houses are built," apparently referring to an Indian town on the river banks
Worchester	Snow Hill	1742	46,543	for the Earl of Worcester

Songs of Our Nation

Who wrote the patriotic songs we sing and why did they do it? There are as many reasons as there are songs.

Our national anthem, "The Star-Spangled Banner," was written by Francis Scott Key. In 1814, this American lawyer watched from a ship as the British attacked Fort McHenry near Baltimore, Maryland. The fight lasted all night. As the morning dawned, Key saw the American flag still flying proudly over the fort. The sight inspired him to write these verses.

"The Star-Spangled Banner"

by Francis Scott Key

O say, can you see, by the dawn's early light,
What so proudly we hailed at the twilight's last gleaming,
Whose broad stripes and bright stars, through the perilous fight,
O'er the ramparts we watched were so gallantly streaming?
And the rockets' red glare, the bombs bursting in air,
Gave proof through the night that our flag was still there
O say, does that Star-Spangled Banner yet wave
O'er the land of the free and the home of the brave?

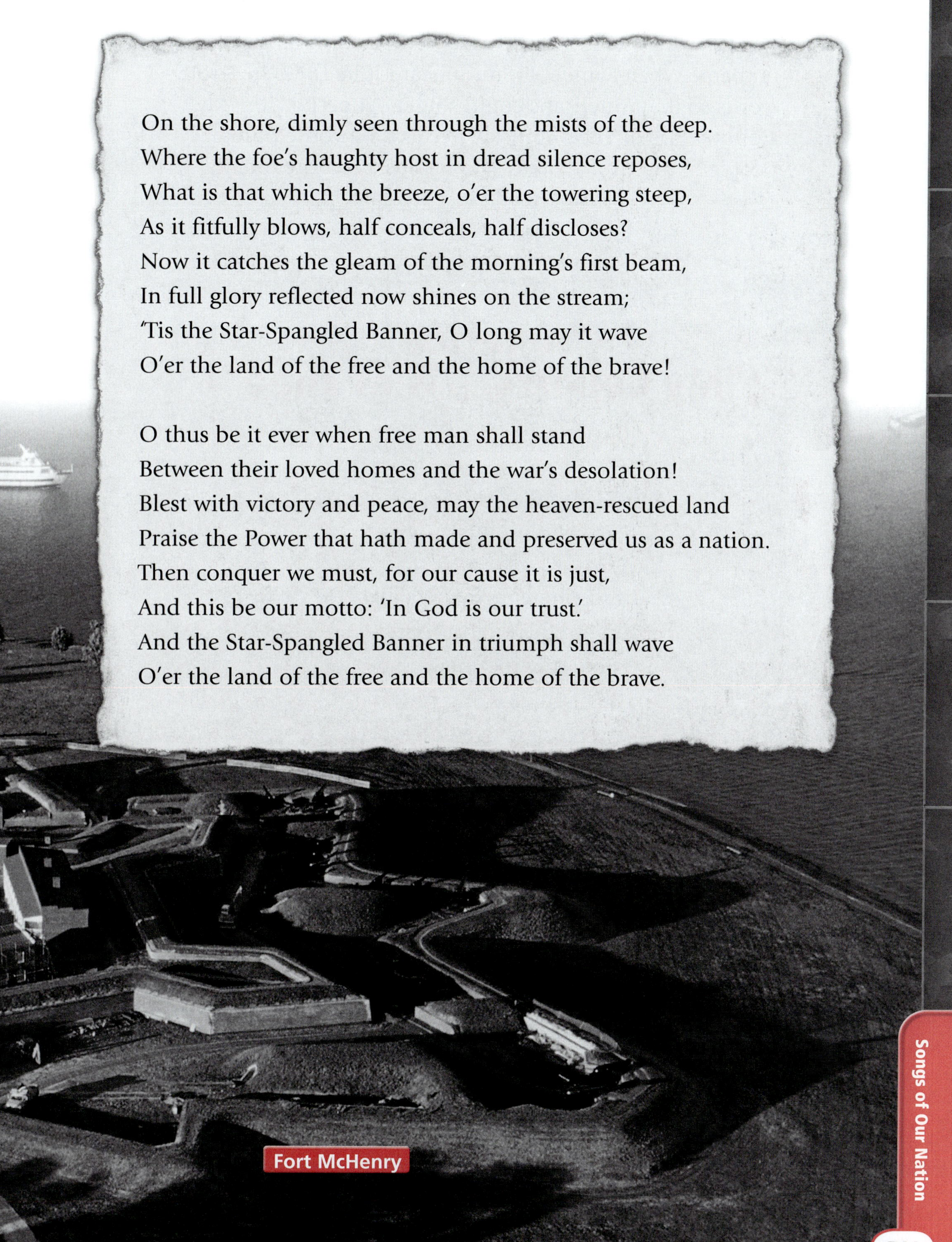

On the shore, dimly seen through the mists of the deep.
Where the foe's haughty host in dread silence reposes,
What is that which the breeze, o'er the towering steep,
As it fitfully blows, half conceals, half discloses?
Now it catches the gleam of the morning's first beam,
In full glory reflected now shines on the stream;
'Tis the Star-Spangled Banner, O long may it wave
O'er the land of the free and the home of the brave!

O thus be it ever when free man shall stand
Between their loved homes and the war's desolation!
Blest with victory and peace, may the heaven-rescued land
Praise the Power that hath made and preserved us as a nation.
Then conquer we must, for our cause it is just,
And this be our motto: 'In God is our trust.'
And the Star-Spangled Banner in triumph shall wave
O'er the land of the free and the home of the brave.

Fort McHenry

Have you ever heard the tune to the British national anthem? When Samuel F. Smith heard it in 1832, he wrote words so that Americans could sing it. "America," or "My Country, 'Tis of Thee," quickly became a favorite of many people in the United States. It remains a favorite today.

"America" ("My Country, 'Tis of Thee")

by Samuel F. Smith

My country, 'tis of thee,
Sweet land of liberty,
   Of thee I sing;
Land where my fathers died,
Land of the Pilgrims' pride,
From every mountain-side
   Let freedom ring.

My native country, thee,
Land of the noble free,
   Thy name I love;
I love thy rocks and rills,
Thy woods and templed hills;
My heart with rapture thrills
   Like that above.

In 1893, a teacher from the east named Katharine Lee Bates took a trip west. She loved the beauty of the United States, its mountains, plains, and open skies. Bates's poem became the words for the song, "America the Beautiful."

"America the Beautiful"

by Katharine Lee Bates

Oh beautiful for spacious skies,
  For amber waves of grain
For purple mountain majesties
  Above the fruited plain.
America! America!
  God shed His grace on thee
And crown thy good with brotherhood
  From sea to shining sea.

O beautiful for patriot dream
  That sees beyond the years
Thine alabaster cities gleam
  Undimmed by human tears.
America! America!
  God shed His grace on thee
And crown thy good with brotherhood
  From sea to shining sea.

Biographical Dictionary

The page number after each entry refers to the place where the person is first mentioned. For more complete references to people, see the Index.

A

Arundel, Anne 1615–1649, wife of Cecil Calvert; the town of Anne Arundel, which later became Annapolis, was named for her (p. 32).

B

Banneker, Benjamin 1731–1806, astronomer, mathemetician (p. 61).

Barton, Clara 1821–1912, reformer; nurse in Civil War (p. 100)

Brent, Margaret 1601–1671, managed money for Maryland Colony after death of Lord Baltimore; first woman in North America to ask for the right to vote (p. 35).

C

Calvert, Benedict Leonard 1679–1715, 4th Lord Baltimore; requested that the Maryland Colony be restored to Calvert proprietorship (p. 36).

Calvert, Cecil 1605–1675, 2nd Lord Baltimore; planned the Maryland Colony in North America (p. 25).

Calvert, George 1580–1632, 1st Lord Baltimore; requested land that was used to establish the Maryland Colony (p. 25).

Calvert, Leonard 1606–1647, brother of Cecil Calvert; established and acted as governor of the Maryland Colony beginning in 1633 (p. 26).

Carroll, Charles 1737–1832, Revolutionary leader; signer of the Declaration of Independence (p. 51).

Charles I 1600–1649, king of England, 1625–1649; granted charter for Maryland Colony (p. 25).

Chase, Samuel 1741–1811, lawyer; patriot; signer of the Declaration of Independence (p. 51).

Clarke, Martha 1944–, ballet dancer and choreographer (p. 179).

Columbus, Christopher 1451–1506, explorer; reached the Americas (p. 24).

Cummings, Elijah E. 1951–, Member of U.S. Congress from Maryland (p. 139).

D

Da Verrazano, Giovanni 1485–1528, Italian explorer who led a French ship along the Atlantic Coast of North America in about 1524 (p. 24).

De Sousa, Matthias 17th c.–?, free African American entrepreneur and member of the General Assembly in the Maryland Colony (p. 31).

Douglass, Frederick 1818–1895, abolitionist and writer; escaped from slavery (p. 86)

Grant, Ulysses S. 1822–1885, general of the Union forces during the Civil War; leader of the Union army at the war's end; 18th president (p. 101).

J

Jefferson, Thomas 1743–1826, wrote Declaration of Independence; 3rd President of the United States, 1801–1809 (p. 55).

Johnson, Thomas 1732–1819, Revolutionary leader; first governor of the state of Maryland, (p. 58).

Key, Francis Scott 1779–1843, lawyer; witnessed the Battle of Baltimore during the War of 1812; wrote a poem that was later set to music and became the U.S. national anthem (p. 72).

King, Martin Luther, Jr. 1929–1968, civil rights leader (p. 123).

Lee, Robert E. 1807–1870, Confederate general in the Civil War (p. 100).

Lincoln, Abraham 1809–1865, 16th President of the United States; issued Emancipation Proclamation (p. 94).

M

Madison, Dolley 1768–1849, wife of President James Madison; first lady during War of 1812; saved important documents in the White House during the burning of the city of Washington, D.C. (p. 71).

Madison, James 1751–1836, 4th President of the United States; led the United States during the War of 1812 (p. 69).

Marshall, Thurgood 1908–1993, civil rights lawyer and Supreme Court justice (p. 123).

McClellan, General George 1826–1885, Union general during the Civil War (p. 100).

Mencken, H.L. 1880–1956, journalist for the *Baltimore Sun* (p. 179).

Myers, Isaac 1835–1891, established a company in Baltimore to provide jobs for African Americans (p. 105).

Paca, William 1740–1799, patriot; signer of the Declaration of Independence (p. 51).

Perry, Oliver Hazard 1785–1819, captain in the United States Navy; defeated the British at the Battle of Lake Erie during the War of 1812 (p. 69).

Pickersgill, Mary 1776–1857, Maryland businessperson; sewed the flag that flew above Fort McHenry during the Battle of Baltimore (p. 72).

Roosevelt, Franklin D. 1882–1945, 32nd President of the United States, 1933–1945 (p. 117).

Seton, Elizabeth 1774–1821, educator and founder of the first free Roman Catholic school for girls in the United States (p. 60).

Smith, Samuel 1752–1839, United States senator from Maryland; led the defense of Baltimore during the War of 1812 (p. 72).

Stone, Thomas 1743–1787, signer of the Declaration of Independence (p. 55).

Tecumseh 1768?–1813 Shawnee leader; allied with British during the War of 1812 (p. 69).

Tubman, Harriet 1820?–1913, helped enslaved African Americans reach freedom in the North (p. 93).

Washington, George 1732–1799, commanded Continental armies during Revolution; 1st President of the United States, 1789–1797 (p. 55).

White, Father Andrew 1579–1656, Jesuit priest who traveled with Leonard Calvert to the Chesapeake Bay; wrote *A Relation of Maryland,* in which he described the experiences of the early colonists. (p. 30).

Geographic Terms

basin
a round area of land surrounded by higher land

bay
part of a lake or ocean that is partially enclosed by land

canyon
a valley with steep cliffs shaped by erosion

cape
a piece of land that points out into a body of water

coast
the land next to a sea or ocean

coastal plain
a flat area of land near an ocean

delta
land that is formed by soil deposited near the mouth of a river

desert
a dry region with little vegetation

fault
a break or crack in the earth's surface

▲ **glacier**
a large ice mass that pushes soil and rocks as it moves

hill
a raised area of land

island
an area of land surrounded by water

isthmus
a narrow piece of land connecting two larger land areas

lake
a large body of water surrounded by land

mountain
a raised mass of land with steep slopes

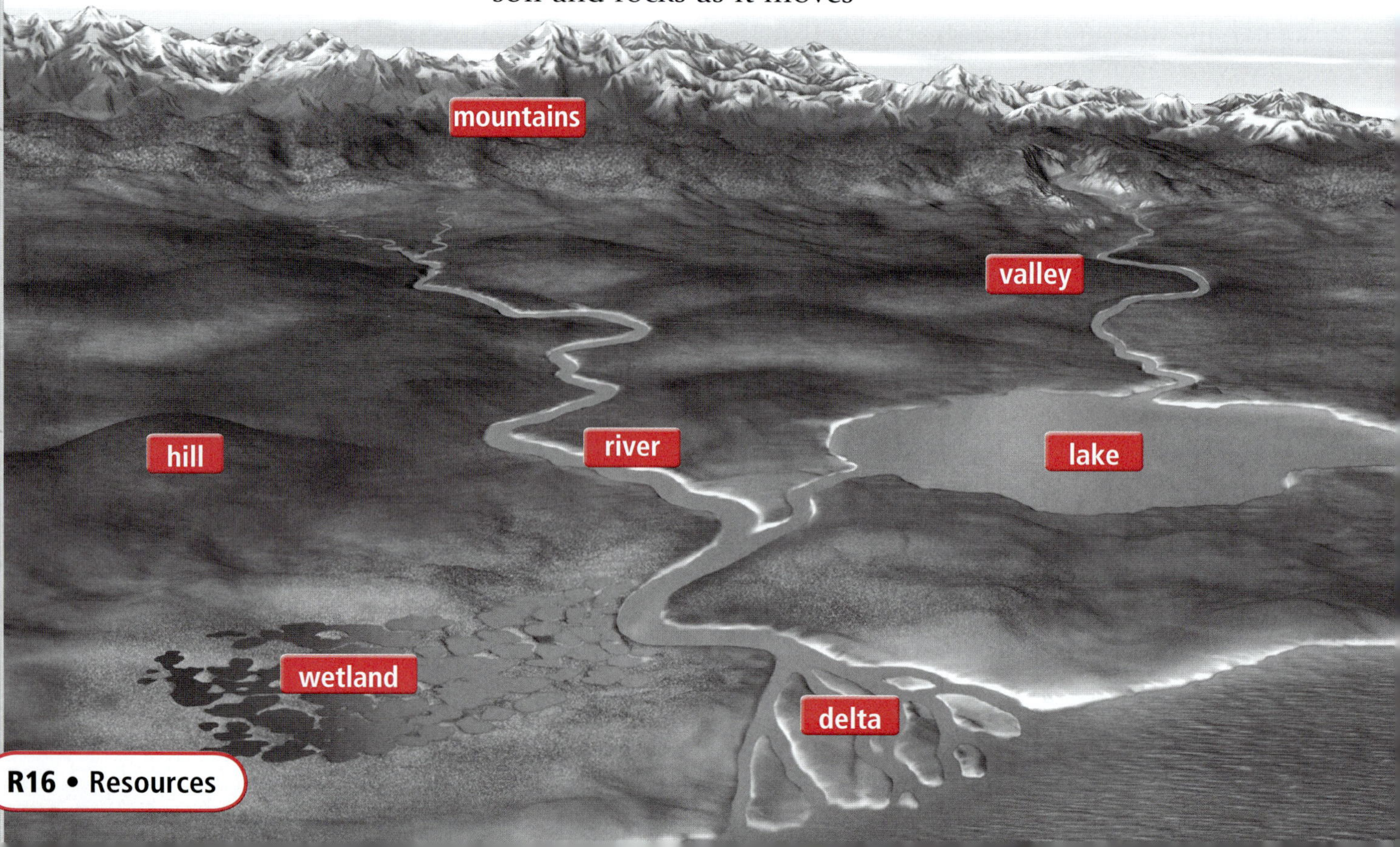

ocean
a large body of salt water that covers much of Earth's surface

peninsula
a strip of land surrounded by water on three sides

plain
a large area of flat land

plateau
a high, flat area of land

port
a sheltered part of a lake or ocean where ships can dock

prairie
a flat area of grassland with few trees

rain forest
a thick forest that receives heavy rainfall throughout the year

river
a body of water that flows from a high area to a lower area

river basin
an area that is drained by a river

tectonic plate
a huge slab of rock in Earth's crust that can cause earthquakes and volcanoes when it moves

tributary
a river or stream that flows into another river

valley
a low area of land between hills or mountains

volcano
an opening in Earth's surface through which melted rock and gases escape

wetland
an area that is soaked with water, such as a marsh or a swamp

Atlas

The World: Political

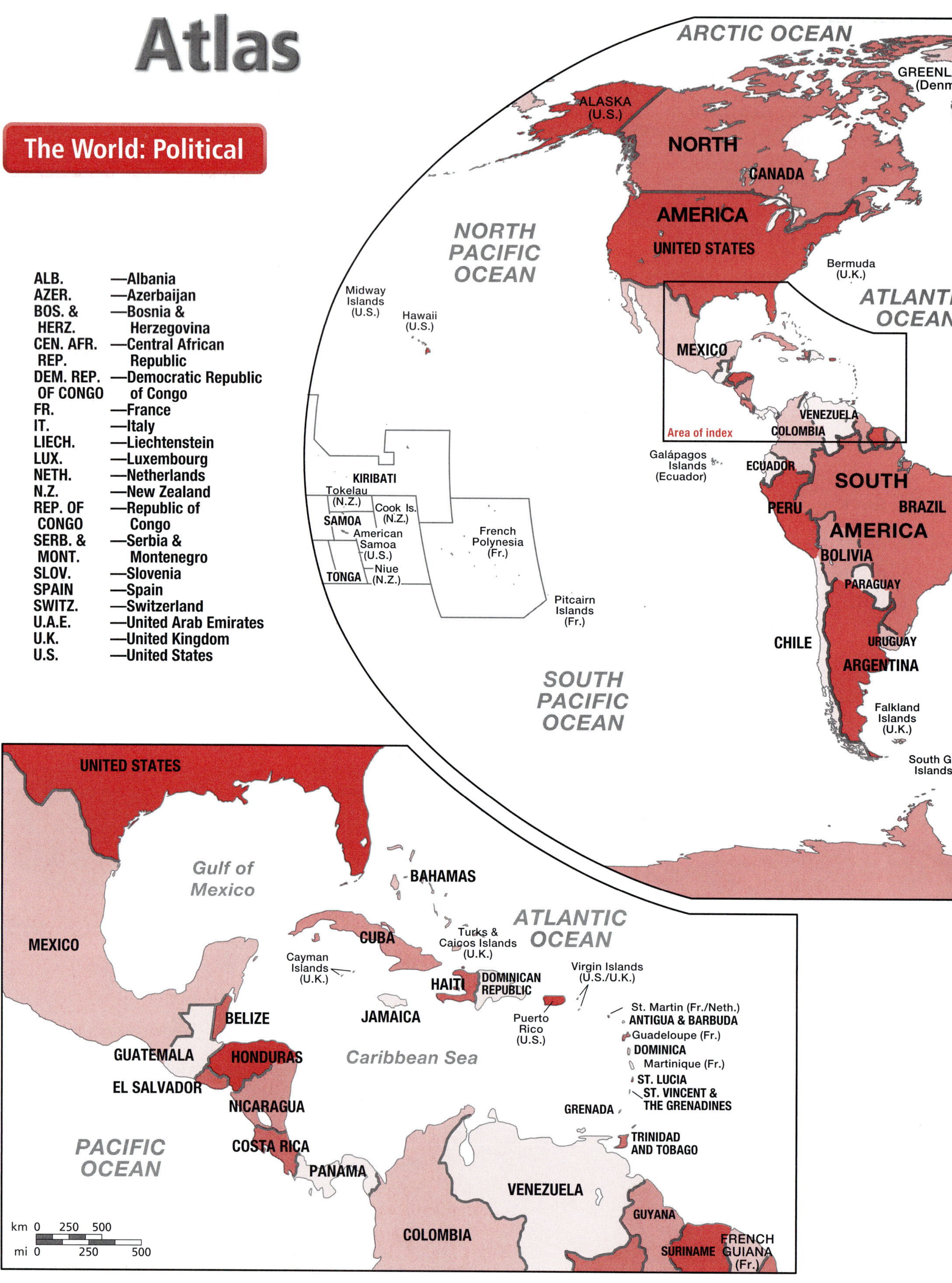

ARCTIC OCEAN
ICELAND
RUSSIA
ASIA
EUROPE
KAZAKHSTAN
MONGOLIA
GEORGIA
ARMENIA
TURKEY
AZER.
UZBEKISTAN
KYRGYZSTAN
TURKMENISTAN
TAJIKISTAN
CHINA
N. KOREA
S. KOREA
JAPAN
PACIFIC OCEAN
Area of index
TUNISIA
CYPRUS
SYRIA
LEBANON
IRAQ
ISRAEL
JORDAN
IRAN
AFGHANISTAN
KUWAIT
PAKISTAN
NEPAL
BHUTAN
BANGLADESH
MOROCCO
ALGERIA
LIBYA
EGYPT
WESTERN SAHARA (Morocco)
QATAR
U. A. E.
SAUDI ARABIA
OMAN
INDIA
MYANMAR
LAOS
TAIWAN
AFRICA
MAURITANIA
MALI
NIGER
CHAD
SUDAN
ERITREA
YEMEN
THAILAND
VIETNAM
CAMBODIA
PHILIPPINES
Northern Mariana Islands (U.S.)
MARSHALL ISLANDS
Guam (U.S.)
FEDERATED STATES OF MICRONESIA
PALAU
KIRIBATI
SENEGAL
GAMBIA
GUINEA BISSAU
GUINEA
SIERRA LEONE
LIBERIA
BURKINA FASO
GHANA
IVORY COAST
TOGO
BENIN
NIGERIA
DJIBOUTI
CEN. AFR. REP.
ETHIOPIA
SOMALIA
SRI LANKA
BRUNEI
MALAYSIA
SINGAPORE
CAMEROON
EQU. GUINEA
SAO TOME AND PRINCIPE
GABON
REP. OF CONGO
DEM. REP. OF CONGO
UGANDA
KENYA
RWANDA
BURUNDI
TANZANIA
MALDIVES
INDONESIA
EAST TIMOR
PAPUA NEW GUINEA
NAURU
SOLOMON ISLANDS
TUVALU
COMOROS
SEYCHELLES
ANGOLA
MALAWI
ZAMBIA
MOZAMBIQUE
ZIMBABWE
BOTSWANA
NAMIBIA
MADAGASCAR
MAURITIUS
Reunion (Fr.)
INDIAN OCEAN
VANUATU
FIJI
New Caledonia (Fr.)
AUSTRALIA
SWAZILAND
LESOTHO
SOUTH AFRICA
km 0 1000 2000
mi 0 1000 2000
NEW ZEALAND
ATLANTIC OCEAN
ANTARCTICA
FINLAND
SWEDEN
NORWAY
RUSSIA
ESTONIA
km 0 150 300
mi 0 150 300
North Sea
LATVIA
LITHUANIA
DENMARK
RUSSIA
UNITED KINGDOM
IRELAND
NETH.
BELARUS
POLAND
GERMANY
BELGIUM
LUX.
CZECH REPUBLIC
UKRAINE
FRANCE
LIECH.
AUSTRIA
SLOVAKIA
HUNGARY
MOLDOVA
ATLANTIC OCEAN
SWITZ.
SLOV.
CROATIA
ROMANIA
SAN MARINO
BOS. & HERZ.
SERB. & MONT.
MONACO
Corsica (Fr.)
BULGARIA
ANDORRA
MACEDONIA
ALB.
ITALY
PORTUGAL
Sardinia (It.)
VATICAN CITY
GREECE
SPAIN
Balearic Islands (Sp.)
TURKEY
Sicily (It.)
GIBRALTAR (U.K.)
Mediterranean Sea
MOROCCO
ALGERIA
TUNISIA

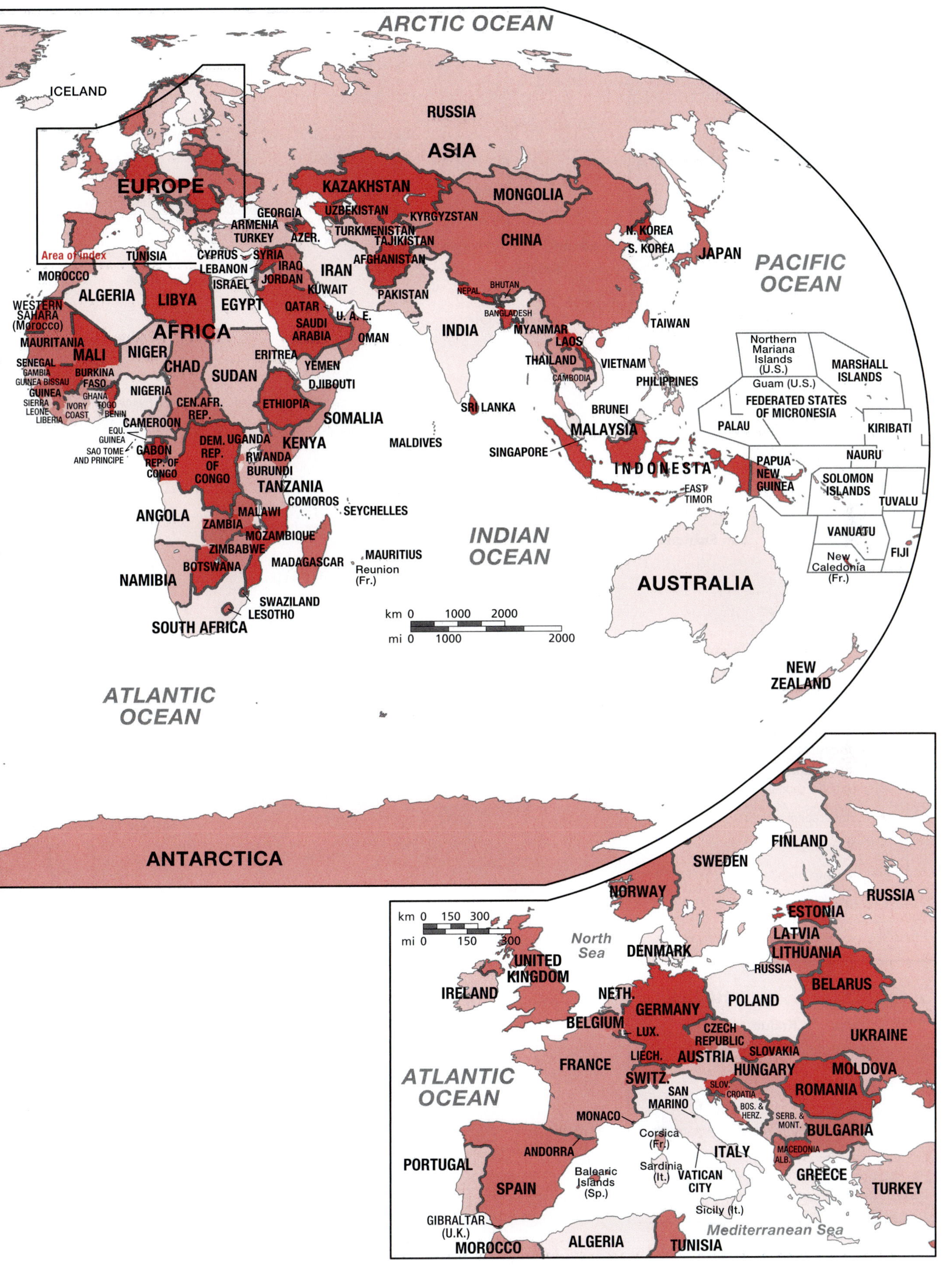

Atlas

United States: Political

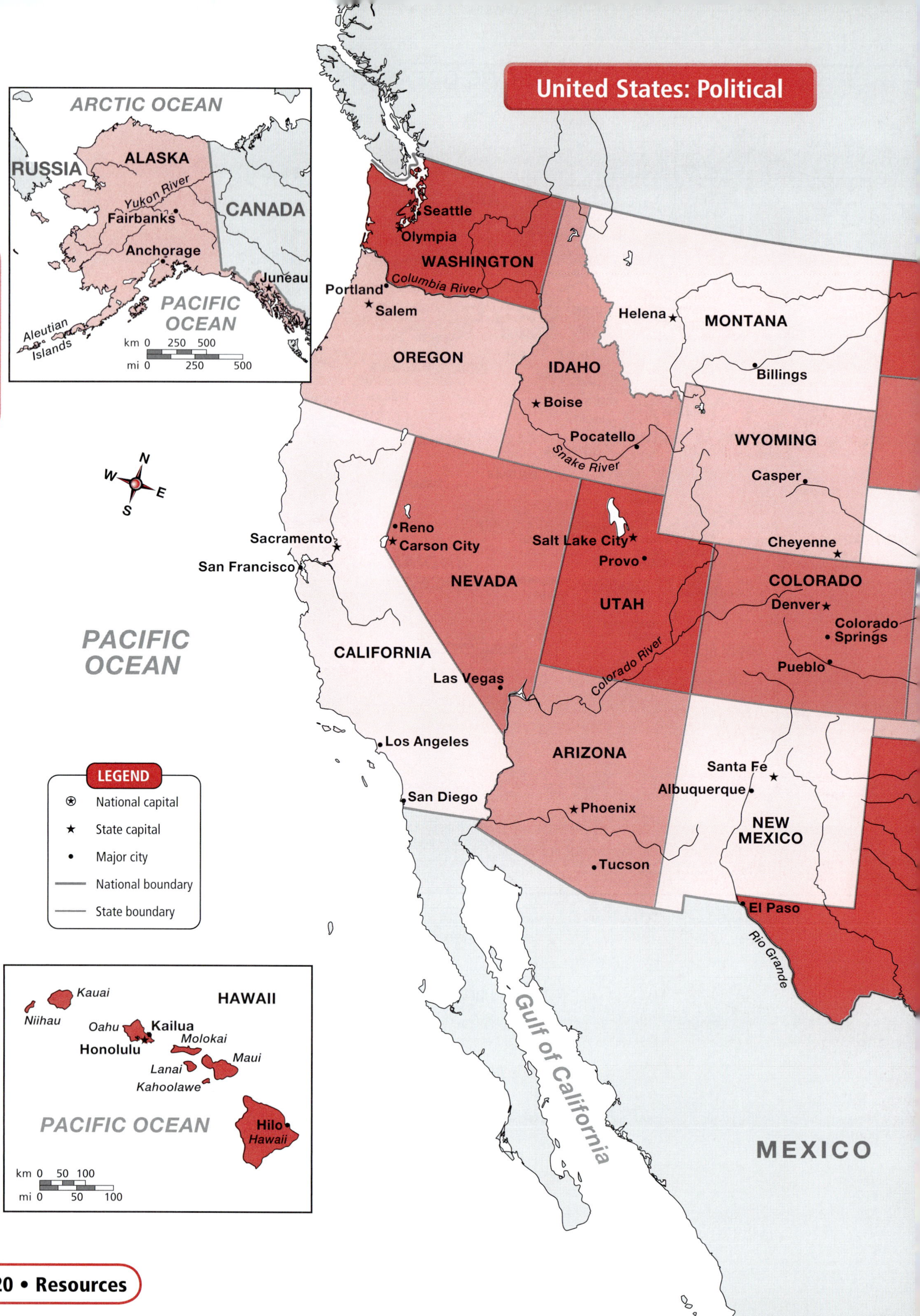

ARCTIC OCEAN
RUSSIA
ALASKA
Yukon River
Fairbanks
CANADA
Anchorage
Juneau
PACIFIC OCEAN
Aleutian Islands
km 0 250 500
mi 0 250 500

Seattle
Olympia
WASHINGTON
Columbia River
Portland
Salem
OREGON
Helena
MONTANA
Billings
IDAHO
Boise
Pocatello
Snake River
WYOMING
Casper
Cheyenne
N
W
E
S
Sacramento
San Francisco
Reno
Carson City
Salt Lake City
Provo
NEVADA
UTAH
COLORADO
Denver
Colorado Springs
Pueblo
PACIFIC OCEAN
CALIFORNIA
Las Vegas
Colorado River
Los Angeles
ARIZONA
San Diego
Phoenix
Tucson
Santa Fe
Albuquerque
NEW MEXICO
El Paso
Rio Grande
Gulf of California
MEXICO

LEGEND

- ⊛ National capital
- ★ State capital
- • Major city
- National boundary
- State boundary

Kauai
Niihau
HAWAII
Oahu
Kailua
Honolulu
Molokai
Maui
Lanai
Kahoolawe
PACIFIC OCEAN
Hilo
Hawaii
km 0 50 100
mi 0 50 100

CANADA

St. Lawrence River

NEW HAMPSHIRE
VERMONT
MAINE
Augusta
Montpelier
Burlington
Portland
Concord
Manchester
Boston
MASSACHUSETTS
Providence
RHODE ISLAND
CONNECTICUT
Hartford
New Haven
NEW YORK
Albany
Rochester
Buffalo
New York
Newark
Trenton
Philadelphia
NEW JERSEY
Dover
DELAWARE
Annapolis
Washington, D.C.
MARYLAND
Baltimore
Harrisburg
Pittsburgh
PENNSYLVANIA
L. Ontario
Lake Erie
Lake Huron
Lake Michigan
Lake Superior

NORTH DAKOTA
Bismarck
Fargo
MINNESOTA
St. Paul
Minneapolis
SOUTH DAKOTA
Pierre
Sioux Falls
WISCONSIN
Madison
Milwaukee
MICHIGAN
Grand Rapids
Lansing
Detroit
Cleveland
OHIO
Columbus
Cincinnati
IOWA
Cedar Rapids
Des Moines
Missouri River
NEBRASKA
Omaha
Lincoln
Chicago
ILLINOIS
Springfield
INDIANA
Indianapolis
WEST VIRGINIA
Charleston
VIRGINIA
Richmond
Norfolk
Kansas City
Topeka
Kansas City
Jefferson City
St. Louis
Louisville
Ohio River
Frankfort
KANSAS
MISSOURI
KENTUCKY
Greensboro
Raleigh
NORTH CAROLINA
Tulsa
Oklahoma City
OKLAHOMA
Fort Smith
ARKANSAS
Little Rock
Mississippi River
Memphis
Nashville
TENNESSEE
Columbia
SOUTH CAROLINA
Charleston
MISSISSIPPI
Birmingham
Atlanta
GEORGIA
Savannah
Dallas
TEXAS
LOUISIANA
Jackson
Montgomery
ALABAMA
ATLANTIC OCEAN
Jacksonville
Mobile
Tallahassee
Austin
Houston
Baton Rouge
New Orleans
San Antonio
Tampa
FLORIDA
Miami
Gulf of Mexico
BAHAMAS
CUBA

km 0 100 200 300 400 500
mi 0 100 200 300 400 500

Atlas

Western Hemisphere: Political

Gazetteer

Africa 2nd largest continent (10°N, 22°E) p. 31

Annapolis Capital of Maryland; located on the Western Shore of the Chesapeake Bay (39°N, 76°W) p. 8

Anne Arundel City that later became Annapolis (39°N, 76°W) p. 32

Appalachian Highlands Region in western Maryland characterized by the Appalachian Mountains (39°N, 78°W) p. 6

Appalachian Mountains Range stretching from Canada to Alabama (37°N, 82°W) p. 8

Appomattox Court House Small town in eastern Virginia; site of Lee's surrender to Grant, ending the Civil War (37°N, 78°W) p. 101

Atlantic Coastal Plain Geographic region in Maryland east of the Fall Line, surrounding the Chesapeake Bay, and along the Atlantic Ocean (35°N, 79°W) p. 7

Atlantic Ocean Extends from the Arctic to the Antarctic; east of the United States (5°S, 25°W) p. 4

B

Backbone Mountain Mountain in western Maryland part of the Allegheny Mountains; highest point in Maryland at 3,360 feet (39°N, 79°W) p. 8

Baltimore Largest city in Maryland; located in north central Maryland along the Chesapeake Bay (39°N, 76°W) p. 8

Belgium Country in western Europe; capital: Brussels (51°N, 3°E) p. 73

Bethesda City in west-central Maryland; home of the Naval Medical Center (39°N, 77°W) p. 118

Bladensburg Town in central Maryland; site of a battle during the War of 1812 (39°N, 77°W) p. 70

Blue Ridge Mountains Area of Appalachian Mountain range that runs though several states, including Maryland (39°N, 77°W) p. 6

Boston Capital of Massachusetts (42°N, 71°W) p. 50

Britain Island country in western Europe made up of England, Wales, Scotland and Ireland; capital: London (51°N, 0°W) p. 48

Canada Country bordering United States on north (50°N, 100°W) p. 68

Cape Cod Area in southeast Massachusetts that extends into the Atlantic Ocean (42°N, 70°W) p. 191

Caribbean Islands Series of islands located throughout the Caribbean Sea in the Western Hemisphere (15°N, 76°W) p. 31

Chesapeake Bay Inlet of the Atlantic Ocean between Virginia and Maryland (38°N, 76°W) p. 4

Chester River River in Maryland (39°N, 76°W) p. 50

Chestertown Town on the Chester River on the Eastern Shore of Maryland; site of the Chestertown Tea Party in 1774 (39°N, 76°W) p. 50

Columbus Capital city of Ohio (40°N, 83°W) p. 77

Concord Site in Massachusetts of first battle in Revolutionary War (42°N, 71°W) p. 55

Cumberland City in western Maryland; located on the routes of the National Road, Chesapeake and Ohio Canal, and Baltimore and Ohio Railroad (40°N, 39°W) p. 8

Delaware 1st state; capital: Dover (39°N, 76°W) p. 8

Detroit City in southwestern Michigan (42°N, 83°W) p. 49

Eastern Shore Eastern area of Maryland that borders the eastern shore of the Chesapeake Bay (39°N, 76°W) p. 4

Emmitsburg Town in western Maryland (39°N, 77°W) p. 60

Gazetteer

England Country in Western Europe; part of Britain (52°N, 2°W) p. 24

Europe 6th largest continent (50°N, 15°E) p. 24

Fort Frederick British fort located near present-day Hagerstown (39°N, 78°W) p. 48

Fort McHenry American fort located in Baltimore Harbor; site of a battle during the War of 1812 (39°N, 76°W) p. 72

Fort Sumter Fort in South Carolina attacked by Confederate soldiers at the start of the Civil War (32°N, 80°W) p. 98

France Country in Western Europe (47°N, 1°E) p. 24

Frederick City in western Maryland (39°N, 77°W) p. 78

Georgetown Town in central Maryland (39°N, 76°W) p. 78

Germany Country in Western Europe (51°N, 10°E) p. 114

Ghent City in Belgium; site of treaty ending the War of 1812 (51°N, 30°E) p. 73

Great Lakes Five freshwater lakes between the United States and Canada (45°N, 83°W) p. 69

Greenbelt Town in central Maryland; one of the planned communities built during the Great Depression (39°N, 77°W) p. 117

Hagerstown City in northwestern Maryland (39°N, 78°W) p. 8

Havre de Grace City in northeastern Maryland (39°N, 76°W) p. 70

Hawaii 50th state; capital: Honolulu (20°N, 158°W) p. 118

Holland Country in western Europe, also called the Netherlands; capital: Amsterdam (52°N, 6°E) p. 24

Ireland Island nation in the North Atlantic Ocean; capital: Dublin (53°N, 6°W) p. 114

Italy County in southern Europe; capital: Rome (44°N, 11°E) p. 24

Jamestown First permanent English settlement in North America; located in present-day Virginia (37°N, 76°W) p. 24

Japan Island nation off east coast of Asia; capital: Tokyo (37°N, 134°E) p. 118

Kent Island Island in Chesapeake Bay off the coast of east-central Maryand (39°N, 76°W) p. 26

Kentucky 15th state; capital: Frankfort (38°N, 88°W) p. 94

Lexington Site in Massachusetts of first battle in Revolutionary War (42°N, 71°W) p. 55

Maryland 7th state; capital: Annapolis (39°N, 76°W) p. 8

Massachusetts 6th state; capital: Boston (42°N, 73°W) p. 55

Montgomery County County in west central Maryland (39°N, 77°W) p. 6

New Jersey 3rd state; capital: Trenton (41°N, 75°W) p. 8

New Orleans City in southern Louisiana; site of a battle during the War of 1812 (30°N, 90°W) p. 73

New York 11th state; capital: Albany (43°N, 78°W) p. 56

New York City City in New York state; largest city in the United States (41°N, 74°W) p. 203

North America Northern continent of Western Hemisphere (45°N, 100°W) p. 10

North Pole Northernmost point on Earth (90°N) p. 18

Ocean City City in eastern Maryland along the Atlantic Ocean (38°N, 75°W) p. 7

Ohio 17th state; capital: Columbus (41°N, 83°W) p. 77

Ohio River Valley Region west of the Appalachian Mountains (37°N, 88°W) p. 48

Patuxent River River that runs through southern Maryland into the Chesapeake Bay (38°N, 76°W) p. 8

Pearl Harbor United States naval base; attacked by Japan (21°N, 158°W) p. 118

Pennsylvania 2nd state; capital: Harrisburg (41°N, 78°W) p. 8

Philadelphia Large port city in Pennsylvania (40°N, 75°W) p. 56

Piedmont Plateau Geographic region of Maryland that lies in the central part of the state (39°N, 77°W) p. 6

Plymouth Town in Massachusetts, site of first Pilgrim settlement (42°N, 71°W) p. 25

Poland Country in eastern Europe; capital: Warsaw (52°N, 21°E) p. 114

Potomac River River that forms the border between Virginia and Maryland; flows into the Chesapeake Bay (38°N 76°W) p. 4

Prince George's County County in central Maryland (39°N, 77°W) p. 150

Princess Anne Town in eastern Maryland (38°N, 75°W) p. 19

Russia Country in eastern Europe; capital: Moscow (61°N, 60°E) p. 114

St. Clement's Island Located off southern Maryland in the Potomac River; site of first settlement of Maryland Colony (38°N, 76°W) p. 26

St. Lawrence River Links Great Lakes to the Atlantic Ocean (49°N, 67°W) p. 25

St. Mary's City Located in southern Maryland; first settlement in and first capital of Maryland (38°N, 76°W) p. 26

Sandy Point Cape in central Maryland located on the Western Shore of Chesapeake Bay; location of one end of the Chesapeake Bay Bridge (39°N, 76°W) p. 124

Sharpsburg Town in western Maryland; site of the Battle of Antietam during the Civil War (39°N, 77°W) p. 100

South America Southern continent of the Western Hemisphere (10°S, 60°W) p. 24

South Carolina 8th state; capital: Columbia (34°N, 81°W) p. 56

Spain Country in Western Europe; capital: Madrid (40°N, 5°W) p. 24

Susquehanna River River that runs through eastern Pennsylvania and northern Maryland into the Chesapeake Bay (39°N, 76°W) p. 8

Talbot County County on the Eastern Shore of Maryland (38°N, 76°W) p. 93

United States Country that lies mostly in central North America; capital: Washington, D.C. (38°N, 110°W) p. 57

Upper Marlboro County seat of Prince George's County (38°N, 76°W) p. 150

Virginia 10th state; capital: Richmond (37°N, 81°W) p. 4

Gazetteer

Washington, D.C. Capital of the United States (39°N, 77°W) p. 8

Western Shore Area of Maryland that is on the western shore of the Chesapeake Bay (38°N, 76°W) p. 4

West Virginia 35th state; capital: Charleston (38°N, 81°W) p. 4

Wheeling City in northern West Virginia (40°N, 80°W) p. 77

Yorktown Town in Virginia; site of last major battle of Revolutionary War (37°N, 77°W) p. 57

Gazetteer

Glossary

A

abolitionist (ab uh LIH shuhn ihst) a person who worked to end slavery. (p. 93)

allies (AL eyez) a person or group that joins with another person or group to work toward a goal. (p. 48)

anthem (AN thihm) a song of praise or loyalty. (p. 72)

artifact (AHR tih fakt) an object made by humans. (p. 11)

atlas (AT luhs) a book that contains many different kinds of maps. (p. 53)

axis (AKS ihs) a vertical or horizontal line on a graph that shows the units of measurement. (p. 120)

B

barter (BAHR tur) to exchange goods without using money. (p. 13)

beltway (BEHLT whey) a major road that travels around a city rather than through it. (p. 125)

blockade (blah KAYD) the use of ships or troops to keep people and goods from entering or leaving an area. (p. 70)

border state (BOHR dur stayt) a state that allowed slavery but chose not to secede from the Union during the Civil War. (p. 99)

boycott (BOY kaht) type of protest in which people refuse to buy, sell, or use certain goods. (p. 50)

canal (kuh NAL) a waterway made by people for traveling and shipping. (p. 78)

candidate (KAN dih dayt) a person trying to win an elected position. (p. 154)

cape (kayp) a point of land that extends into the water. (p. 191)

capital resource (KAP ih tuhl REE sawrs) a tool, machine, or building that people use to produce goods and services. (p. 169)

capitol (KAP ih tuhl) the building in which lawmakers or legislators in a state or nation meet (p. 204)

casualty (KAZH oo uhl tee) a soldier who is killed or wounded. (p. 100)

cause (kawz) an event that makes another event happen. (p. 38)

charter (CHAHR tur) a plan for a business or an organization. (p. 25)

citizen (SIHT ih zuhn) someone who is born in a country or who promises to be loyal to that country. (p. 136)

civil rights (SIHV uhl ryts) the rights that the government guarantees its citizens. (p. 122)

civil war (SIHV uhl wawr) a war between two groups or regions within a nation. (p. 98)

climate (KLY miht) the weather over time. (p. 4)

colony (KAHL uh nee) a settlement ruled by another country. (p. 24)

common good (KAHM uhn guhd) the good of the whole population. (p. 136)

compass rose (KUHM puhs rohz) a part of a map that shows the cardinal and intermediate directions. (p. 9)

compromise (KAHM pruh myz) a plan that everyone agrees on. (p. 126)

conflict (KAHN flihkt) a disagreement. (p. 126)

constitution (kahn stih TOO shuhn) a written plan for government. (p. 58)

consumer (kuhn SOOM uhr) a person or company that uses goods or services. (p. 163)

county (KOWN tee) a unit of local government. (p. 148)

culture (KUHL chur) a way of life shared by a group of people. (p. 14)

custom (KUHS tuhm) a way of doing something that is shared by a group. (p. 14)

data (DA tuh) facts or numbers. (p. 120)

delegate (DEHL ih giht) someone chosen to speak and act for others. (p. 144)

demand (dih MAND) the desire for something and the willingness to buy it for a certain price. (p. 165)

democracy (dih MAHK ruh see) a form of government in which people hold the power of government. (p. 137)

depression (dih PREHSH uhn) a period when businesses fail, prices drop, and jobs are hard to find. (p. 117)

diplomacy (dih PLO mah see) the management of international relations. (p. 118)

dredge (dredj) to drag large baskets along the bottom of a body of water to collect oysters. (p. 113)

due process (doo PRAHS ehs) the protected legal rights of anyone who goes to court. (p. 141)

economy (ih KAHN uh mee) the way people run businesses and make money in an area. (p. 30)

effect (ih FEHKT) the event or action that is the result of a cause. (p. 38)

election (ih LEHK shuhn) the way voters choose people to serve in government. (p. 137)

elevation (ehl uh VAY shuhn) height above sea level. (p. 5)

encyclopedia (ehn sy kluh PEE dee uh) a set of books that have information about people, places, and events. (p. 53)

fact (fakt) information that can be proved true. (p. 106)

factors of production (FAK tuhrs uhv pruh DUHK shuhn) the people and materials needed to make goods or provide services. (p. 198)

Freedmen's Bureau (FREED muhnz byor oh) an organization that provided food, clothing, and advice to poor African Americans after the Civil War. (p. 103)

frontier (fruhn TEER) the edge of a country or settled region. (p. 76)

glacier (GLAY shur) a huge, slowly moving sheet of ice. (p. 191)

heritage (HEHR ih tihj) the traditions that people have honored for many years. (p. 210)

human resource (HYOO muhn REE sawrs) a worker and the skills and knowledge that the worker brings to a job. (p. 169)

immigrant (IHM ih gruhnt) a person who moves to a new country. (p. 114)

indentured servant (ihn DEHN churd SUHR vuhnt) persons who agree to work for a certain time period without pay in order to pay off a debt. (p. 31)

index (IHN dehks) an alphabetical listing of the topics in a book. (p. 53)

integration (ihn tuh GRAY shun) bringing together people of different races. (p. 123)

independence (ihn dih PEHN duhns) freedom from being ruled by someone else. (p. 55)

interdependence (ihn tur dih PEHN duhns) a relationship in which people depend on one another. (p. 209)

jury (JUR ee) a group of citizens who decide a case in court. (p. 141)

L

landform (LAND fohrm) a feature of the Earth's surface. (p. 4)

legend (LEHJ uhnd) a part of a map that explains what the colors, symbols, and lines on the map represent. (p. 9)

legislature (LEHJ ih slay chuhr) a group of people who make laws. (p. 61)

line graph (LYN grahf) a chart showing changes in data over time. (p. 120)

lines of latitude (LAT ih tood) imaginary lines that run east and west on a map. (p. 18)

lines of longitude (LAHN jih tood) imaginary lines that run north and south on a map. (p. 18)

longhouse (LAWNG hows) a large, rectangular house with a frame of wood poles covered with sheets of bark used by most Eastern Woodland Indians. (p. 16)

Loyalist (LOY uh lihst) a colonist who stayed loyal to the British king. (p. 54)

M

manufacturing (man yuh FAK chuhr ihng) using machinery to make goods. (p. 169)

map scale (map skayl) a part of a map that compares distance on the map to distance in the real world. (p. 9)

mass transit (mas TRANS iht) a system, such as a railroad or subway that provides transportation for many people at once. (p. 203)

metropolitan area (meh truh PAHL ih tuhn AIR ree uh) a region that includes at least one city and the surrounding suburbs. (p. 175)

multicultural (muhl tee KUHL chuhr uhl) representing or having many cultures. (p. 176)

municipality (myoo nihs uh PAL ih tee) a city or town that has its own government. (p. 148)

N

natural resource (NACH ur uhl REE sawrs) something found in nature that is useful to people. (p. 12)

O

opinion (uh PIHN yuhn) a belief or a feeling. (p. 106)

P

Parliament (PAHR luh mehnt) group that makes most of the laws in England. (p. 34)

Patriot (PAY tree uht) a colonist who opposed British rule and wanted the colonies to be free from British rule. (p. 54)

plantation (plan TAY shuhn) a large farm on which crops are grown by workers who live there. (p. 31)

point of view (poynt uhv VYOO) the way that someone looks at a situation, an event, or a person. (p. 96)

port (pohrt) a place where ships and boats can dock, load, and unload products. (p. 36)

prehistoric (pree hih STOR ihk) people and things that existed before writing was invented. (p. 11)

primary source (PRY mehr ee sawrs) a firsthand account of an event. (p. 28)

privateer (PRY vuh teer) a privately owned ship that attacked British ships during the Revolutionary War. (p. 56)

producer (pruh DOOS ur) a person or company that supplies goods for other people or companies. (p. 163)

profit (PRAHF iht) the money left over after a business pays its expenses. (p. 196)

proprietor (pruh PRY ih tuhr) a person who owns and controls the land of a colony. (p. 25)

prosperity (prah SPEHR ih tee) wealth and success. (p. 210)

ratify (RAT uh fy) to accept. (p. 59)

rebellion (rih BEHL yuhn) an attempt to overthrow a government or change it by force. (p. 35)

Reconstruction (ree kuhn STRUHK shuhn) the period during which the South rejoined the Union after the Civil War. (p. 102)

reform (rih FAWRM) a change that makes something better. (p. 114)

region (REE juhn) an area that has one or more features in common. (p. 6)

report (ri PAWRT) a piece of writing that provides information about a topic. (p. 146)

representative (rehp rih ZEHNT uh tihv) a person who speaks for other people in government. (p. 59)

responsibility (rih spahn suh BIHL ih tee) a duty that a person is expected to perform. (p. 154)

rights (ryts) freedoms protected by the government. (p. 55)

route (root) a way of going from one place to another. (p. 80)

rule of law (ROOL uhv lawh) the idea that laws should apply to everyone in the same way. (p. 138)

scarcity (SKAIR sih tee) a situation in which resources are hard to find. (p. 164)

search engine (SURCH ehn jihn) a website that finds other websites related to key words. (p. 53)

secede (sih SEED) to leave or break off from a country. (p. 94)

secondary source (SEHK uhn dehr ee sawrs) information written by someone who was not present at an event. (p. 28)

segregation (sehg rih GAY shuhn) the separation of people on the basis of their race. (p. 104)

slavery (SLAY vuh ree) a system in which people can be bought and sold and made to work without pay. (p. 31)

skyscraper (SKY skray pur) a very tall building. (p. 203)

suburb (SUHB urb) a community outside a city. (p. 119)

summary (SUHM uh ree) a short way of telling what something is about. (p. 74)

supply (suh PLY) the amount of a product or service that is available for trade or sale (p. 165)

surrender (suh REHN dur) to give up. (p. 72)

tax (taks) money that people or businesses pay to their government in return for services. (p. 49)

technology (tehk NAHL uh jee) the use of scientific knowledge and tools to do things better and more rapidly. (p. 168)

temperate (TEHM pur iht) without extremes. (p. 192)

tolerance (TAHL ur uhns) allowing people to do or to believe as they wish. (p. 25)

trade (trayd) the exchange of goods or products. (p. 13)

tradition (truh DIH shuhn) a way of doing things that has been passed down through the years. (p. 176)

turnpike (TURN pyk) a road on which a toll is collected from travelers. (p. 77)

unemployment (uhn ehm PLOY muhnt) the condition of being without a job. (p. 117)

Union (YOON yuhn) another name for the United States. (p. 95)

volunteer (vahl uhn TEER) someone who helps other people without being paid. (p. 154)

website (WEHB syt) a source of information that can be found by using a computer. (p. 53)

wetland (WET land) land that is covered by water part of the year, such as a swamp or marsh. (p. 5)

Index

Page numbers followed by m refer to maps. Page numbers in *italic* type refer to photographs, illustrations, or charts.

B

Index

Index

Acknowledgments

Acknowledgments

For each of the selections listed below, grateful acknowledgment is made for permission to excerpt and/or reprint original or copyrighted material, as follows:

Photography

title/cover Patti McConville/Image Finders. **ii** One Mile Up, Inc. **iii** (tl) Jan Butchofsky-Houser/CORBIS, (cl) Leszczynski, Zigmund/Animals Animals/Earth Scenes, (cr) Dale C. Spartas/CORBIS, (br) Richard Hamilton Smith/ CORBIS, (bl) Arthur Morris/CORBIS, (tr) Joseph Sohm; ChromoSohm Inc./CORBIS. **(kids)** (b) HMCo/Angela Coppola. **(globe)** (bkgd) Photdisc/Getty Images. **xii** (tl) Marylyn "Angel" Wynn/Nativestock, (b) Maryland Historical Society, Baltimore, Maryland. **xiii** (tl) CORBIS, (b) Photo by MPI/Getty Images. **xiv** (tl) From the Penn Center School Collection. Permission granted by Penn Center Inc., St. Helena Island, SC, (bl) Maryland Historical Society, Baltimore, Maryland. **xv** (tl) Tom Carter/PhotoEdit, (b) James L. Amos/CORBIS. **xvi** Tom Carter/PhotoEdit. **xvii** National Geographic Collection/Getty Images. **xix** Ray Boudreau. **0** (cr) Courtesy of the Maryland Commission on Artistic Property, of the Maryland State Archives. (br) One Mile Up, Inc. **1** (cr) Anne Arundel County Historical Society. (cl) Image courtesy of Historic St. Mary's City. (br) Image provided by www. EarlyAmerican.com. (bl) Cincinnati Medical Center, University of Cincinnati. **2** (cl) © Tyler Campbell/Mire. com. All Rights Reserved. (cr) Richard A. Cooke/CORBIS. **3** Bettmann/CORBIS. **4–5** © Tyler Campbell/Mira.com. All Rights reserved. **5** National Geographic Collection/Getty Images. **6** Peter Evans/Alamy. **7** Kevin Fleming/CORBIS. **9** Ray Boudreau. **10** Troop of Mammoths (oil on canvas), Burian, Zdenek (1905-81)/Musee de l'Histoire Naturelle, Archives Charmet;/Bridgeman Art Library. **11** (cl) Ohio Historical Society. (tc) Ohio Historical Society. (tr) Richard A. Cooke/CORBIS. **12** (bc) Bettmann/CORBIS. (t) Cameron Davidson/IPN/Aurora Photos. **13** Image Source Limited/ Index Stock Imagery. **14** North Wind Picture Archives. **15** Marilyn "Angel" Wynn/nativestock.com (208)788-0144. **17** John Harrington/National Museum of the American Indian, Smithsonian Institute. **18** Ray Boudreau. **22** (cl) Image Courtesy of Historic St. Mary's City. (cr) Georgetown University, Special Collections. **23** (cr) Maryland Historical Society, Baltimore, Maryland. (cl) Bettmann/CORBIS. **25** Mary Evans Picture Library. **26** Image Courtesy of Historic St. Mary's City. **27** Virginia Department of Historic Resources. **29** Ray Boudreau. **30** Aldo Tutino/Art Resource, NY. **31** Bettmann/CORBIS. **32** (bl) Paul A. Souders/CORBIS. (tr) Ann Arundel County Historical Society. **34** © North Wind/North Wind Picture Archives – All rights reserved. **35** National Geographic Society. **36** (cr) Enoch Pratt Free Library. (b) Maryland Historical Society, Baltimore, Maryland. **44** (cr) Bettmann/ CORBIS. (br) Courtesy of the Maryland State Archives. **45** (cl) National Portrait Gallery, Smithsonian Institution / Art Resource, NY. (bl) © SuperStock, Inc. /SuperStock. (br) Images.com/CORBIS. (cr) Stock Montage/Getty Images. **46** (cl) © North Wind/North Wind Picture Archives – All rights reserved. (cr) Courtesy of the Maryland Commission on the Artistic Property of the Maryland State Archives. **47** (cl) CORBIS. (cr) Courtesy of the Maryland State Archives, Maryland State Papers. **48** Cameron Davidson/ IPN/Aurora Photos. **50** (br) Courtesy of the Maryland Commission on the Artistic Property of the Maryland State Archives. **51** © North Wind/North Wind Picture Archives – All rights reserved. **52** Ray Boudreau. **54** Photo form the collection of the Lexington, Massachusetts Historical Society. **55** CORBIS. **56** The Maryland Historical Society, Baltimore, Maryland. **57** Three Lions/Getty Images. **58** Mary Evans Picture Library. **59** Bettmann/CORBIS. **60** (b) Photo courtesy of Enoch Pratt Free Library/State Library Resource Center, Baltimore, Maryland. (br) Courtesy of Pride, Inc., the non-profit organization that operates Pride of Baltimore II, a replica of an 1812 era topsail schooner. (cr) The Granger Collection, New York. **61** The Granger Collection, New York. **63** Ray Boudreau. **66** (cl) Peabody Essex Museum, Salem, Massachusetts/ Bridgeman Art Library. (cr) Bettmann/CORBIS. **67** (cl) The Maryland Historical Society, Baltimore, Maryland. (cr) The Mariners Museum/CORBIS. **68** Photo courtesy of the Military & Historical Image Bank, www. historicalimagebank.com. **69** Bettmann/CORBIS. **70** © Peabody Essex Museum, Salem, Massachusetts, USA French, out of copyright/Bridgeman Art Library. **71** Photo by MPI/Hulton Archive/Getty Images. **72** Bettmann/CORBIS. **76** Library of Congress Prints and Photographs Division, Washington, D.C. 20540. USA **78** © SuperStock, Inc./SuperStock. **79** Photo by MPI/ Hulton Archive/Getty Images. **81** Ray Boudreau. **86** (cr) CORBIS. (br) Photo by D.A. Pearson ©2005. **87** (cl) Art Archive/National Archives Washington, DC. (bl) Library of Congress, Prints and Manuscripts Division. (cr) CORBIS. (br) Underwood & Underwood/CORBIS. **88** (all) CORBIS. **89** (cr) CORBIS. (cl) Bettmann/CORBIS. **90** Scala/Art Resource. **92** (t) Maryland Historical Society, Baltimore, Maryland. (c) Courtesy of First Baptist Church, Baltimore, Maryland. **93** (bl) Brown Brothers Sterling, PA 18463. **94** (b) State Historical Society of Illinois, Chicago, IL, USA/Bridgeman Art Library. **96** (all) Ray Boudreau. **98** Bettmann/CORBIS. **99** Private Collection/Bridgeman Art Library. **100** CORBIS. **101** The Granger Collection, New York. **102** Bettmann/CORBIS. **103** (tr) CORBIS. (tl) From the Penn School Collection. Permission granted by Penn Center, Inc., St. Helena Island, SC. **104** (tr) The Maryland Historical Society, Baltimore, Maryland. (tl) The Mariners' Museum/CORBIS. **106** Bettmann/CORBIS. **110** (cr) Maryland Historical Society, Baltimore, Maryland. (cl) The Mariners' Museum, Newport News, Virginia. **111** (cl) Library of Congress. (cr) Bettmann/CORBIS. **112** Special Collections/Courtesy of the Maryland State Archives. **113** Chesapeake Bay Maritime Museum. **114** (tl) Maryland Historical Society, Baltimore Maryland. (br) Library of Congress Prints and Photographs Division Washington D.C. 20540. USA. **116** Library of Congress. **117** CORBIS. **118** (bl) The Maryland Historical Society, Baltimore, Maryland. (b) Bettmann/CORBIS. **119** Library of Congress. **122** Library of Congress Prints and Photographs Division Washington D.C. 20540. **123** (b) Hulton-Deutsch Collection/CORBIS. (tr) Bettmann/ CORBIS. **125** Paul S. Souders/CORBIS. **127** Ray Boudreau. **132** (br) Bettmann/CORBIS. (cr) Enoch Pratt Free Library. **133** (br) Photodisc Green/Getty Images. (bl) Ingram Publishing/Alamy. (cr) Robbie Jack/CORBIS. (cl) Bettmann/ CORBIS. **134** (all) AP/Wide World Photos. **135** (cl) Stock Connection Blue/Alamy. (cr) Tom Carter/PhotoEdit. **136** AP/Wide World Photos. **137** AP/Wide World Photos. **140** Lowell Georgia/CORBIS. **142** AP/Wide World Photos. **142–143** (bkgd) Lowell Georgia/CORBIS. **143** (all) AP/ Wide World Photos. **144** Paul Conklin/Photo Edit. **145** Tom Carter/PhotoEdit. **147** MAGMA, Artbase, Inc. **148** Tom Carter/PhotoEdit. **150** (b) Catherine Karnow/ CORBIS. (tr) Tom Carter/PhotoEdit. **151** Michael Newman/ Photo Edit. **152** Paul A. Souders/CORBIS. **153** (cr) Tom Carter/Photo Edit. (t) Richard T. Nowitz/CORBIS. **154** Tom Carter/Photo Edit. **157** Ray Boudreau. **160** (cr) James L. Amos/CORBIS. (cl) Paul A. Souders/ CORBIS. **161** (cl) Joseph Sohm; Visions of America/ CORBIS. (cr) Folio, Inc. **162** Unknown Photographer/Grant Heilman Photography. **163** Paul S. Souders/CORBIS. **165** Paul A. Souders/CORBIS. **167** Brand X Pictures/Getty Images. **168** Richard T. Nowitz/CORBIS. **169** James L. Amos/CORBIS. **170** Paul A. Souders/CORBIS. **173** Paul A. Souders/CORBIS. **174–175** (b) Joseph Sohm;Visions of America/CORBIS. **175** (cr) ©IKE GEIB/Heilmanphoto. **176** (tl) Middleton Evans. (tr) Folio, Inc. **177** (cr), (b) Joseph Sohm;ChromoSohm Inc./CORBIS. **178** (bl) Benno Friedman/Time Life Pictures/Getty Images. (tr) The Granger Collection, New York. **179** Photo by Gjon Mili/Time Life Pictures/Getty Images. **181** Ray Boudreau. **188** (cl) Theo Allofs/CORBIS. (cr) David Young-Wolff/PhotoEdit. **189** (cl) Richard T. Nowitz/CORBIS. (cr) Tom Carter/PhotoEdit. **190** Grant Heilman Photography, Inc. **192** Reuters NewMedia, Inc./CORBIS. **193** Joe McDonald/CORBIS. **195** Rudi Von Briel/PhotoEdit. **196** Elizabeth Hathon/ CORBIS. **197** Toni Freeman/PhotoEdit. **198** (cl) Grant Heilman Photography, Inc. (bc) Arthur C. Smith III/Grant Heilman Photography, Inc. (cr) PhotoDisc/Getty Images. (br) Roy Morsch/CORBIS. **199** David Young-Wolff/ PhotoEdit. **201** LWA-JDC/CORBIS. **202–203** Alan Schein Photography/CORBIS. **204** Richard T. Nowitz/CORBIS. **208** Michael Macor/San Francisco Chronical/CORBIS. **210** (b) Artbase, Inc. (cr) Jack Hollingsworth/Getty Images. **211** Bernd Obermann/CORBIS. **R0–1** James Blank/Index Stock Imagery. **R1** Panoramic Images/Getty Images. **R4** (br) Bettmann/CORBIS. (cl) Underwood & Underwood/ CORBIS.

Map Credits

Maps by Mapping Specialists, Ltd.

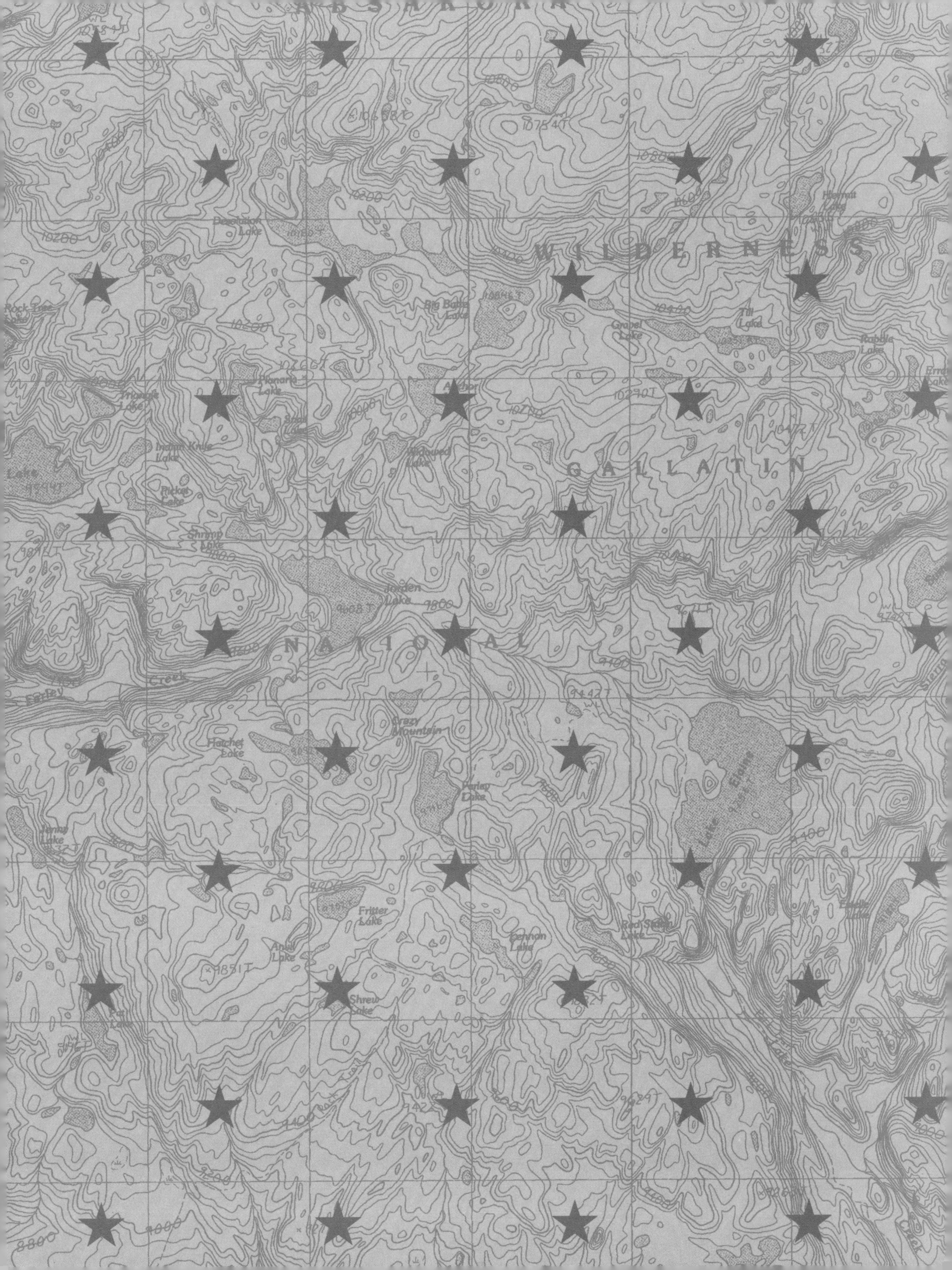
WILDERNESS
GALLATIN
NATIONAL
Desolation Lake
Gravel Lake
Till Lake
Indian Knife Lake
Pickup Lake
Jorden Lake
Crazy Mountain
Hatchet Lake
Parley Lake
Fritter Lake
Shrew Lake
Lake Elaine

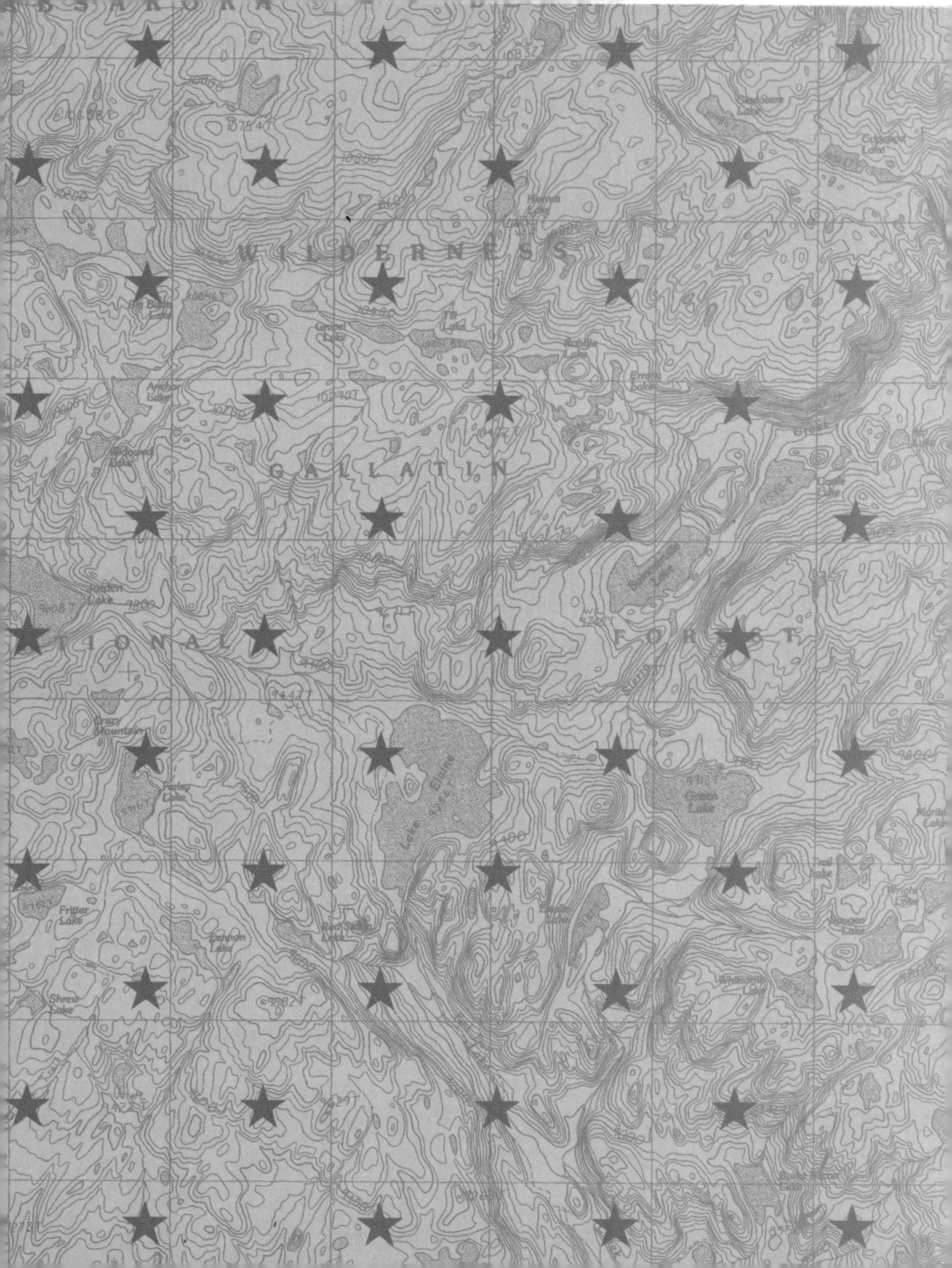

WILDERNESS
GALLATIN
Anchor Lake
Jorden Lake
Crazy Mountain
Farley Lake
Fritter Lake
Shrew Lake
Lake Elaine
Green Lake
Trail Lake
Wright Lake